THE BELLEWS OF MOUNT BELLEW

The Bellews of Mount Bellew

*A Catholic Gentry Family
in Eighteenth-Century Ireland*

Karen J. Harvey

FOUR COURTS PRESS

Set in 10.5 on 13 point Times for
FOUR COURTS PRESS LTD
Fumbally Lane, Dublin 8, Ireland
e-mail: info@four-courts-press.ie
and in North America for
FOUR COURTS PRESS
c/o ISBS, 5804 N.E. Hassalo Street, Portland, OR 97213.

A catalogue record for this title
is available from the British Library.

ISBN 1-85182-351-4

Printed and bound in Great Britain by
MPG Books Ltd, Bodmin, Cornwall

For Paul and the Menagerie

Contents

LIST OF FIGURES

Preface

There are many persons who have helped me in the preparation of this book: to all, thanks are owed.

I am indebted to the following institutions and their staffs for their help and co-operation: the John Carter Brown Library in Providence, RI, the William L. Clements Library in Ann Arbor, MI, and, in Dublin, the National Archives, the Registry of Deeds, the library of Trinity College, and, especially, the National Library of Ireland, the depository for the Bellew papers. (My particular thanks to Ms Colette O'Flaherty of the NLI for her kindness in providing me with a draft version of the re-sorting and cataloguing of the Bellew family papers.) The facsimile of the 1767 map of a portion of the Bellew estate is reproduced courtesy of the National Library of Ireland. Thanks also are due to Lock Haven University of Pennsylvania for granting me academic leave to complete research and writing.

I owe a great deal to academic mentors at both Brown University and the Pennsylvania State University. In addition, my debt to L.M. Cullen, as is that of all who research and write about eighteenth-century Ireland, is immense, as will be seen in both end notes and bibliography. My thanks to Professor Cullen as well for his gracious and sound advice. My thanks also to Michael Adams, Martin Healy, and Martin Fanning of Four Courts Press for their encouragement and patience. All errors in this work, whether factual or interpretive, are, of course, my own.

I have also appreciated the forebearance of family, friends, and colleagues, who have heard all too much about the preparation and writing of this book. My greatest debt, as always, is to Paul, without whose help, encouragement, and gentle prodding this work would never have been completed, and to whom it is dedicated.

Introduction

In April of 1767, Andrew French, a Galway merchant visiting Montpellier, wrote to his brother-in-law in Ireland who had expressed interest in living conditions in France:

> You say you have some thoughts of settling your family in this kingdom – to preserve the religion of our posterity is what every good Catholic might endeavour to do ... I hope God will incline the hearts of our rulers, to mitigate the Penal Laws, and thereby make us useful subjects, and not compel us to the dreadful necessity to emigrate from our beloved country.[1]

At first glance, this letter would appear to confirm a long-held view of Catholics in eighteenth-century Ireland – as helpless victims of an oppressive legal code from which emigration was one of the few salvations. Yet, the recipient of French's letter, Michael Bellew of county Galway, was far from down-trodden. A member of the east Galway gentry, he had a prosperous estate: his son would eventually become heir to approximately 10,000 acres and £5000 a year. Indeed, in the same month the letter was written, Bellew was completing an imposing country house. A profound contradiction appears to exist between the sentiments of French's letter and the reality of Bellew's circumstances.

To explain this contradiction is one purpose of this book. Its topic – the Catholic gentry – is only one among many that historians of eighteenth-century Ireland have begun to explore in their reassessment of the nature of the Catholic community. Beginning with Maureen Wall's innovative analyses in publications of the 1950s and 1960s, two succeeding generations of historians have not only taken different approaches to Irish Catholic history from those of an earlier period, but, in producing important works on the economic, cultural, and social contexts of Catholic life, have also significantly altered our view of the eighteenth century.

One major trend in current scholarship has been a reassessment of the pe-

11

nal laws and their impact on Irish Catholics. A series of acts passed by the Irish parliament in the late seventeenth and early eighteenth centuries, the penal laws limited the civil, political, religious, and economic rights of Roman Catholics. Irish Catholics were deprived of seats in the Irish parliament and eventually the parliamentary suffrage itelf, and excluded from corporations, the army, and most professions. A Catholic education, either clerical or lay, was forbidden. Land ownership was restricted in a variety of ways: a Catholic was prohibited from renting or purchasing lands for terms longer than thirty-one years, or holding mortgages or judgments on them. He was not permitted to inherit lands from a Protestant: the inheritance was to pass to the nearest Protestant relative, debarring any Catholic heirs. If a Catholic secretly purchased lands or had them purchased in trust, a Protestant who 'discovered' such an arrangement could obtain the lands for himself. In addition, the descent by entail of the lands of a Catholic to the eldest of his sons was forbidden. Inheritable lands were to be left equally to all sons; if there were no sons, lands were to be divided equally among the daughters. Moreover, incentives were offered to promote conformity to the Protestant faith: a Catholic eldest son was allowed full inheritance rights if he changed his religion; younger sons and wives, upon conversion, could claim a portion of the estate.

The penal laws issued from a parliament dominated by a Protestant elite rooted in settlement, conquest, and the established religion. Because the laws' passage consolidated the power of a Protestant minority over an overwhelming Catholic majority, they have provided a handy referent for frequently controversial interpretations of a series of relationships: those between religion and power, between Protestant and Catholic, even between Ireland and Great Britain. As a result, interpretations of the impact of the penal laws have often been coloured by nineteenth and early twentieth-century historians' sectarian loyalties or political allegiances.[2] In the historiography of the period, the penal laws had long been characterized as harsh and degrading, tending to crush the influential and vigorous elements in Irish Catholic society. Recent research, particularly in the last fifteen years, has significantly modified the traditional interpretation, showing that the impact of the laws has been exaggerated. The editors of a 1990 collection of essays on Catholics in the eighteenth century stated, 'No longer can we accept without substantial qualification the traditional picture of eighteenth-century catholicism as one of unmitigated persecution and servitude'.[3] Moreover, S.J. Connolly, in a recent work analyzing the consolidation of the power of the Protestant landed classes, asserts that the penal laws were only a part, 'and not the most important part', of a long process of transferring wealth from Catholics to Protestants; the laws did not, in themselves, significantly restructure Irish society. He also notes the continuing use of the term 'penal era' to characterize the eighteenth century, a usage, one can infer, that he prefers to jettison.[4]

Certainly, any contention that the penal laws were, or indeed that any legal code could be, the sole determinant of the social construct of eighteenth-century Ireland would be a misguided one. Nonetheless, the reality of the laws' broad scope and their *intent* to encompass almost every field of Catholic economic, social, and civil activity remain. Whether the burden of argument is that enforcement of the laws was rigorous or lax, that their impact on a particular group or class was devastating or negligible, because of the laws' pervasiveness, any analysis of the eighteenth-century Catholic experience must take them into account. This is particularly so in the case of the Catholic gentry.

As the research of Wall, John Brady, and others has shown, the eighteenth-century practice of the Catholic faith was not seriously threatened; by mid-century, after the threat of Jacobite invasion had waned, the clergy were relatively unmolested.[5] The Catholic mercantile classes, although excluded from corporate guilds, were affected by few of the penal laws in their economic pursuits.[6] The bulk of the peasant class would have remained untouched by the landowning restrictions. However, the same degree of de facto toleration or relaxation of the laws, or a corresponding lack of statutory regulation, is not as evident in regard to the gentry. There were good reasons for this circumstance, above all security.

Confiscation and plantation as government policy in response to Catholic rebellion, whether on the vast scale of the Cromwellian settlement or by the relatively mild terms of the Williamite settlement, ended in 1703. Henceforth, the main thrust of penal legislation was designed to ensure that Catholics would never again occupy a position of strength from which to threaten the Protestant establishment. The most effective method of guaranteeing this was to eliminate Catholic access to the indispensable foundation of political and social power: land ownership. The restrictions thus placed on the inheritance, purchase, and leasing of lands should be considered the keystone of the penal structure.[7] These restrictions were certainly regarded as the most pernicious of the disabilities incurred by those gentry who remained in the Catholic faith.

The intent of the laws would seem clear: for a gentry family remaining Catholic, the division of lands into smaller and smaller parcels by the equal division of the estate among the sons, or the diminishing of the unentailed estate by land or money settlements to members of the family willing to conform. The carrot, as opposed to the stick, was total freedom in land use and disposal upon conversion. Realization of the intent of the penal legislation should have made 'Catholic gentry' a contradiction in terms, and many historians from the nineteenth century onwards have held the laws accountable for the decline in Catholic landholding in the eighteenth century. The statistics are familiar: by 1776, the Catholic share of lands, estimated at some 14 per cent in 1703, had dwindled to 5 per cent.[8] Wall, in her study of the penal laws, asserted that they 'operated effectively in practically destroying the landed classes'.[9] However, the estimate of Catholic land-holding in 1776 is impressionistic at best. Moreover, that estimate considers lands held only in fee simple; as will be seen, Catholics could build up a landed interest with other forms of possession. Nor does it distinguish lands lost by factors having nothing to do with the impact of the penal laws: poor management and indebtedness, for example.

The focus of this study is those Catholics who resisted the pressures to conform: those who kept their religion, and maintained their estates and gentry status. Despite the statistical implications, however interpreted, there were Catholic gentry families who prospered during the eighteenth century.

However, any attempts to generalize concerning the factors which enabled them to do so encounter two complex and interlocking problems. First, as recent studies have convincingly shown, the Draconian letter of the law was frequently at variance with the efficacy of its enforcement. Instances of successful circumvention, through successful litigation; judicious use of trustees or discovery by collusion, that is, a friendly Protestant bringing action to forestall a genuine discovery (both of which would account for the statistical decline of lands in 'Catholic' hands)[10] can be observed. So, too, however, can instances where gentry families became entangled in the laws' provisions and lost lands. Second, regional differences could also have had their effect on observation of the laws. Variables such as the proportion of Catholic gentry to Protestant and the attitudes of the latter are obviously important factors. In short, the situation of the Catholic gentry in Tipperary was not always that of the Catholic gentry in Galway, or in Ulster.

Given these problems and qualifications, the reassessment of the impact of the penal laws on the Catholic gentry would continue to profit from a regional[11] and individual approach: that is, examination of the particular conditions within a region and the individual experiences of specific landed families. This study will examine one family in one county, the Bellews of Mount Bellew in county Galway. Galway had one of the highest concentrations of Catholic gentry and the Bellew family is an excellent representative of one regional group, those families with roots dating back to the Norman settlement in the thirteenth century, who were transplanted to Galway in the seventeenth century from other parts of Ireland. The Bellews had estates of significant size, thus subjecting them to the landownership provisions of the penal laws, and they were active in the movement to dismantle them, thus providing them with notable status in

Catholic affairs. Moreover, the Bellew family papers provide sufficient correspondence and estate records to evaluate their position as Catholic gentry and assess the impact of the penal laws on the family unit. I make no claim for the Bellews as paradigmatic of the eighteenth-century Irish Catholic gentry. However, an examination of the Bellews' status and their success in maintaining it provides an opportunity to relate, and sometimes contrast, specific experiences to general interpretations of the situation of the Catholic gentry of the period.

This study, I emphasize, will not provide a detailed legal analysis of the penal laws themselves,[12] rather an analysis of their impact on one particular family. Moreover, although this study is a species of family history, it is not simply an antiquarian exercise in genealogy. Family history, subject to proper methods of analysis, can reflect in microcosm the social, religious, and economic environment of a particular period. Thus, in addition to tracing the effects of the penal laws on a Catholic gentry family, this study will also place the Bellews in the broader context of eighteenth-century Irish country life, emphasizing the related aspects of landownership, landlord-tenant relationships, land use and management, and the gentry's place in the economic structure of their region. It will also explore the means by which a Catholic gentry family could provide avenues for advancement of younger sons – a paradoxical problem created by success in avoiding the land divisions called for by the penal laws – and also how it could expand its resources by participation in domestic business and foreign trade, two endeavours often intertwined.

The central themes that will be developed in the following chapters are these: the means by which a Catholic gentry family could evade the laws and preserve their estates intact; the factors – regional and familial – which permitted them to do so; and, perhaps most important, the psychological as well as the material impact of the penal laws. Discussion of a psychological dimension of the penal structure may seem, at first glance, odd, in the case of this particular family. The Bellews prospered, despite the penal laws: they maintained their estates, their lands provided them with a good living, and they were a prominent family in their region. Yet, as I hope to show, the family did not remain untouched. Accommodation to the penal structure was necessary and can be seen in almost every area of the Bellews' endeavours. The penal laws resulted in a life which was rarely, if ever, uncomfortable, but it was one that could never be completely settled, or 'normal' in terms of their Protestant counterparts. It was most certainly not one of oppression, but it was one of accommodation and frustration. The goal of the laws to eliminate Catholic gentry was never met, yet they shaped the lives of those gentry in important, if unquantifiable, ways.

Few recent studies (least of all, as will be seen, this one) would contest that the material aspect of the laws has been exaggerated. Indeed, the continuing reassessment of the Catholic community during the eighteenth century is a healthy one, enabling us to view the lives and actions of distinguishable classes and groups in their own right rather than lumping them together as helpless victims. Such a reassessment not only moves us away from overly subjective 'victim history', but also is a further step in avoiding what Nancy Curtin has aptly termed 'the unhelpful eight-hundred-years-of-unrelieved-oppression mode of analysis'.[13] Yet, we might pause before constructing a new interpretation that suggests the laws' impact was at worst *minimal*, particularly in the case of the gentry. To maintain, as does S.J. Connolly, that because of the inequality of eighteenth-century Irish society and the elite nature of power, only a few new faces would have made their appearance among the ruling class if the penal laws had been removed,[14] is, despite its inherent logic, an *argumentum ex silentio* and perhaps an overly objective one at that. Examinations of the penal laws that stress only statistical success or relative loss tend to omit an important, human, dimension of a legal system's impact – one this study hopes to restore.

'In Open Rebellion':
The Seventeenth-Century Background

The Bellews, like most of their gentry neighbours in county Galway, were of 'Old English' ancestry, that is, descendants of pre-Elizabethan settlers. By the seventeenth century, some 2,000 Old English families owned approximately 2¼ million acres, or almost one third of the profitable land in Ireland.[1] They were concentrated in the counties of the old Pale (Dublin, Louth, Meath, and Kildare); in the counties of Kilkenny, Westmeath, and Wexford; and, in the west, in the town of Galway as well as its environs. Until the late Tudor period and subsequent changes in English policy based on religion and national security, this influential group held county offices, served in the Irish government, and sat in the Irish parliament; indeed, they had been the mainstay of English authority in Ireland. However, despite their ancestry, landholding, and political influence, the continued adherence of a majority of the Old English to Catholicism after the Reformation resulted in their gradual displacement from positions in central authority. Their alliance with the native Irish in the rebellion of 1641 was even more costly, as many were removed from their estates, transplanted elsewhere, and in future regarded as part of the general Irish Catholic community to be controlled and regulated. Finally, following their unsuccessful support of James II in 1689–90, they were completely excluded from power – barred from purchasing lands and participating in government.

A recounting of the seventeenth-century history of the Bellews, as members of this group of Old English landowners, is thus key to understanding their later circumstances. For it was their political allegiances as well as their Catholicism that resulted, first, in their arrival in eastern Galway, and, second, their status as landholders there by the eighteenth century.

The Norman family of Belleau had accompanied William the Conqueror to England. Sometime after the twelfth-century Anglo-Norman conquest of Ireland under Henry II, they settled in Louth and Meath, where by the thirteenth century, their name had been anglicized to Bellew. They played a prominent role in their counties, serving as sheriffs and members of parliament, and marrying into leading families of the Pale – the Plunketts, Barnewalls, and Dillons.[2]

As with any other close-knit social group, these family connections were both intricate and extremely important for patronage and advancement.

Sir John Bellew, Knight of Bellewstown, the Roche, and Castletown, county Meath, succeeded his grandfather in 1542 as the head of the Bellewstown family. From him descended the holders of the seventeenth-century barony of Duleek and baronetcy of Barmeath and the nineteenth-century baronetcy of Mount Bellew and barony of Barmeath (Figure 1). The founder of the Barmeath and Mount Bellew branches of the family, with whom this study is concerned, was his great-grandson, John Bellew of Lisrenny and Graftonstown, county Louth.

John Bellew was born in 1606, the eldest son of Patrick Bellew of Lisrenny and Grafton and Mary Warren of Warrenstown Castle. His early life reflects the usual training and pursuits of a member of the Old English landed class. In 1627, when he was 21, his name was entered on the admissions register of Grey's Inn;[3] this was a period in which many of the children of the Irish nobility and gentry were sent to England for schooling, often including the study of English law. In an earlier period, this knowledge prepared them for administrative office and advancement;[4] in the more unsettled years of the early seventeenth century, to be described shortly, it became extremely useful in defending land titles.[5] By 1632, Bellew was back in Ireland, where he purchased the estate of Willistown in county Louth; he would henceforth be known and referred to in the contemporary records as John Bellew of Willistown. In 1634, he married Mary Dillon, daughter of Galway landowner Robert Dillon of Clonbrock, a member of another Old English family with branches in the Pale and the west of Ireland. His marriage into a Galway family was an ironic foreshadowing of a much closer association with the west, as Bellew and his Louth relatives would be caught up in the complex civil and religious affairs of Ireland under Charles I which would eventually lead to their removal to Connacht.[6]

Despite their loyalty to the Crown during the Nine Years' War, an allegiance prompted as well by distrust of the native Irish, the Old English rapidly found themselves threatened in the opening decades of the seventeenth century by the same government policies which had been applied to their conquered Gaelic co-religionists. Like their English gentry and aristocrat counterparts under Elizabeth and James I, the Old English were able to reconcile temporal allegiance to the Crown with spiritual allegiance to the Roman church. However, the English government, concerned about the attractiveness of a predominantly Catholic Ireland as a potential base for continental Catholic foes, regarded this divided loyalty with suspicion and initiated its policies accordingly.

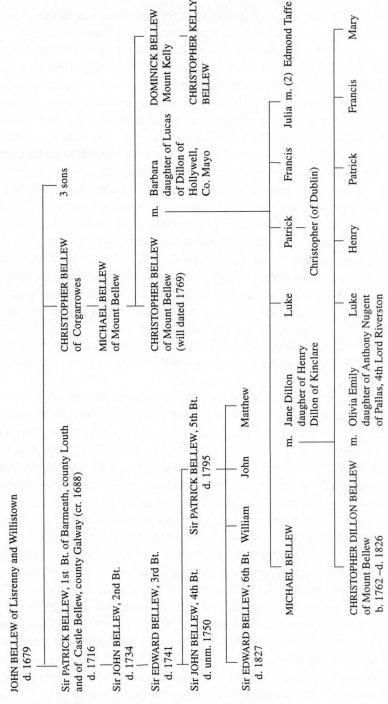

Figure 1: Bellew Family Genealogy

First, there was a more rigorous enforcement of the Elizabethan statutes requiring religious conformity and the institution of an Irish court of wards, in which Protestant guardians were appointed for Catholic minors. It could be argued that the primary motive behind these actions was financial as well as religious, since the recusancy fines and the income from wardships were extremely useful to the financially-pressed Stuart government. Moreover, James i's religious policies were often tempered by his desire for a Spanish alliance, which resulted in a certain degree of circumspection concerning the treatment of his Catholic subjects. Nonetheless, the Catholic Old English found the sterner side of this vacillating religious policy both irritating and worrisome,[7] particularly when it was encouraged by elements in the Irish administration in Dublin whose composition was changing in ways unfavourable to Catholics.

For although they still played an important role in local government, the Old English found themselves supplanted in central government posts and positions of influence and profit by 'New English' families, primarily Protestant, who had settled in Ireland during the Elizabethan and Jacobean periods. As well, the parliamentary influence the Old English were accustomed to wielding was being undermined, as seats from forty new boroughs were added to the Irish parliament, resulting in Protestant majorities.

In the 1620s, the Old English found themselves facing another, even more ominous, development: the renewal of a policy of plantation. Most earlier confiscation and plantation had been at the expense of the native Irish.[8] Any confiscation directed against the Old English had been as a result of direct participation in rebellion, for example, the plantation of the lands of the Munster Desmonds after the rebellion of Tyrone. Now the holdings of the loyal Old English were being threatened as part of a Stuart policy of challenging land titles in an attempt to recover revenue for the crown. While plantation did not mean total confiscation – usually only one quarter of the land was planted and the remainder regranted – it did mean financial, as well as property, loss for the owner, since it necessitated a fine for a new title and a crown rent.[9] More important, it continued the steady erosion of the Old English position.

In the 1620s, a solution to the dilemma of Stuart insolvency and Old English insecurity seemed at hand. War with Spain required the financing of troops for Ireland's defense; while the loyalty of the Old English was questioned, the value of their money was not, and a bargain was struck with Charles i. In 1628, in return for payments of £120,000 over a period of three years, Irish landowners were to be granted concessions in the form of the 'Graces'. Among them were several of paramount importance to the Old English: no future royal claims on titles more than sixty years old, relaxation of religious tests and recusancy fines, and guarantees for land titles in Connacht and Ulster.[10]

The subsidies were soon spent, but official enactment of the Graces was not to be forthcoming. With foreign wars concluded and the arrival of Thomas Wentworth as Lord Deputy in 1633, the policies that had threatened the Old English were renewed with not only vengeance but efficiency.[11] In the Irish parliament which met in 1634, Wentworth, after successfully obtaining subsidies for the Crown in the first session, refused to enact the key Graces in the second. The attack on defective land titles was also renewed, particularly in the west of Ireland, hitherto unaffected. Despite the large landholdings in Galway of the influential Old English earl of Clanrickard, Wentworth's bullying of grand juries in Mayo, Roscommon, and Galway led in 1637 to the 'submission of Connacht', the finding of the king's claim to title. Although no wholesale plantation was to be initiated under Wentworth's regime, the implications of his policy were clear:

> The plantation of Connaught was the fearfully anticipated point of qualitative change in government policy: the point at which the Old English and the Irish became, without differentiation, simply so many papists.[12]

However, Wentworth's policies of centralization and 'thorough' in Ireland were perceived as threatening not just by the Old English, but by almost every influential Protestant segment of society. His investigation into land titles and tactics of revenue-raising, including recoveries of church lands and fees, affected the New English as well, and his attempts to bring the Church of Ireland into doctrinal line with the Laudian English church offended many Irish Protestants who favoured a more Calvinistic theology. The situation came to a head with the departure of Wentworth, now Lord Strafford, for England in 1639 and the summoning of an Irish parliament in 1640 to aid the king in his war with the Scots. A parliamentary alliance of Catholic Old English and Protestant New English was formed, united only in its opposition to Strafford and a desire to overturn his policies. John Bellew, as one of the members of parliament for county Louth, was to figure in this brief union of parties and their relations with their opposites in the English parliament.

In early November of 1640, the Irish Commons drew up a Humble and Just Remonstrance; despite the opposition of the Irish government, a committee was appointed to travel to London to represent Irish grievances to the king. A letter was also written to the English Commons requesting them to present the Remonstrance to Charles. Its delivery, along with an annexed petition signed by 84 MPs, was entrusted to John Bellew and Oliver Cashel. They were introduced to the House on 30 November, and the contents of the letter they carried were used in the preparation of articles of impeachment against Strafford.[13]

Bellew would also play an increasing role on Commons committees after many of the initial leaders of 1640 had left for London. In February 1641, for example, he was a member of the committee appointed to prepare articles of impeachment against the Irish lord chancellor and chief justice and the bishop of Derry, in an attempt to discredit potential defenders of Strafford at his trial.[14]

The fruits of parliamentary alliance and intrigue followed in rapid succession: after negotiations with the Irish parliamentary representatives in England, Charles at last conceded the Graces in April of 1641; Strafford was executed in May; and, in exchange for subsidies, the king made further concessions to the Old English in July. The Old English had been successful in pressuring Charles to grant them what they wanted, but their victory came too late and at too great a price. The Graces were never to go into effect, and it soon became apparent that the Old English had committed a tactical error. Their former allies in the Irish parliament were now in league with the English parliament and in a position to enforce recusancy laws with new severity. Moreover, their attempts to undermine the policies of the king's representative, distasteful as they were, with the aid of the English parliament had enhanced parliamentary power at the expense of the royal prerogative. That prerogative was the only guarantor not just of the continued tolerance of their religion, but of their very status in Ireland.[15] The question of their future bargaining position both with the Crown and the Irish parliament in maintaining their status and their religion would, however, become moot as Ireland and then England were shortly plunged into revolt and civil war.

The outbreak of insurrection in Ulster on 23 October 1641 was precipitated by events in Britain – the fall of Strafford and the increasing hostility of Parliament toward Charles, both of which weakened the Irish government – and the successful example of the Scottish revolt against English religious policy. Its root cause, however, lay in the English program of plantation and the resultant cultural and economic dislocation that affected Irish gentry as well as tenants.[16]

Once initiated, the rebellion spread rapidly through the North; the response of the Old English would be of decisive importance in its success or failure. This was a fact appreciated by the Lords Justices in their report to the Lord Lieutenant two days after the outbreak of violence:

> All the hope we have here is that the Old English of the Pale and some other parts will continue constant to the King in their fidelity, as they did in former rebellions.[17]

One of the Justices' first acts after securing Dublin was to send letters to the sheriffs of the five counties of the Pale, 'to consult of the best way and means of their preservation'. Shortly afterwards, they issued commissions of martial law to 'the most active gentlemen, though all Papists, inhabiting in the several counties' and appointed prominent Old English lords and gentry in the Pale to levy forces.[18] The Bellews, as one of the leading gentry families in Louth, figured in these plans for defense: John Bellew was sheriff of Louth, one of those issued a commission of martial law;[19] his cousin Sir Christopher Bellew was one of those chosen to raise troops in the county.

Whatever the degree of involvement – if any – of some of their members in plotting against the Irish government to protect Catholicism during the uncertain period after the fall of Strafford,[20] the initial response of the Old English in October was supportive. On 24 October, the Lords of the Pale came before the Council, professing their loyalty and requesting arms for their defense. Although sufficient arms for almost 10,000 men were at their disposal, the Lords Justices, unwilling at this point to be almost totally dependent on Catholic aid, temporized, professing uncertainty as to sufficient supply for the protection of even Dublin. Nevertheless, they said they were prepared to issue a small supply of arms to those whose estates were in the greatest danger.[21] By the end of October and early November, the Ulster rebels had reached Dundalk and Ardee in Louth; Colonel Brian MacMahon, commander of forces from Monagahan, summoned the gentry and, according to later depositions, persuaded many, including the Barnewalls and Bellews, to join them.[22] In the meantime, proclamations were issued barring all non-residents from Dublin. While ensuring that the countryside would not be totally without leadership for its defense, these orders also effectively banished the Old English to their estates to face the approaching rebels with little means of resistance. Moreover, the Irish government delayed the issuing of weapons until 10 November, when arms to equip 300 men were sent to each of the counties of Westmeath, Louth, Dublin, and Kildare.[23]

How strong was the commitment of the Louth gentry to the rebels, in the face of thousands of their troops, can only be conjectured. Sir Christopher Bellew refused an appointment as colonel-general of forces to be raised in Louth. John Bellew appears to have hoped for parliamentary negotiation and reconciliation of Irish grievances. The depositions given before the chancellor of the exchequer in 1642 which recount Bellew's joining with the rebels are not specific regarding the date of that action. That given by William Moore of Barmeath, a justice of the peace for Louth, states simply that it occurred 'sometime after the sitting of the parliament at Dublin about Allhallowstide last past'. On 16 November, the Irish parliament, which had been prorogued, sat for one day to draw up a proclamation against the rebellion and appoint a committee to deliver it and a letter from the Lords Justices to the rebels in an attempt at negotiation. The committee contained eighteen Catholics out of twenty-seven members, including John Bellew from Louth. The parliamentary mission, however, was refused by the rebels: 'they tore the order and letter in pieces and rejected the treaty'.[24]

For Bellew and the Old English who had attended parliament and taken part in negotiations, this rebuff was followed by another. On their return to their estates, they found themselves without arms once more. On 17 November, those allocated for the defence of Meath had been removed from Lord Gormanston's house on the order of the government during his attendance at parliament; those for Louth, the most exposed of the counties, were taken by Viscount Moore of Drogheda, who suspected treachery.[25]

The outcome of decades of mutual suspicion between the Old English and the Irish government was perhaps inevitable. Forbidden the safety of Dublin and fearing the intentions of the Lords Justices, with insufficient arms for their defence, many of the Palesmen opened their estates to the advancing army of the rebels. It may well have been at this point that, in the words of William Moore's deposition, 'John Bellew of Willistown ... began to bestir himself and to raise forces to join ... in the said rebellion, by whose example and labour others of the said county did join ...'. In turn, the Justices were confirmed in their suspicion of the loyalty of the Old English, complaining on 22 November that:

> In the county of Louth (one of the five counties of the English Pale, which in all the defections of former rebellions here, stood firm to the Crown of England) the rebels are harboured and lodged in the gentlemen's houses as freely as if they were good subjects ...[26]

For John Bellew and the other Catholic landholders of Louth, any hopes of dissociating themselves from rebellion had come to an end. On 25 November, the Irish government reported that 'the whole county of Louth, both gentry and others, are joined with the rebels, and that the sheriff of that county, one John Bellew, Esq., is likewise with them'.[27] This intelligence came from Viscount Moore and Sir Henry Tichborne, the government commander of the garrison at Drogheda.

Lord Moore, whose estate of Mellifont was within two miles of Drogheda, had gone to the town on 26 October to prepare resistance against the rebels; Tichborne joined him there on 4 November. They reported to the Lords Justices that an alderman of the town who had joined the rebels came into Drogheda on protection accompanied by the sheriff of Louth, who was a member of parliament.[28] The two were said to have advised Moore to return to Mellifont, where his father had remained safely all through Tyrone's rebellion, and suggested that he might have a command if he wished. Nonetheless, since this meeting took place prior to the parliamentary negotiations with the rebels, in which Bellew took part, it would seem he had not yet made a firm decision to join with them, despite the Justices' conclusion. Moreover, on 10 December, Moore and Tichborne gave Bellew and James Bath of Athcairn a safe conduct pass to enable them to travel between Drogheda and Dublin, 'it being thought good that they should travel to Dublin upon special occasions concerning the peace and quietness of the commonwealth'.[29]

This pledge of safety may have been part of an attempt by the Irish government to confer with the Palesmen one last time. On 3 December, the Lords Justices summoned the Lords of the Pale to a meeting in Dublin on 8 December to discuss the state of affairs. Fearing the government's intentions, only one Catholic, Lord Viscount Fitzwilliam, joined the Protestant earl of Kildare and Lord Howth. The Justices deferred the conference to 17 December; however, by the second week of December, events had overtaken any further attempts at negotiation.

In late November, the Old English of Louth and Meath had been in contact with Rory O'More, a landowner in the Pale and a relative through marriage of the influential Barnewall family, who had approached them on behalf of the rebels.[30] Assured by O'More that the Irish were fighting for the king and his royal rights against parliament and in defense of the Catholic religion, the Old English made common cause with the northerners. Arrangements were made for formal and public meetings of the nobility and gentry with O'More and leaders of the northern rebels. In early December, the Old English gathered at the hill of Bellewstown, then moved to the arranged meeting place at the hill of Crofty where a formal union with the rebels was concluded. Among the lords and leading gentry in attendance were the earl of Fingall; the lords Gormanston, Louth, Slane and Trimbleston; the Barnewalls; Sir Christopher Bellew; and James Bath of Athcairn, who would shortly receive, with Bellew, the safe conduct pass, now meaningless, to Dublin.[31] A further meeting was held at the hill of Tara on 7 December; there military assistance and provisioning for the Ulster army was organized. Soon systematic arrangements for the raising of forces from the Pale itself would follow. Those who refused to join the alliance or provide aid were to be treated as enemies, a threat implicit in a letter of 5 December from Christopher Barnewall of Rathasket to Sir Christopher Bellew:

I pray you be here tomorrow with such forces of horse and foot as you can possibly make, whereof if you fail there is a course to be taken for the ruin of yourself and your estate, which I advise you to prevent.[32]

By the end of the year, an 'army of the Pale' was organized; Lord Gormanston was appointed its commander-in-chief in January 1642. The Old English
were initially reluctant, despite their alliance, to assimilate themselves into
'the Catholic army' of the rebels: they tried to keep their forces under
Gormanston, and, although their leaders met with the rebel army besieging
Drogheda, there is no record of a Palesman leading troops there.[33] Soon, however, events were to force them into a closer union.

By early 1642, the rebellion had spread to most parts of Ireland. Nevertheless, Sir Charles Coote and the marquis of Ormond held Dublin, which they
used as a base for successful raids against the insurgents; by the end of March,
their forces had relieved Drogheda and driven the Irish from the Pale. In the
north, the Scottish troops raised by the Irish government met with notable
success against the rebels and were joined in April by 2,500 fresh troops from
Scotland.

Dealings with the civil arm of the government – in both England and Ireland – were no more successful. In December, the Old English had sent a
petition to Charles, explaining the reasons for their taking arms and joining the
Irish. In February, a royal proclamation of January reached Ireland: those in
arms were to be considered rebels and traitors and were commanded to sub-
mit. However, attempts at negotiation with the Irish government were rejected,
and the treatment of the few Palesmen who submitted in obedience to the royal
proclamation – they were imprisoned, interrogated, and in some instances,
racked – was little encouragement to others who may have wished to surrender
themselves.[34] Finally, the response of the English parliament in March of 1642
was decisive. It took the form of the Adventurers' Act, which proposed to raise
money to suppress the rebellion on the security of 2½ million acres of Irish
land to be confiscated from all four provinces.

This final action made further negotiations with the Irish government or the
English parliament seem futile; however, for the Old English it reinforced their
stated reason for taking arms: loyalty to the king and defense of his prerogative
against an encroaching, and to the Old English inimical, parliament.

By mid-1642, the need to establish contact with the king, their only perceived protector, now at war with his parliament, became apparent. Moreover,
some central authority was necessary to administer internal affairs of the territory under the insurgents' control and direct what promised to be a protracted
military campaign. The Irish clergy, after initial meetings among themselves,
invited prominent lay Catholics, the majority from Leinster and Munster, to
Kilkenny where a provisional government was organized, one in which no
distinction was to be made between Gaelic Irish and Old English. Consisting
of an elected general assembly and a supreme council, bound by an oath of

association, it met at Kilkenny in its first formal session in October of 1642.

There, John Bellew, expelled from the Irish parliament in June along with his cousin Sir Christopher Bellew and thirty-nine others as 'rotten and unprofitable members', 'either in open rebellion, or [who] stand indicted of high treason', took the oath of the 'confederate Catholics of Ireland'.[35] At the same time, he joined the Confederate army. Whether Bellew had joined the earlier army of the Pale is uncertain; however, his commission, dated 14 October, was signed by Lord Gormanston, its former commander. It appointed him Lieutenant-General (that is, lieutenant) of Artillery in the Confederate Army of Leinster; a list of his troops, raised by himself, records Richard Bellew as lieutenant and is endorsed 'Capt. John Bellew ... a list ... Jesus, Maria'.[36]

The same month Bellew was appointed to his post, the Confederate army of Leinster – 6,000 foot and 600 horse – was put under the command of Colonel Thomas Preston, an uncle of Lord Gormanston. Preston had recently returned to Ireland from service in the army of Spain. Although his military career had not been without some success, he was nonetheless referred to as 'the Drum' (heard often in defeat).[37] More important for the future of the Confederate cause, however, were his relations with Owen Roe O'Neill, who had preceded him to Ireland just one month before, to take command of the Ulster provincial army. Both had served the Spanish army in Flanders, and their rivalry had soon developed into hostility. This personal enmity between the Old English Preston and O'Neill did not augur well for unified action; moreover, it would soon serve as an unfortunate focus to the different outlooks toward, and expectations of, the war by the predominantly Old English Leinster forces and the predominantly Irish Ulster troops.

The Old English shared a common religion and a common fear of government policy with the Irish rebels, but these commonalities were deceptive. In religion, the acceptance of Tridentine continental Catholicism by most of the Old English clashed with native Irish religious localism and practices.[38] They also had different reasons for fighting. The natural loyalties of the Old English lay with the king, their only hope for protection against a Protestant parliament and Irish establishment. They were always willing to seek accommodation and compromise with the marquis of Ormond, Charles' representative in negotiations, to ensure their landholdings and a practical toleration of their religion. The Irish, on the other hand, having experienced direct confiscation of their lands, wanted an end to plantation and were more willing to ally with the Roman clergy to seek a definitive religious settlement that would make Catholicism the established church in Ireland. These divisions could at times be papered over, but with the arrival of papal representatives to the Confederacy, committed to a peace treaty re-establishing Catholicism in Ireland, these essential differences often split the Confederates into two discernible groups: the Old English supporters of Ormond and accommodation and the Irish supporters of O'Neill and the papal representative Rinuccini.

The complexities of the period that followed have been accurately described in terms of an 'endless on-off war with shifting alliances, wandering detachments, often at cross-purposes with one another, bewildering kaleidoscopes of alliances ... and sudden changes of sides'.[39] The focus here will be on John Bellew's actions and allegiances. As might be expected, he was firmly attached to the Old English policies just described, and his name appears frequently in the contemporary sources. The material available is worthy of extended commentary, for his activities during his six years of service to the Confederate cause reflect something of the internal rivalries and divisions in the Confederacy itself and the financing and supply of its army.

Payments made to the Confederate forces came from county applotments, often in arrears, and the rents of confiscated estates. For example, in December 1645, the receiver of county Wicklow, by order of the Leinster assembly, was to pay £10 8s. 'out of the rents of enemies' estates in the County Wicklow to John Bellew, Esq., and the officers of his company of artillery', and an account of April 1647 records payments made to the army from enemies' rents in Carlow in 1646. Bellew received £15 11s. 9d.

Financial records also indicate the size of Bellew's company. At a muster at Sigginstown, county Kildare in November 1646, payments were made to the train of artillery: 'John Bellew's guard of 83, a lieutenant ensign, 2 sergeants, 3 corporals, and a drum ... £15 14s. 0d.'. In June 1647, payments made to the army in camp included £14 10s. 6d. to the Lieutenant-General of the artillery 'for self, officers, and company [for one week] ... being 71 soldiers and 3 corporals'.

Nonetheless, among the routine orders for deliveries of artillery necessities (spades, axes, bandoliers) are communications concerning shortages of funds and supplies. A petition of April 1647 to the Commissioners General of the Confederate Catholics for the Leinster Army from Torlogh O'Duffe and four others, carpenters of the artillery, stated, 'The means due to petitioners since last November have not been paid for by the Lieutenant-General of the Artillery' and was accompanied by a certificate of its accuracy signed by John Bellew, commander of the artillery. As well, Bellew's communications to Preston frequently mention shortages in supplies or difficulties in obtaining them. In the same month of the carpenters' petition, he reported on supplies of cannon shot, bullets, and 'all the pikes that could be had here, viz., 700 or 800 and some old cloth – the best I could get for cartridge ...'. The following month, he wrote that 'the carpenters sought everywhere hereabouts for befitting timber, but could get none, so I sent three of them to Kilkenny yesterday. In the woods there they will get all they want'. Another communication from the Leinster Committee to General Preston hints at an additional financial problem – peculation and profiteering:

> We have written to Lieutenant-General Bellew to find whether the Quartermaster of the Artillery can be spared, and that he intends the public should be eased of that charge. We shall not dismiss Quartermaster Plunkett till misdemeanor has been proved against him.[40]

As for Bellew's military actions, the fighting between the Confederacy and their opposites, the Scots and the Irish government army led by Ormond, from 1642 through 1645 was sporadic. Action by the Confederates against the latter was suspended by the cessation negotiated by Ormond in 1643. Bellew's participation, if any, in Preston's campaigns during this period – an unsuccessful foray against Ormond north of Dublin, the successful siege of Ballinakil early in 1643, his expeditions in King's County in the summer of 1643, or his reduction of the garrison at Duncannon in March 1645[41] – is unrecorded. However, he may have been nearby during O'Neill's victory over the army of Lord Moore and Colonel Coote at Portlester, county Meath on 12 September 1643. Both Preston and O'Neill had been sent into the Pale to secure the harvest. When the Scots threatened to move southward to join with the forces of Moore and Coote, O'Neill was sent to prevent the junction, with Preston and Sir James Dillon to provide reinforcements if necessary. When Moore and Coote attacked him at Portlesterford, O'Neill handily won the battle, capturing Portlester. The Old English reinforcements arrived a day later; their leader Sir James Dillon was supposedly greeted by O'Neill with the remark, 'I think glory awaits you in the drawing rooms'. Bellew might have been part of these reinforcements, as the family papers contain a copy of an apparently face-saving letter from O'Neill at Portlester dated 14 September on behalf of Lieutenant-General Bellew. It states that 'he did behave himself like a valiant and expert gentleman' and performed the 'said duty of his place, as well as any man could have done'.[42]

In 1646, Bellew accompanied Preston on an expedition to Connacht; an army roll of Leinster officers and regiments mustered there on July 18, 1646, lists two Bellews as captains in Preston's regiment and John Bellew as the commander of the artillery with his company of ninety-one. The description of the artillery, ammunition, and supplies for the expedition provides an interesting glimpse of seventeenth-century warfare and an illustration of a new development in Irish campaigning, armies with their own artillery trains.[43] Bellew's consisted of:

Six score and three oxen, eight great wagons covered; a brass cannon; a
brass culverin; two quarter cannons mounted on their carriages, and a
sledge for the cannon; twenty-eight casks of powder, weighing three thousand weight; three thousand weight of match; three thousand weight of
lead bullets; 204 shovels and spades; 92 pickaxes; 60 bill-hooks; 40 axes;
6 iron crows; 153 snap-sacks; 19 iron chains; 100 iron bullets.[44]

The Confederate forces were successful in Roscommon – capturing the county
capital, Clunibrun, and other castles in the area – but were unable to attack
Sligo, an enemy stronghold; they had exhausted their ammunition, and they
had no means for transporting the guns over the Curlew hills.[45] Even the victory at Roscommon was bittersweet for Preston and his Leinster forces, since
it was overshadowed by O'Neill's spectacular triumph over the Scots at Benburb
the same month.

Bellew was also present in the Leinster force collected by Preston later in
the year to join with O'Neill in an attempt on Dublin. It was abandoned when
the two generals fell out, O'Neill returning to winter quarters while Preston
flirted with negotiations for a settlement with Ormond. Preston and his officers, in consultation with the earl of Clanricard, agreed to observe the peace
treaty concluded with Ormond in March 1646, but rejected by the papal nun-
cio Rinuccini and a national synod of the clergy in August. Only the strictures
of the Supreme Council, then the threat of excommunication by Rinuccini
brought Preston and his troops back to Kilkenny for a reconciliation.[46]

Although Dublin was spared attack by the dissension within the Confederate camp, the position of Ormond became rapidly untenable. With no hope of
assistance from Charles, and aid offered from Parliament only in exchange for
submission, Ormond chose the English parliament over the Irish rebels, and
on 19 June 1647, handed over Dublin to the parliamentary commander Colonel Michael Jones. In August, Preston was routed at Dungan Hill by Jones, and
in November, the Confederate army of Munster, under the command of Taaffe,
was destroyed at Knockmanuss. With the fortunes of the Confederate army at
low ebb in 1648, negotiations were begun for the return of Ormond and a
royalist alliance.

Ormond landed at Cork on 30 September 1648. His ensuing negotiations
with the Confederates resulted in a treaty on 17 January 1649, just thirteen
days before the execution of Charles i. The Confederate government was dissolved; leadership of areas under Catholic control was assigned to twelve Commissioners of Trust and Ormond as the Lord Lieutenant of the newly proclaimed Charles ii. By the terms of the treaty, the Commissioners were to supply Ormond with an army of 15,000 foot and 2,500 horse, and the marquis was

soon in contact with the Old English officers of the former Confederation army who would form the new Loyalist force. In January, a group of Leinster officers, including John Bellew, addressed Ormond, stating their compliance with his orders to consult with the Commissioners of Trust concerning 'the reformation of officers'. In a politic move, they sent Sir Robert Talbot, a long-time supporter of Ormond, to 'deliver our sense in that and other affairs concerning the army'.[47] Bellew's commission from Ormond, dated 1 February 1649, appointed him Lieutenant-General of the Ordinance and to the command of a company of 100 men and officers as a guard for the train of artillery; his cousin Lord Taaffe was soon to be appointed Master of the Ordinance.[48] Bellew's name also appears on a list of the Leinster army in early 1649; it states – reflecting what was a chronic problem with the Confederate and later Royalist forces – that 'captain John Bellew's company, upon delinquents', was not mustered.[49]

In the late summer of 1649, Bellew's company was part of the force of 7,000 foot and 1,700 horse assembled by Ormond to attempt the recovery of Dublin from the parliamentary forces. Leaving Lord Dillon with 2,500 men to press a siege from the north, Ormond crossed the Liffey and camped at Rathmines to the south. While Ormond's force was weakened by the removal of two regiments to the south where it was rumoured the landing of an English army under Cromwell was imminent, the parliamentary forces in Dublin were strengthened by the arrival of reinforcements from England, making the two forces almost equal in number. When the Royalists moved toward the castle of Baggotrath to cut off pasture for the parliamentary horse, they were surprised by Colonel Michael Jones with a force from the garrison. In the resulting 'breach of Rathmines' on August 2, Ormond's army was routed.[50] The consequences of this major defeat were more than just the number of Royalists killed, wounded, and captured: ten days later, Oliver Cromwell, with an army of 12,000 men, landed in Dublin unopposed.

John Bellew was among the more than one hundred officers taken prisoner at Rathmines. After paying a heavy indemnity, he secured a pass from Colonel Jones dated 24 September, ensuring his safe passage, with a horse and a boy, to 'Irish quarters without let or disturbance'.[51]

After the end of September, however, 'Irish quarters' would become increasingly constricted. After his arrival in Dublin, Cromwell subdued one Irish town after another, beginning on 3 September with Drogheda, where Bellew's uncle Colonel Warren was among those massacred;[52] through Wexford, Ross, Youghal, Kinsale; taking Kilkenny itself in March of 1650; and ending with Clonmel in May. Ormond's tactics during this period were predicated on harsh reality: his army, deficient as it was in not only leadership but equipment, was no match for Cromwell's, although virtually equal in numbers. Besides being militarily less effective, the army's divisions between Irish and Old English made it difficult for Ormond to assemble one large dependable force. Thus, Ormond's strategy was to garrison towns and castles, while keeping a small army in reserve.[53]

After his release from Dublin, Bellew appears to have moved south to re-join Ormond's retreating army and eventually became part of the forces garri-soning the few Royalist strongholds left after Cromwell returned to England in May of 1650. Cromwell's military successor Henry Ireton immediately began the reduction of the remaining Loyalist posts east of the Shannon. John Bellew was stationed in one of these garrisons, Tecroghan in the southwestern corner of Meath.

A fortified castle by the headwaters of the Boyne, Tecroghan was called 'one of the pillars of Ireland'. In mid-May of 1650, the fort was besieged by a parliamentary force under Colonel Reynolds and Sir Theophilus Jones. At-tempts were made to relieve the fortress by the earl of Castlehaven, but the terrain was boggy and the troops unreliable – the Irish rear guard deserted under fire – and no further Royalist action was taken to lift the siege.[54] The garrison's commander, Sir Robert Talbot, appointed John Bellew to negotiate the surrender of the fort with Reynolds. The parliamentarians offered Talbot and Bellew their estates on surrender if they would quit the king's service and retire to their homes.[55] Both refused, but the garrison was granted honourable terms and marched out of Tecroghan on 25 June.

Ireton continued mopping-up operations in the east, then turned to the west. After protracted sieges, Limerick and finally Galway in April 1652 capitu-lated. The remnants of Royalist forces followed soon after. The men of the Leinster army, including John Bellew, surrendered at Kilkenny on 12 May under the promise of continuance on their lands, if they had not been confis-cated, until 'the pleasure of Parliament be known', and most important, under the promise of enjoyment of 'such moderate parcels of estates as may make their lives comfortable' if they stayed in Ireland.[56]

John Bellew's loyalties throughout this long period of intermittent warfare were clear, and were those of most of his class. Serving under Preston and later Ormond, he was consistently allied with those seeking accommodation and settlement, fighting a losing battle to re-establish the status quo of some fifty years before – when the Old English were substantial landowners in positions of power and influence, entrusted with the affairs of Ireland by an English government willing to acknowledge civil loyalty and disregard religious non-conformity. That, after eleven years of rebellion and civil war, was no longer possible, and the policy of the victorious Cromwellians was to be the first step in an attempt to destroy the basis for any future restoration of that power and influence.

On 12 August 1652, the Commonwealth Parliament in *An Act for the Settling of Ireland* established degrees of guilt in the rebellion of 1641. Eight qualifications were determined with appropriate penalties for persons comprehended in each. These ranged from death and confiscation for the first five qualifications to proportional forfeiture of estates and removal to other parts of Ireland.[57] The latter two qualifications introduced what was to be the policy of dealing with the rebellious Irish, particularly those with estates – transplantation, or the removal of Catholic landowners to accommodate and compensate the Cromwellian soldiers and officers and the 'Adventurers' of 1642. In July 1653, Connacht was designated as the place of transplantation; there, transplanted landowners were to receive a proportion of their former estates. A committee was appointed at Loughrea, county Galway in January of 1654 to set out and distribute lands according to the qualification of the transplantee; in December of the same year, the Athlone Court of Qualifications began to hear and determine claims.

Although 'John Bellew of Willystown in the County of Louth Esquire' was among 105 specifically exempted by name from pardon of life and estate, this qualification was soon abandoned as government policy toward the defeated evolved and exigencies of the period dictated,[58] and he and many of the 105 named were included in the ranks of those ordered to transplant. Bellew and other Old English, Richard Barnewall, Laurence Dowdall, and Patrick Netterville, began a series of petitions in March 1655 to Colonels Sankey and Lawrence and Lord Jones, members of the standing committee in Dublin who managed transplantation policy.[59] They argued that transplantation was a violation of the articles of Kilkenny under which they had submitted. While they thanked the government for the continuation of the rents and profits of their estates while they had awaited the pleasure of Parliament, they stated that the articles entitled them to enjoy such a remnant of their estates as should make their lives comfortable, a condition transplantation would obviously hinder. Moreover, the estates themselves were construed when they surrendered as their original holdings, not a proportional compensation in other parts of Ireland, 'transplantation at that time being no more thought of by your petitioners than their removal into America'.[60] John Bellew also appealed on additional grounds: Cecily Jones, wife of either Colonel Michael or Colonel Oliver Jones, signed a petition stating that during the rebellion, she had been provided with refuge at Willistown and that Bellew had saved the lives of herself and her companions, 'civilly entertained them', and conveyed them safely to Tredagh [Drogheda]. She 'did then observe that the said Mr. Bellew and all his family were as much for the preservation of the English as any could be'.[61]

Both petitions were of no avail. On 3 April, Bellew and the other petition-ers were ordered to transplant at or before the fifteenth of April 1655, and make application to the Commission at Athlone to determine their claims to estates and the Commission at Loughrea to set out their due proportion of estates. One further petition was made; in it, the Old English families appear to have accepted the committee's verdict, but had questions concerning the unencumbered disposal of their corn in Leinster, the collection of rent from their tenants, and their accountability for any arrears of taxes on their new lands. The Council's reply on 12 April was final: transplanation was to take place, although the petitioners' wives and children could continue in their former residence until 20 May. Their Leinster corn could be disposed of and arrears on rent from 29 July 1653 would be paid at Athlone after taxes were deducted. Although the petitioners were granted a stay until 1 May, presumably to settle estate affairs, they were to have no additional time to search records in Dublin, but ordered to leave the city.

Having already forfeited some 800 acres of his properties in Louth, includ-ing parts of Lisrenny and Grafton, John Bellew, in accordance with this final order, removed to Connacht. This action was apparently within the time limit specified, since on 16 June the Council at Athlone ordered the Commissioner General of the Revenues to ensure that persons employed by John Bellew to reap his corn on his lands in Leinster not be molested, in compliance with his petition, 'in regard that he has transplanted himself according to orders and in consideration of the report thereon by Sir Charles Coote, Sir Hardress Waller ...'.[62]

On 12 June 1655, the Commission sitting at Athlone adjudged Bellew to have lands in Galway to the value of one-third of his estates on their assess-ment. He received approximately 800 acres: some 650 in the barony of Tiaquin, including the lands of Clonoran, Carrowboe, and Clonoranoughter; 133 in the barony of Killian at Corgarrowes; and 3 in the barony of Ballymoe. Other lands were granted in western county Galway, in the baronies of Ross and Ballynahinch, but possession appears never to have been taken.[63] The lands may indeed have been set out, but there was much confusion and difficulty in determining claims, the demands of transplanters often outstripped the avail-able land supply, and since transplantation had been going on from 1654, there were often problems in obtaining lands to satisfy the decrees given to those who transplanted late. In any event, Restoration land records do not show lands in these baronies in the Bellews' possession. The majority of Bellew's new estate came from lands confiscated from the Gaelic Irish Kellys.

Two other Bellews had lands set out in county Galway following transplantation orders: John Bellew of Castletown, son of Sir Christopher Bellew, received substantial grants in eastern Galway in the baronies of Ballymoe and Tiaquin, although he seems never to have taken possession of the majority of the lands;[64] and Roger Bellew of Thomastown received 300 acres in the parish of Moylough in Tiaquin.[65]

John Bellew established a residence on his Galway property, but with the Restoration, immediately joined the ranks of the Catholic gentry and aristocracy who had fought for the Stuart cause under Ormond in seeking the recovery of the lands they had lost. Bellew was more successful than many, and his success is an excellent illustration of the continued strength and importance of family and patronage ties among the Old English families.

From 1661 to 1668, Bellew served as agent, in both Ireland and England, for Theobald, Viscount Taaffe, his cousin and patron. Taaffe, who had been a commander in the Confederate army, Ormond's Master of the Ordinance, and an active participant in diplomatic affairs on behalf of Charles during his exile, had recently been created earl of Carlingford and was also a devoted adherent of the Duke of York. These familial and political relationships would be instrumental in Bellew's restoration to, or reprisal for, much of his property in Louth and the confirmation of his holdings in Connacht.

A month after the return of Charles II to England, Bellew petitioned the king for the restoration of his Louth properties. He cited his imprisonment and ransom after Rathmines, his loans in the king's cause, his refusal of the parliamentary offer of estates to give up his service to Charles, and the devoted service of his family to the Stuarts. He stated that he had been exempted by 'the usurped government' from life and estate, 'compounded upon pain of death to transplant and apply himself to the several judicatures of Athlone and Loughrea for lands in Connaught'. Since the 'pittance given petitioner in Connaught was in order to Articles made with the usurped power', he asked that he 'forthwith be restored unto his Estate'.[66]

This petition was backed by certificates from Ormond, then Lord Lieutenant, testifying to his military service for the king, and Lord Taaffe, who, endorsing Ormond's statements, added that Bellew had expended his own money furnishing a guard for his train of artillery and never been reimbursed. Bellew received yet another certificate from Sir Thomas Stanley. This came at the request of Sir Robert Talbot, the commander at Tecroghan and brother of Richard Talbot, another follower of the Duke of York, who would make him earl of Tyrconnell in 1685. Of Old English background, Richard Talbot had fought with Preston, then Ormond. He would be instrumental in helping Catholics in the Court of Claims appealed to by those who sought restoration; Louth and county Dublin landowners in particular would benefit from his aid.[67] Stanley's certificate affirmed Bellew's refusal to quit the king's service during the siege of Tecroghan, despite the parliamentary commanders' offers to ensure him his estates.[68]

The petition and testimonials resulted in royal attention, if not immediate restoration. From Whitehall on 7 March 1661, Charles stated his satisfaction with Bellew's service and loyalty: 'He was lieutenant of the Ordinance in Ireland, and was forced to transplant ... but did not do so of his own free will'. He instructed the Lords Justices that Bellew be put into his Louth estates, 'such of the lands as are in the king's hands', including Lisrenny and Graftonston; if he was unable to get the lands, he was to be granted reprisals, or lands elsewhere.[69] Charles' directive was followed by a letter from the Duke of York on Bellew's behalf. He wrote on 5 April that

> The Lords Justices having understood by the testimony of the Duke of Ormonde the great zeal which John Bellew hath heretofore manifested to the king's service, and having myself observed the same in some of his nearest relations under my own command [apparently a reference to Taaffe], I have thought it fit to recommend him to your favour and protection, desiring you to afford it to him as often as his occasions shall require it, and that it shall be agreeable to justice.[70]

A number of such royal letters were issued immediately after Charles' restoration, but not all were successful for the petitioner;[71] moreover, they also called for the reprisal of those already in possession of forfeited estates. John Bellew was among those loyal Catholics who were caught between Charles' desire to compensate his followers and his politic reluctance to disregard the rights of both the Irish Protestants and the Cromwellian settlers. This presented obvious problems, summed up best by Ormond: 'There must be new discoveries of a new Ireland, for the old will not serve to satisfy these engagements'.[72] The Act of Settlement of 1662 and the Act of Explanation of 1665 seemed to offer Catholic landowners firmer hopes than royal grants of regaining their forfeited estates. The Court of Claims set up by the Acts was to hear cases of those who considered themselves unfairly deprived of lands. Those deemed 'innocent' (defined in a variety of ways) were to be restored.

The first Court of Claims, however, which sat from January to August 1663, was of no use to Bellew. As a Connacht transplanter, he would have been among those last in line to be heard, since the Court's policy was to restore first innocents who had not transplanted.[73] To make matters worse, Bellew's title to his lands in Connacht was hardly secure, since the lands had been granted by the Cromwellian commissioners. His dilemma was resolved ultimately by his loyal, and indefatigable, service to Taaffe.

The family papers contain the account of the disbursements and transactions made by Bellew during his eight years as Taaffe's agent, and they are extensive, indicative of the time and effort expended in his patron's behalf.[74] He oversaw Taaffe's dealings with the Courts of Claims – which granted the Earl a decree of innocence in 1663 and ultimately some 9,637 acres in Louth – and the Exchequer (the account also records the sums necessary for the greasing of palms to guarantee access to both). He searched legal records, contended with sheriffs, and let Taaffe's lands as well. The latter activity was particularly complex, as Taaffe was heir to lands in Louth and Sligo, and had been given claims to lands that had been held by Hardress Waller in Limerick. Indeed, looking after Taaffe's business was a Bellew family enterprise. His eldest son Patrick visited Sligo, his third son Christopher went on Taaffe's affairs to Louth, and both took trips to Limerick.

The role of Bellew's wife Mary in both Bellew and Taaffe affairs was also important. During her husband's and sons' lengthy absences, she appears to have been in large measure responsible for managing the Galway properties. In June 1662, she wrote to John from Clonoran of business and estate matters, the sale of oxen and wool, and problems with the sheriff – 'My opinion ... is that he is a knave'. But the outcome of his suit for restoration was of equal importance; the sales, she hoped, 'will make another hundred pounds, so that your business cannot starve for want of monies'.[75] She also assisted her husband's patron: one payment recorded in Bellew's account was 'to such as I was engaged unto for his lordship's occasions when I went to England and to herself [Mary] when she followed his lordship's business in Dublin by my direction'.

Bellew's efforts on behalf of Taaffe in England in 1667, while the latter went to Vienna as the English ambassador, did not go unnoticed by Charles. In a communication to Ormond concerning Taaffe's lands, he directed that 'at the request of the Earl and of John Bellew, who has been in attendance on us concerning matters relating to his lordship ... Bellew suffer nothing in respect of his claim during the time of his attendance here'.[76]

This service resulted in an apparent bargain between Bellew and Taaffe:[77] with little hope of being heard by the first Court of Claims, Bellew seems to have permitted the lands in Louth apportioned to him by his petition to Charles incorporated into Taaffe's Louth property which had been awarded to him by the Courts (a measure in and of itself of Bellew's success on his patron's behalf). In 1671, Taaffe then conveyed to Bellew Barmeath, Graftonstown, and other lands in county Louth. Bellew never regained Lisrenny and some of his other former lands, but Willistown was his again, and Barmeath would henceforth be the seat of the Bellew holdings in Louth. As for the Galway properties,

Taaffe at one point sought the aid of the earl of Orrery in seeking a good title for Bellew. Firm title to the properties would not come, however, until the end of the decade. A commission had been appointed in 1676 to review titles to lands apportioned by the Commonwealth to transplanters; ultimately letters patent were granted to John Bellew and his eldest son and heir Patrick in 1677 and 1678.

John Bellew's will, dated 17 February 1672, bequeathed his lands in both Louth and Galway to Patrick, with one exception to be discussed shortly. The Galway lands had been expanded since Bellew's entry in the 1650s, apparently added to by purchase or lease. An acquisition of interest is illustrated in articles of agreement between John Bellew and his friend John Hadsor of Capoge, county Louth, drawn up in 1657. Hadsor, 'through disability', was unable to transplant on the date decreed, and Bellew was to serve as his agent in Galway. Hadsor conveyed 40 acres of land to Bellew from 'such land as the said John Hadsor shall or is to obtain...in order to his decree according unto and as lands have hitherto been usually given out unto transplanted persons by the Commission of Transplantation sitting at Loughrea'. In return, Bellew was to 'find out for the said John Hadsor his heirs or assignees 400 acres' from the lands given him as part of his transplantation decree.[78]

By the time Patrick Bellew came into his inheritance on his father's death in 1679, the Bellew estates in county Galway consisted of some 2,520 acres, the majority in the baronies of Tiaquin and Killian, with smaller holdings in Ballymoe and Dunkellin baronies, all in the eastern part of the county. There were also small, scattered Bellew holdings in Kilmaine barony, county Mayo and Moycarnan barony, county Roscommon.[79] The senior branch of John Bellew's descendants through his son Patrick would reside at Barmeath in county Louth with the seat of their Galway holdings at Clonoran or Clonoranoughter; it would come to be known as Castle Bellew.[80]

Nonetheless, a cadet line through his third son Christopher would continue to reside in Galway and establish a seat there. In John Bellew's will, a clause provides that

> Whereupon my going into England a while since I left an authority with my said wife to prefer my said son Christopher Bellew who was much in my thoughts for his attendance and care of my concerns on all occasions, and what she should engage or do in my behalf I would make good the same and therefore and in persuance thereof I do now hereby ... give, grant, demise, and confirm unto him the said Christopher ... the towns and lands of both the Corgarrowes with the mills and all other their appurtenances.

Whatever the circumstances behind this bequest to an apparently favorite third son (presumably for the services rendered both Taaffe and Mary Bellew), a lease was passed for 1,000 years by John Bellew to Sir Nicholas Plunkett of Dublin and Nicholas Bellew of Barmeath in trust for Christopher. This 'savings' was also recorded in the letters patent issued in 1678.[81]

Christopher was henceforth referred to as Christopher Bellew of Corgarrowes, and he added to his holdings in county Galway. Besides the 133 acres of the Corgarrowes,[82] he had 34 acres in Liscloonemeltog and 31 in Treanreagh, all in Moylough parish, Tiaquin barony. By the late 1680s he had established himself in what would come to be known as Mount Bellew[83] and acquired lands which he would pass on to his Galway descendants.

While the Bellews had been notably successful in weathering the Interregnum and the land settlement that followed, the hopes many Catholics had entertained at the Restoration had been for the most part unfulfilled. Despite Charles' good intentions, many of his supporters had recovered only a portion of their estates or none at all; despite his Catholic sympathies, Protestants continued to staff important civil and military positions.

However, the accession of the Catholic James II and the policies of his deputy Tyrconnell – including the installation of Catholics in the army, judiciary, and county administration – once again raised gentry hopes of regaining both their accustomed status and their lands. For the Bellew familes of Louth, it was a brief period of assumption of their former influence. John Bellew of Castletown, who had been knighted under Charles II, was created Baron Bellew of Duleek in 1686 and made a member of the Irish Privy Council; Patrick Bellew of Barmeath and Castle Bellew was made high sheriff of Louth in 1687 – the oath of supremacy was waived[84] – and created first Baronet of Barmeath in December of 1688.

After James' overthrow in England and his subsequent flight to Ireland, Patrick Bellew was also appointed commissioner for arranging monthly levies of £20,000 from Louth to support the royal army raised for the Stuart cause.[85] Lord Bellew was made Lord Lieutenant and Governor of the county of Louth early in 1689 and sat in the Jacobite Parliament which overturned the Acts of Settlement and Explanation.[86]

With the arrival of William in Ireland and the ensuing War of the Two Kings, however, the Bellew family was to share in the military misfortunes of the Stuarts once more. Bellews of Barmeath, Mount Bellew, and Duleek all served in King James' Irish army. Lord Bellew was commissioned colonel of a regiment of foot, part of the rapidly improvised army which took the field in the spring of 1689.[87] John Bellew, eldest son of Sir Patrick Bellew of Barmeath, held a brief commission in James' army, and Christopher Bellew of Mount

Bellew held the rank of captain in Colonel Oliver O'Gara's regiment of foot.[88]

It was the Bellew branch of Duleek, however, that suffered the most in the Stuart cause, in loss of both property and life. Lord Bellew's seat at Castle Bellew served as a staging area for the Jacobite army centering on Dundalk in June 1689. When the Stuart army moved south, it was then garrisoned by the Williamite commander Schomberg in September, after his landing in Ulster; 2,000 of Bellew's sheep were used for provisioning Schomberg's army and his orchard trees were cut down for fuel.[89] As to military losses, although Lord Bellew's brother Matthew of Rogerstown was killed at the Boyne, it was at Aughrim in 1691, a battle in which the Irish nobility and gentry suffered appalling losses, that the Duleek family was virtually decimated.

In command of his regiment of foot, Lord Duleek was wounded and taken prisoner; he died of his wounds the following January. His eldest son and successor, Walter, captain of a troop of horse in Tyrconnell's Regiment, fought to the war's conclusion; however, he died in 1694, also as a result of wounds suffered at Aughrim. His second son Richard, captain of a troop of dragoons in the earl of Limerick's regiment, became its commander at the age of twenty, after the death of Colonel Walter Nugent in the battle.[90]

The Williamite settlement of Ireland, after the Jacobite disaster at Aughrim and the final capitulations of Galway and Limerick, the remaining rebel strongholds in the west, was, in comparison with the Cromwellian settlement, relatively lenient. The stiff Irish resistance after the battle of the Boyne, marked by William's initial failure to take Limerick, led the king to fear a protracted campaign. His desire to free himself for action in Europe against Louis xiv resulted in favourable terms being offered by his commander Ginkel to the Irish who remained in rebellion after Aughrim. William's eagerness to negotiate was matched by the eagerness of many of the Catholic gentry to accept favourable terms for surrender. After the battles of the Boyne and Aughrim, hopes of recovering ancestral estates held out by the repeal of the Act of Settlement vanished, and were replaced by a desire to save as much of their lands as possible. An Irish peace party, comprised of those landowners whose titles to at least part of their estates had been confirmed by the Restoration land settlement and those who had purchased lands after it and thus been opposed to its repeal, entered into active negotiation with Ginkel.[91] Under the Articles of Galway and Limerick, submittees were promised retention of their estates – a promise for the most part kept – and many royal pardons were subsequently granted as well. The Bellews, under both the former and latter policies, were successful in keeping their estates.[92]

Lord Duleek was outlawed in February 1690 and his estates granted to

Viscount Sidney, but his successor Walter, in the garrison at Limerick, was within the Articles. By forgiving Sydney some £3400 received from the estates while in his possession, Walter was able to recover the lands, which were restored to his younger brother Richard on his succession to the barony.[93] Richard, who had taken advantage of the article in the Limerick treaty allowing those soldiers who wished passage to France, came back to Ireland, obtained a pardon, and, having conformed to the established religion, passed on the estates and title to his son.[94]

Sir Patrick Bellew was one of those affected by the repeal of the Acts of Settlement and Explanation. An undated petition by Bellew to the commissioners of the revenue states that he had lost more than 5,000 acres in Louth and Galway 'all which the old proprietors have entered upon during his being on his majesty's service in the north'.[95] Both Sir Patrick and his younger sons came within the articles of Limerick,[96] but his eldest son John, the heir to the Barmeath estates, had been outlawed. The Calendar of State Papers contains an entry concerning a warrant for the reversal of his outlawry, and the circumstances reflect the concern of the Catholic gentry, despite their adherence to the Stuart cause, to retain their lands when that cause appeared lost. The entry states that Bellew

> laid down his commission in the Irish army and has never since borne employment; in obediance to the declaration of August 1690, he quitted the Irish quarters, and lived peaceably in Dublin; in May, 1691, he was sent back by the Lords Justices to do a considerable piece of service to the government in the Irish quarters, but, contrary to promise, was outlawed during his absence, and at the same time was suspected by the enemy, and clapped into prison, where he remained till the battle of Aughrim.[97]

He was subsequently granted a pardon on 18 September 1693.[98]

A record of the royal pardons granted after the end of the war provides a fuller story: John Bellew 'was outlawed by his own consent to prevent the enemies having any suspicion of the services he was doing for their majesties in enemies quarters, and pardoned persuant to a promise made him by the government'.[99] The services were presumably to aid the Irish peace party in negotiations, and, it seems safe to assume, to ensure his entry into the Barmeath and Galway estates after the war's conclusion.

Captain Christopher Bellew of Mount Bellew shared in the success of his nephew John Bellew of Barmeath. Comprised within the articles of Limerick,[100] he retained his lands in Galway to be passed on to his son Michael.

The relatively secure position of the Bellews and gentry families like them in the aftermath of two seventeenth-century rebellions should not be underestimated in an assessment of their success in maintaining their estates in the eighteenth century. For it was the Cromwellian and Williamite confiscations that accounted for most of the massive decline in Catholic landownership, from an estimated 59 per cent of the land in 1641 to 14 per cent in 1703.[101] Catholic families, primarily those of Old English ancestry, who had kept their estates intact and unencumbered in this period would be better able to meet the challenge of future government policies, as confiscation ended and new means were devised to ensure that Catholics would never again regain a position of strength and influence. The chief of these would take the form of legislation designed to eliminate access to the traditional basis for political and social power – landholding.

'The Gavel, that Infernal Act': The Land, the Law and the Catholic Landed Gentry

If, as I have maintained, the restrictions on the ownership, rental, and transfer of land should be considered the keystone of the penal structure, it is necessary to examine at least the letter of the law before analyzing its impact on the Bellews. As will be seen, the penal laws concerning land tenure were indeed comprehensive.

The *Act to Prevent the Further Growth of Popery* of 1704 and subsequent legislation of 1709 sharply curtailed the freedom of Catholics to purchase, rent, and dispose of lands. The descent by entail of the lands of a Catholic to the eldest son was forbidden. Fee-simple lands were to be left equally to all sons, a procedure known as gavelkind, or as Sir Patrick Bellew referred to it, 'the gavel, that Infernal Act'.[1] If there were no sons, lands were to be left equally among the daughters. However, should the eldest son convert, the estate was entailed, and he became heir to it in its entirety. Settlements for younger Catholic children were not permitted except by the permission and direction of the Court of Chancery; even these, if allowed, were not to exceed one-third of the inheritance. Any younger son who conformed could compel his father to disclose, on oath, the value of his estate in Chancery. He could then obtain a portion such as the Court considered suitable for his maintenance. A wife, on conforming, could follow the same procedure and obtain a portion of the inheritance up to one-third of the estate, with full power to assign it.

A Catholic could not purchase lands free-hold, nor could he hold mortgages or judgments on them. He was not permitted to inherit lands from a Protestant; the inheritance was to pass to the nearest Protestant relative, debarring any closer Catholic heirs. Land might be leased by Catholics, but no leases beyond a period of 31 years were allowed. If the land produced a profit greater than one-third of the rent and he did not pay a proportional increase, his right in the land ceased. If a Catholic secretly purchased lands or had them purchased in trust, or violated the laws regarding their lease, a Protestant who discovered such an arrangement could be awarded the land or lease for the terms of the unlawful conveyance.

Further, no Catholic could be guardian to a child. If a Catholic heir was a minor at the death of his father, a Protestant guardian was to be appointed by the Lord Chancellor. This meant, in many cases, that the child would be brought up (indeed, the law directed that he be) in the Protestant faith.

As to the degree of both efficacy and enforcement of the penal laws regarding land, the evidence is mixed. Certainly, there was successful circumvention of the laws; otherwise, there would have been no Catholic gentry. Estates were reconveyed through a process called 'fine and recovery', although this was expressly invalidated by the legislation of 1709. Discovery by collusion was also practiced, for both leases and conveyances, in which a 'discoverer' was set up to take action to forestall a genuine discovery. Litigation, too, could be successful; indeed, growing numbers of Irish lawyers, many of them converts, specialized in tactics designed to protect Catholic landownership.[2] Examples can also be given of the compassion of the Court of Chancery towards Catholic landowners in adjudicating claims made against them by family members who had converted for the sole purpose of acquiring land.[3] On the other hand, there were instances in which Catholics did lose lands, surely with a chilling effect on those who retained them. Moreover, the prospect of lengthy and expensive litigation if ownership was challenged must have been daunting, regardless of the outcome.

The legislation described above remained, with one minor change,[4] in effect until 1778, when almost all of the limitations on rentals and inheritances were repealed. Catholics could henceforth, upon taking an oath of allegiance and a prescribed declaration, hold leases for 999 years (although they still could not purchase land freehold). Lands could be disposed of freely, estates could pass to eldest sons entailed, and no further provisions were made by Chancery to family members who conformed. Finally, in 1782, the last restrictions on land acquisition were eliminated when complete freedom to purchase lands was granted.

How effective had the penal laws restricting land tenure been in promoting conformity? It is of course impossible to enumerate conversions according to motive and it should be remembered that they could also be prompted by a desire to enter a profession such as law or to hold office. The political climate could also be an influence (the cases of conformity following the Jacobite threats of 1715 and 1745, for example). Nonetheless, a government official in the early 1780s saw the threat to estates posed by the legislation of 1704 and 1709 as instrumental in bringing about the conformity of many landed Catholics in the first quarter of the century.[5]

In Connacht, one might expect that the pressure of the laws was especially strong, simply because, as a result of the Cromwellian transplantation and the prior purchase of lands by Galway merchants, there were, by the eighteenth century, more Catholic landowners there than in any other part of Ireland. Through the course of the century, a significant number of these conformed. From 1703 to 1800, approximately 5,797 names of converts were enrolled in the Court of Chancery, and, as might be expected, where accurate county locations can be ascertained, most came from the west.[6]

Conversion to the Protestant faith was made for a variety of reasons: The son of Sir Walter Burke of county Galway conformed to strengthen his position in a lawsuit against his father. Robert Martin Dangan of Galway was suspected of Jacobitism in 1745 and, circumspectly, converted.[7] The operation of the penal laws concerning guardianship can be seen in the case of John Browne of Westport, county Mayo. His Catholic father died when John was sixteen; as heir, he was provided with Protestant guardians who brought him up in that faith and sent him to Oxford, 'that he may be secure from the insinuating attempts of his Popish kindred'.[8] Browne became the first earl of Altamont in 1771 and his heirs would be the nineteenth-century Protestant marquesses of Sligo.

Yet, the primary reason for conformity appears to have been the desire of an heir to keep an estate intact – or for a junior family member to obtain part of it for himself. The latter motive is illustrated in the history of the O'Conors, an old Irish family. Once 'kings of Connacht', with landholdings of an estimated 6,000 acres, they had been left after the Cromwellian confiscation with several hundred encumbered acres. Of the county Roscommon branch, Hugh O'Conor, younger brother of Charles O'Conor of Belanagare, conformed in 1756 and promptly filed a bill of discovery to obtain the land from his brother. Even though his claim had to take second place to that of a Protestant family with mortgages on a part of the inheritance, he still received some portion of a settlement; the O'Conor family, on the other hand, was left with the expenses of a lawsuit and further encumbrances on the estate.[9] DeLatocnaye, a Frenchman on a tour of Ireland in the 1790s, considered the desire for political office, but above all, the desire to keep their lands safe, to have been the chief factor that had motivated Catholics to convert. To emphasize the latter, he reported the story told him of the owner of the estate of Oranmore in county Galway, who decided to conform. When the former Catholic was asked by a Protestant clergyman what had led him to the faith, his answer was simple – 'Oranmore'.[10]

The number of Galway names on the convert rolls approaches 400, the highest county total. Of these, approximately 80 are styled as 'Mr.', 'Gent.', or 'Esq.'.[11] Included are some of the most prominent of the Bellews' neighbors in central and eastern county Galway: the Mahons of Castlegar, the Dillons of Clonbrock, the Dalys of Carrownekelly, and the Frenches of Monivea. Conformity must in many cases be related to particular family circumstances, but it sometimes reflects the cumulative effect of the vicissitudes endured by many Catholic landowners through the Cromwellian confiscations and the uncertainties of the period following the War of the Two Kings, capped by the penal laws of 1704 and 1709.

The histories of the Frenches of Monivea and the Dillons of Clonbrock provide good examples of the desire for security. The Frenches of Monivea were a branch of the French family of the town of Galway and were descended from Robuck French, the sixteenth-century mayor. Patrick French had purchased the castle of Monivea and other lands in the barony of Tiaquin in the first quarter of the seventeenth century. His grandson Patrick French, once MP from Galway, was deprived of Monivea in 1658 and transplanted to part of the earl of Clanrickard's estates; in turn Monivea was granted to Lord Trimleston, who had been transplanted to Galway from Meath. After the accession of Charles II, Clanricard's lands were returned to him, and French forced to leave. In the meantime, Lord Trimleston received a decree for reinstatement at Trim; however, the Cromwellian grantee in possession refused to leave until he was given an adequate reprisal elsewhere. It was not until 1676 that Patrick French was able to re-purchase the castle and lands of Monivea and begin the process of dislodging the Trimleston interest.[12] He died in 1701; his heir, his grandson Patrick, to safeguard the estate (and continue to practice as a barrister) conformed in 1709.[13]

The Dillons were one of the first Old English families to settle in Westmeath; their descendants moved into nearby counties, including Galway, where Thomas Dillon bought the castle of Clonbrock in the reign of Elizabeth. (The Clonbrock family were, as mentioned previously, relatives of the Bellews: John Bellew of Willistown had married Mary, daughter of Robert Dillon of Clonbrock, in 1634.) This branch of the Dillon family escaped the Cromwellian confiscation: Robert Dillon's son and heir Richard was declared an 'innocent Papist' capable of holding land.[14] However, Richard's heirs, Robert, then his son Luke, suffered through anxious moments in 1696 in the aftermath of the War of the Two Kings. Although the family was entitled to the articles of Limerick, they encountered some difficulties in maintaining their status – and possibly their lands – during the course of investigations into the estates of those in rebellion by commissions from the Courts of Chancery and the Exchequer. When Richard Dillon's greatgrandson Robert came into the estate in 1717, he would put any future uncertainties concerning Clonbrock to rest. Among the Dillon family papers are his sacramental certificate issued from the parish of St Nicholas in Dublin in 1725 and a copy of a confirmation certificate issued to Robert Dillon in the same year.[15]

SECURING THE LAND

Despite the various pressures placed on Catholic landed families to conform, there were many who resisted and kept their estates intact, the Bellews of Mount Bellew among them. How were the penal laws circumvented and the estate passed on? An inspection of the land transfers between three generations of Bellews reveals a combination of fortuitous circumstances which allowed them to do so successfully.

Of the Bellews' succession to the lands of Mount Bellew acquired by Christopher, the third son of John Bellew of Willistown, it is possible to trace every transfer that would have been affected by the penal laws save one. Christopher Bellew had the good fortune to have only one male heir, Michael. Thus, there were no legal impediments to his inheritance. The circumstances of the transfer of lands to Michael's son Christopher in the next generation are less definitive. Michael Bellew, who died in 1742, had married twice: his first marriage was into the Barnewall family, the second into the Kelly family of Mount Kelly.[16] He had a son and heir, Christopher, by his first wife, but appears to have had one other son, Dominick, by his second.[17] What arrangements, if any, made with this second son are not clear. Dominick had his seat at Mount Kelly, on the road from the village of Creggs to Tuam; he also had title to the approximately 250 acres of Cregane, or Barnewall's Grove, which was adjacent to the desmesne of Mount Bellew.[18]

Much more is known about the last land transfer, that from Christopher Bellew to his eldest son Michael, for an abstract of Christopher's Prerogative Will exists.[19] Dated 13 June 1769, it was proved 2 February 1770 by Michael as executor. Christopher Bellew had three other sons beside Michael; in such a case, the law required the lands to be gavelled. Bellew seems to have employed two stratagems to prevent this: First, there was an acknowledgment of the law in the will. As a modern legal scholar has noted, 'Articles in Catholic family settlements that bore on their face no trace of conflict with the philosophy of the gavelling clause might manage as before to pass muster'.[20] Second, the terms concerning his younger sons appear designed to discourage the possibility of their insisting on a portion of the estate.

There is no specific mention of the disposal of real estate (which obviously went to Michael), just the brief statement bequeathing 'to my eldest son Michael Bellew all my effects which I shall die possessed of'. Provisions were made for his wife Barbara and only daughter Julia: by a series of indentured deeds, Michael Bellew was to provide an annuity of £70 to his mother and a flat sum of £1000 for his sister. As for his three younger sons, Christopher Bellew, with the assistance again of his son Michael, paid them the following sums: to his second son Luke, £840; to his third son Patrick, £430; and to his fourth son Francis, £430 – a total of £1800. What then follows would appear to be the negative incentive by which he hoped to keep the estate intact: 'I direct that in case any of my younger sons shall set up a right to gavel my said real estate, that in such case the said sum of £1800 to be paid to them shall be charged upon and shall be raised out of my said real estate'. Likewise, in case of an attempt to have the estate gavelled, his daughter Julia's £1000 settlement was also to be taken from the real estate.

In these terms, it may be possible to see the implicit threat of encumbering, and lessening the value of, the estate if a challenge was made by a younger son. At the very least, it presented, for that younger son who might consider claiming his right to a portion, the prospect of possible and uncertain litigation (not to mention familial discord) rather than the certainty of assured payments. Whatever the intent, the inheritance remained intact. Michael Bellew entered into possession; his younger brothers used their settlements to establish themselves in mercantile careers.

The success of the Bellews in preserving their lands was due, in some measure, to good fortune: there was a single male heir in the first two generations to be affected by the legislation of 1704 and 1709, so prominent in the conformity of Catholics with significant estates, and no challenge by a younger son in the third. Their success should also be placed in a regional context, as eighteenth-century Galway provided perhaps the most favourable conditions for Catholic landed families in Ireland.

On the one hand, the concentration of Catholics ensured occasional governmental scrutiny, particularly when invasion from France threatened. As well, there were a number of Protestant families – the Gores, Trenches, and Eyres – who had settled in the sixteenth and seventeenth centuries and could be counted on to maintain the Protestant interest. In particular, Colonel Stratford Eyre, whose father had been governor of Galway in 1715, was sent to govern Galway in 1747 and served as an aggressive Protestant watchdog for some years after, informing Dublin Castle, in tones best described as cranky, of Catholic affairs and influence.[21]

Nevertheless, the willingness of Protestant neighbours and family members who had converted to hold lands in trust, and the general protection afforded by recent convert families to their collateral branches who remained Catholic, were key factors in sustaining a Catholic gentry. Thus the Burkes of Creggeen, despite their official forfeiture under Cromwell, remained in possession of their lands through the protection of the Masons of Masonbrook. John Burke, profiting from the provisions trade in the 1770s, built a new house, improved the lands, and gave a new name to Creggeen, Marble Hill.[22] The

conformity of the Dalys of Carrownekelly and the Frenches of Monivea shel-
tered such Catholic branches as the Dalys of Dalysgrove and the Frenches of
Castlefrench. For example, James Daly of Carrownekelly, who had conformed
in 1729, led the opposition to Stratford Eyre in Galway;[23] both the Frenches
and the Dalys would assist the Catholic political cause as it developed through
the course of the century. Collusive bills of discovery filed by Protestant family members and timely conformities (and then reversion to Catholicism) shel-
tered the Galway estates of the Tower Hill Blakes.[24] Indeed, for many of these
gentry families of Galway who remained Catholic, the greatest threat posed by
the penal laws at the time of land transfers was perhaps not from without, that
is, a genuine Protestant discoverer, but from within – the discontented younger
son.

Nonetheless, the penal laws were a fact of Catholic life, and their effect can
be observed in a wide range of other matters concerning landownership and
rental. Two examples in particular are indicative of both the complexity of
land dealings and the potential for family division occasioned by their structure.

The first is Michael Bellew's acquisition of the Dillon lands of Kinclare
and Lisnagree, an estate of some 1,000 acres to the southeast of Mount Bellew.[25]
These lands, originally granted to John Bellew of Willistown, had been placed
in trust for Thomas Dillon, a member of the Clonbrock family, in 1677.[26] By
the eighteenth century, Henry Dillon was in possession of the lands. He had
two daughters, but no immediate male heirs. One daughter, Sibby Mary, married Andrew French of Rahoon, county Galway; the other, Jane, married Michael
Bellew in 1760. Under the terms of the penal laws, the estate would pass equally
to both.

There were, however, several complicating factors: Henry Dillon had a
cousin german, Gerald Dillon of Dublin, who had a claim to part of the estate,
dating back to John Bellew of Willistown's setting aside of 45 acres to Dillon's
ancestor Garrett in accordance with Dillon's marriage articles.[27] Moreover,
there was some question as to the religion of Gerald Dillon's father and hence,
the religion of Gerald himself.[28] If he was, or if it could be proved that he was,
Protestant, the entire estate would pass to him. Henry Dillon further wished to
keep his estate intact, and, if he married again, there was the possibility of a
male heir of his own. Finally, although he had given his consent to his daughter
Sibby's marriage to Andrew French, if the Bellews' side of the story is to be
believed, the marriage was 'much against the inclination of her father'. Dillon's
draft will of February 1763 appears to reflect these concerns. Despite a later
claim by Andrew French that Henry Dillon had intended to use 'fine and recovery' to bar Gerald Dillon and pass the estate to his daughters and their
children, he did not devise his real property to his daughters, only his personal

fortune of £2600–£1300 to each. In 1763, his assumption, which is borne out by Michael Bellew's later summary of the case, seems to have been that the estate would pass to his cousin, with encumbrances for his daughters.

The likelihood of the estate passing to this male heir, if Henry Dillon died without male issue, was a source of concern to both Andrew French and Michael Bellew. They recognized Dillon's desire to entail the estate, but were relieved that he was willing to encumber it; nonetheless, as Andrew French warned, 'he ought not by doing so to endanger the religion of his children or remainder' – a clear reference to the temptation offered to his children of inheriting far more with a change of religion.

Meanwhile, whatever the resolution of the question of Gerald Dillon's religious affiliation, Andrew French and Michael Bellew must have thought his case was not a strong one. The brothers-in-law began lengthy litigation against his claim to reversion to the estate if Henry Dillon died without a direct male heir. In 1774, Gerald Dillon agreed to a compromise to save further legal expense. French and Bellew agreed to secure to him the sum of £1000 payable on the death of Henry Dillon with interest during his lifetime; each took out bonds of £500. This settlement met with the approval of Henry Dillon, who seems to have been concerned to make some provision for his cousin. It also secured at least a portion of the Dillon estate for the wives of French and Bellew, although, as they knew, there was always the chance Henry Dillon might marry again. Nonetheless, it was an artificial settlement at best, since it sidestepped the delicate issue of Henry Dillon's apparent antipathy toward Andrew French and his obvious desire to keep his lands intact. Indeed, he 'often lamented that one moiety of his estate must descend to them [his daughters] (as the laws then stood, the parties being all Roman Catholic) ...'

The settlement was, in fact, a gamble – one that Michael Bellew won and Andrew French lost. French's wife and two daughters died in Henry Dillon's lifetime, and his attempts to get additional money from Dillon and assistance in paying Gerald Dillon the interest on his bond were unsuccessful. Moreover, in 1778, the penal laws that required Dillon's estate to pass equally to Catholic heirs were repealed. Henry Dillon changed his will and bequeathed the entire estate of Kinclare to his son-in-law Michael Bellew, touching off recriminations from Andrew French that lasted well after Bellew's death.

A second example of the effect of the penal laws concerns the lands of Bovinion and Treanrevagh, a property of some 350 acres to the east of Mount Bellew; in this case, the laws would entangle both Louth and Galway branches of the Bellews.[29] The land had originally been granted to a member of a collateral branch of the seventeenth-century Bellew families of Louth and Meath, Roger Bellew of Thomastown, who had been transplanted to Connacht. He regained possession of the Thomastown properties, only to lose the fee simple ownership again after 1690, despite being comprised in the articles of Limerick. Nonetheless, he retained a rent charge out of the property. Roger Bellew died in 1701, and his sons died without issue. Roger's will directed, in that case, that his interests in Louth and Galway pass to his daughters, Ursula and Mary, provided they marry a Bellew. If they did not, they were to be paid £200 apiece from John Bellew of Castlebellew (later second baronet of Barmeath), who was left in reversion of the estate. Ursula died without issue and Mary married a man named Fleming, by whom she had a daughter, Mary, who married Philemon McCartan of county Down in 1720. John Bellew, thinking that the will might have given Roger's daughters and their issue the estate, despite the conditional limitation, persuaded Mary and Philemon McCartan to sign a deed in which they confirmed the remainder to him, and at the same time, accepted an estate for life only in lieu of what they might get from a reinterpretation of the will. John's heir, Sir Edward Bellew, sought legal counsel in 1735 to determine how the penal laws might affect this complex inheritance.

His concerns were two, since all parties were Catholic: First, if the deed of 1734 was 'discoverable by the Popery acts', that is, whether any greater estate had passed to John Bellew by deed than was limited to him by a will made before the acts. Second, whether Edward Bellew, if he were to sell his interest, could take an assignment of turnpike security 'as a purchase for the same, being a Roman Catholic'. The attorney's opinion as to the first concern was that, since John Bellew did not acquire any *new* estate by the deed, there was no foundation for a discovery. As for the second, he was advised not to take the turnpike security, rather, 'it would be prudent in a Protestant purchaser under Sir Edward Bellew to procure a fine [a sum payable on conveyance] from McCartan and his wife'. A resolution of the issue, at least as far as the Louth interest, appears to have been reached by an agreement that granted McCartan part of it, which he disposed of in 1736. The Bovinion property in Galway passed to Ursula, apparently the daughter of Mary McCartan. She married James Savage, by whom she had a single son Philip. When Savage died, she remarried, to William Strafford, by whom she had another son, Nicholas.

The Bellews of Mount Bellew had, in the meantime, acquired a long-term interest in the nearby property. A lease, originally a mortgage, was taken on parts of Bovinion and Treanrevagh by Michael Bellew's greatgrandfather Christopher in 1699, by his grandfather Michael, and his father Christopher in 1749. The latter lease was apparently for 31 years, the maximum allowable under the penal laws of the time, for in 1780, Michael Bellew renewed the lease from Ursula and William Strafford.[30] Ironically, the effects of the penal laws were soon to complicate Michael Bellew's interest in the lands, even though those provisions affecting the bulk of land transfers had been repealed some two years earlier. At some point in the 1760s, Ursula Strafford apparently wished to see her interest in Bovinion and Treanrevagh descend to her son by her second marriage, Nicholas Strafford. She threatened to bring Nicholas up as a Protestant, cutting out Philip Savage, her son by her first marriage. Philip responded in 1763 by conforming himself and, in 1781, disposed of his interest in the land outright to Michael Bellew.

What then ensued was a lengthy squabble between Savage, the Straffords, Michael Bellew, and his heir Christopher Dillon Bellew. At one point, the Catholic Bellews, contesting their co-religionists, the Straffords, found themselves in the position of enlisting legal counsel to establish the Protestantism of Philip Savage, since the roll of 1763 on which Savage had signed his name as a Protestant convert was thought to have been lost.[31] A final settlement between the contesting parties was delayed until the early nineteenth century, when Christopher Dillon Bellew bought the property.

It was obviously possible, for the Bellews and others, to emerge from the period in which the penal laws were in effect relatively unscathed. The Bellews' lands were passed on successfully, although their acquisition and rental of lands was complicated by the law. Their Protestant neighbors were at the least noninterfering, at the most, sympathetic. Some brief references in the family correspondence show how helpful they could be in overcoming the obstacles posed by the penal laws in obtaining leases. In 1769, before their falling-out over the Dillon estates, Michael Bellew and Andrew French were interested in obtaining a lease on some property. While little detail of the land or its owner is given, the method proposed of renting it is worthy of note. Concerning Bellew's upcoming meeting with a Mr Falkiner, French wrote:

> ... let him know that I will make him a genteel present to serve me with Mr. Whalley who I am told is in a dying way, there's no time to be lost, and if you find that he can settle or get a lease, I will get a Protestant friend to take one for me, or you may find out one ...[32]

The practice of obtaining a 'Protestant friend' or even hiring one as a professional discoverer to facilitate land conveyancing was not uncommon,[33] as seen in the dealings of Edward Bellew with the McCartans. It may also be referred to in letters of 1772 from Edmond Taaffe to Michael Bellew, his brother-in-law. When the latter was interested in obtaining an interest in Dillon lands in Mayo, Taaffe referred to 'the Bill of Discovery necessary to be [filed?] against the purchase' and a 'Bill of Discovery or any method that would better secure the purchase' of a lease.[34]

Despite all of these factors, however, a review of the family correspond-ence leads to the conclusion that the mere presence of the penal laws was oppressive. The laws could be circumvented; nonetheless, they had to be taken into consideration in each and every transaction involving the land – the basis of their economic and social status. The essential point is that the penal laws did not force the Bellews to dismember their estates, nor did they force them to conform, but they did force them into technically illegal actions and complex litigation. The time-consuming, expensive machinations involved must surely have been not only annoying, but psychologically draining: references to the laws in letters between family members are often couched in tones of frustra-tion and despair that the penal structure would ever be changed. Such refer-ences should serve as a reminder that a discriminatory legal system can have a far greater impact than that of the material penalties imposed on those who violate it.

PROFITING FROM THE LAND

The estate of Mount Bellew expanded significantly during the eighteenth-cen-tury; by 1800, it approached 10,000 acres.[35] There is no specific indication of its total acreage in the early 1700s, only references to particular pieces of land. However, judging from maps and leases,[36] the estate, originating in the Corgarrowes grant to Christopher Bellew, expanded to the northeast, south, and east (the lands directly to the west were those of the Louth Bellews). These records would seem to indicate a landed interest of at least 1,000+ acres by mid-century. It should also be remembered that such an interest could be com-prised of more than just land in fee simple, particularly for Catholics after the prohibitions imposed by the penal laws on land purchase. The Bellew estate records show a complicated pattern of leasehold lands and purchases of lease-hold interests. Bellews in Galway rented from each other, from collateral fam-ily branches (for example, the Straffords in Bovinion), and from local families such as the Dillons and Mahons. For example, in the 1730s, Christopher Bellew, Michael's father, held 203 acres from the Mahons at a yearly rent of £78 13s. 3d. and in the 1740s, 184 acres from one of the properties of the Bellews of Barmeath at a bargain rent of £23 11s.[37]

Major acquisitions were made by Michael Bellew shortly after the repeal of the penal laws restricting the purchase and inheritance of lands in 1778 and 1782. His inheritance of the Kinclare estate of his father-in-law Henry Dillon in 1782 brought him approximately 1,000 acres.[38] Moreover, if a reference by a relative in a letter of 1783 is accurate, Bellew also purchased some £7,000

worth of lands at about the same time.[39] In August of 1786, he made his largest
acquisition: the Galway lands of Sir Patrick Bellew of Barmeath, county Louth.
The lands of Castle Bellew were those of John Bellew's original Galway estate
built up after his transplantation and handed down to his eldest son Patrick, Sir
Patrick Bellew's greatgrandfather. The estate, adjacent to Mount Bellew, was
approximately 2400 acres with an estimated rental value of over £2,000 yearly.[40]
Michael Bellew, with the assistance of his eldest son Christopher Dillon, paid
£23,000 for the land and an additional £10,600 in further consideration to Sir
Patrick.[41] He would make further land purchases in Caltra in the 1790s.

With Michael Bellew's acquisitions, Mount Bellew was now a substantial
estate. His son Christopher Dillon was referred to in 1793 as the heir to £5,000
a year;[42] he would be the future possessor of lands extending from Moylough
in the north to beyond Caltra in the southeast (Figure 2). Thus it can be seen
that the lands of Mount Bellew provided their eighteenth-century owners with
considerable status in county Galway as well as an income, one supplemented
by commercial activities,[43] that enabled Michael Bellew to embark on his ambitious program of expansion after 1782.[44]

The uses to which the Bellews' land was put were dictated, obviously, by
climate and topography. Land usage was also influenced by equally important
external factors: the inevitable dominance of England as a market for Irish
products and Ireland's favourable position for trans-Atlantic trade.

The area of eastern Galway in which the Bellews had their holdings is part
of the extensive central lowlands of Ireland. In contrast to the barren, stony soil
to the west, the soil in the east is relatively fertile and was usually regarded by
contemporaries as among the better in county Galway. John Wesley, on one of
his frequent proselytizing visits to Ireland in 1756, was favourably impressed
by the area:

> We took horse about ten, and rode through the fruitful and pleasant county
> of Galway. After having heard so much of the barrenness of this county I
> was surprised, in riding almost the whole length of it, from south-east to
> north-west, to find only four or five miles of rocky ground, like the west
> of Cornwall; all the rest exceeded most that I have seen in Ireland.[45]

The duke of Rutland, Lord Lieutenant of Ireland from 1784 to 1787, had
much the same observations after his tour through the northwest in 1787:

> The whole county is flat, but the land is good, and it produces greater
> quantities of cattle than any other county ... [from Tuam and Loughrea]
> the country remains good all the way to Ballinasloe.[46]

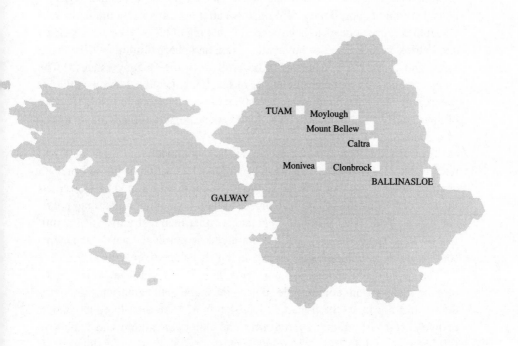

Figure 2: Bellew Estate, *c*.1793

The limestone soil of the region provided for good grassland and hence good grazing lands; even where the stratum of limestone was so near to the surface as to make areas unsuitable for tillage, the land still provided excellent pasture.[47] Moreover, the mild, wet climate allowed the pasturing of cattle and sheep out-of-doors all year round. The raising of livestock in these near-ideal conditions was a key – and traditional – element in the economy. A major consideration of John Bellew of Willistown after his transplantation in the seventeenth century appears to have been the stocking of his new lands. His eldest son Patrick was directed to buy cattle, oxen, and sheep – some 100 lambs, 2 rams, and 2 ewes – in Munster to be brought to the Galway estates.[48] The eighteenth-century Bellews of Galway raised, bought, and sold both cattle and sheep, and their participation and investment in the livestock industry, like that of their gentry neighbors, was on a significant scale, providing a major source of income.

The Irish livestock industry, as well as the manufacture of its products, had been influenced in a variety of ways by English legislation of the seventeenth century, notably the Woollen and Cattle Acts. These acts should be viewed, as modern economic historians have urged, in their economic, rather than political, aspect. They were primarily regulatory rather than restrictive; their result was to shape segments of the Irish economy to first protect, then, by the eighteenth century, to complement the expanding British economy.

The seventeenth century statutes concerning sheep and wool would structure the trade in both commodities during the eighteenth century towards production for a primary Irish market. Legislation of 1666 prohibited the export of live sheep to England; shortly after, the export of mutton and lamb was forbidden as well. In 1699, as a result of pressure from the woollen interests of the southwest, the export of wool and woollen manufactures to any country save England was prohibited; even this trade was dampened by heavy import duties on Irish woollen cloth. However, impetus was given to the production of woollen yarn when English import duties were repealed in 1739, and from the 1740s, much Irish wool was spun into yarn for this English market.[49] Repeal of the Woollen Act came in 1799, but by then it was difficult for Irish woollens to compete, either in labour costs or quality, with those produced in England, and little was exported. By the 1790s, even the export of woollen yarn had dropped precipitously.[50] Nevertheless, the industry in Ireland continued to expand, with an increase in domestic use of woollen products by a rising population; in 1776, Arthur Young noted the higher prices wool commanded in Ireland as compared with those in England.[51]

As for sheep, the prohibition of their export, as well as that of mutton and lamb, was ended in 1759. Some sheep were raised for an English market, but the trade in general would not assume the proportion of that in beef (mutton was unsuited for the provisions trade). The Irish market for mutton was primarily in Dublin; little was consumed in the country. Only from the mid-1780s, would raising sheep for mutton become more important.[52]

Thus, for most of the eighteenth century, sheep were raised primarily for their wool, and woven woollen cloth was produced for an almost exclusively Irish market. Galway, Clare, and Roscommon were the chief sheepbreeding and grazing areas, but the fattening of the animals took place in the eastern regions of these counties, especially in Roscommon. Sheep constituted the principal stock in many areas of central and eastern Galway, and within the county itself, there was a similar pattern for 'finishing' the sheep. In central Galway, winter farms were maintained; for summer feeding and fattening, the sheep were taken to the richer lands in the eastern part of the county. There, landlords rented tracts of land to graziers, but also kept flocks themselves. For example, Frederick Trench of Woodlawn had a flock of 930.[53] To the north, the Bellews also had herds of sheep on their estates; part of Michael Bellew's property, acquired from his father-in-law Henry Dillon, was known as the sheepwalk of Kinclare.

Bellew family accounts record sales of sheep and the proceeds, and letters from relatives and friends reflect the importance of the sales in estate economy. The prime sheep were raised and sold for breeding purposes; wethers too were fattened, then sold. A section of an account book from 7 May 1777 lists buyers, mainly Galway neighbours, and the proceeds:[54]

Ewes	Lambs	Price	Buyers	Security	£ s. d.
50	50	@12s.11d.	Bart & Coll Dillon	- - - -	32. 5.10
50	50	@12s.	Mr Edmond Moore	Garrett Moore, Esq.	30
50	Hoggrells [2 or 3 year-olds]	@ 9s.	John Bodkin, Esq.	ready money	22. 10
40	Do.	@ 7s.	Corns.O'Kelly	Garrett Moore,	14. 0
6	old wedders [wethers]	@ 7s. 6d.	Mr Will Dillon	ready money	2. 5

Total proceeds from the complete list were £442.6s.7d.

The figures bear out the description of the system of grazing and the price structure given to Arthur Young by Robert French of Monivea and Frederick Trench of Woodlawn in 1776: Yearlings were bought for 35s. to £3 3s. and sold at 4 years old for £4 4s.–£6 6s.; sometimes they were sold at 3 years old, wethers of that age going for 15–25s. each. Culled ewes sold at approximately 15s. each.[55] The account books do not indicate the Bellew flock totals, but sales records from 1777 and other years, show numbers ranging from 800–900 head.

Sales were conducted at fairs throughout Connacht. Michael Bellew's brother-in-law Edmond Taaffe of Woodfield, county Mayo sold a number of his sheep at the fair at Castle Plunkett, county Roscommon;[56] in Galway, the main fair was in May and October at Ballinasloe, some sixteen miles from Mount Bellew. There both local buyers and graziers from Meath and Leinster bid on stock.[57]

The strain of the native Irish sheep remained pure during most of the eighteenth century; there was little interbreeding before the introduction of Leicester rams in the early nineteenth century, although Arthur Young mentions the efforts of Mr Gore of Ballina, county Mayo to import rams from England.[58] Hely Dutton's survey of Galway, published in 1824, provides a description of the native Connacht sheep:

> I was not a little surprised at seeing such multitudes of thick legs, booted with coarse wool down to their heels, and such a bushy wig of coarse wool on their heads, that you could scarcely perceive their eyes; at present they have nearly all disappeared ...[59]

As evident from this description, the Irish sheep produced wool in quantity; the fleece weighed 4–5 pounds. Its annual value in the third quarter of the eighteenth century was between 25–50 per cent of that of the sheep itself.[60]

The wool was marketed at fairs; in Galway, the central fair was at Ballinasloe in July of each year. Both the Bellews and their tenants sold fleeces there. In 1788, a year in which demand was slack, bags were selling at 16–17s.[61] The wool was bought, then combed, and sent out to country people to spin. The Ballinasloe fair supplied many of the spinners in county Cork, and the increased demand for wool from the market in the 1770s resulted in a rise in sales. There were also shipments of wool to Dublin, the center of the manufacture of 'old drapery', a coarser, heavier cloth than the newer worsteds.[62] The Bellews engaged in this trade as well; Patrick Bellew, Michael Bellew's merchant brother in Dublin, referred in his correspondence to such shipments. They were not without their occasional problems, presumably the work of larcenous carmen. In 1788, he remarked that a bag had been 'dishonestly made up' with 'wet sand stuffed within a hand of the wool', to make the required weight.[63]

The other component of the Irish livestock industry, one far more historically important in the Irish economy, particularly in export trade, was that of cattle-raising. This too was affected by regulatory English legislation, which determined its structure from the first three-quarters of the eighteenth century. The export of Irish cattle to England for fattening and slaughter had been a rapidly growing trade; by mid-seventeenth century, it was one of considerable magnitude in both volume and value. Protests by English breeders, however, resulted in, first, prohibitive import duties in 1664, then the total ban on the import of cattle and beef from Ireland in the Cattle Act of 1667. Cut off from its primary market, the Irish cattle industry then oriented itself to the development of a provisions trade in salt beef with the continent and European colonies in America, a trade that would become extremely lucrative in the first half of the eighteenth century. Growing demand from England for cattle products resulted in the suspension of the prohibition on cattle in 1758 and that on beef in 1759, and finally its repeal in 1776. In the last quarter of the eighteenth century, Irish exports of both live cattle and beef to England grew rapidly, and the trade resumed its normal channels.[64]

The chief grazing and fattening counties in Ireland were Meath, Westmeath, and Tipperary in the east, and Roscommon, Mayo, Galway, and Limerick in the west. Of the latter area, Galway and Roscommon were reputed to produce the best stock of cattle in Ireland. In the eighteenth century, the breed was almost entirely long-horned, whether from native Irish stock or from interbreeding with Bakewells from England, of considerable size and hardy. The Connacht stock was described by an observer in 1812 as excellent and 'fully equal to any in England'.[65]

The most important cattle market in the west was at Ballinasloe. In October, fat cattle of four years were sold for slaughter in Limerick or Cork, the centers of the provisions trade, or for transport to the Dublin market. In May, stocks of younger lean cattle were put up for purchase by local graziers who would sell them later or by graziers from Tipperary and Meath for fattening in Leinster before their slaughter in Dublin or their live shipment to Liverpool and the English market.[66] In the 1770s, yearlings brought from 30 to 50s., two year-olds from 55 to 60s. Fatter three year-olds were sold at an increase of 40s. and four year-olds were sold from £5–6.[67]

The rising prices of cattle from the second quarter of the eighteenth century onward made investment in livestock farming increasingly profitable; in 1763, an estimate of the personal estate of Ross Mahon of Castlegar included not only sheep valued at £2,500 but cattle herds at £2,400.[68] Although sheep constituted their principal stock, most of the landlords of eastern Galway – among them, the Eyres and Trenches, as well as the Mahons – supplemented their incomes with cattle sales, mostly at Ballinasloe, although other, smaller fairs provided outlets as well. For example, the Bellews raised some cattle for sales at fairs in Castle Plunkett, county Roscommon and Castle Blakeney and Dunmore in Galway, as well as Ballinasloe. A list of 'black cattle' from January of 1767 shows some of the estate stock and its value, as well as cattle marked for sale at fairs in May, probably at Ballinasloe.[69] The list is an interesting illustration of both the increase in cattle prices from the 1760s to those of the 1770s noted above, and the kind of stock kept on landed estates:

13 milch cows at 4:11	60. 5. 9
20 in-calf heifers at 4:11	91. 0. 0
3 heifers 3-year-old at 2.8.3	10. 4. 9
4 Do. 2-year-old at 2:10	10. 0. 0
3 bulls	14.15. 9
6 plow bullocks at 6:10	39
13 4-year-old bullocks at May @5	65
18 2-year-old Do. at May at 2:15	49.10. 0
3 fat cows - one of which I'll keep till May @	5.13. 9
8 yearlings at May @2:5:6	18. 4. 0
	£363.14. 0

The Bellew livestock accounts also include, indicative of the growing interest in animal husbandry and improvement (albeit through primitive means), an 'infalliable cure for the disorder in horned cattle called the Big Gall' taken from the *Connaught Mercury* of May 1769. Reputed to be efficacious for the 'black rot' in sheep as well, it consisted of dissolving half an ounce of Castile soap in a quart of water, 'the beast being drenched therewith 4 days successively completes a cure'.

Despite the importance of the livestock industry in eastern Galway, in terms of sales and leases to graziers, rents from agricultural lands remained a considerable part of landlords' incomes: indeed, ownership and rentals of such land defined them as a class, socially as well as economically. From mid-century on, these rents began to rise. Arthur Young concluded, from the data gathered on his tour in 1776, that rents had doubled in the past twenty-five years.[70] Generalizations for rent increases in Galway must of course be tentative; however, what figures are available from estate records tend to support Young's estimation. The rentals for the Galway estates of the Dillons of Clonbrook show substantial increases. In 1735, rents are 4s.6 to 10s. per acre with a total income of £1,737.14s.7½d. In 1767, rents are 4s. to 12s. per acre with a total of £2,083.15s.4½d. By 1780, rents have risen to 10s. to 22s.9d. per acre, with a gross rental income of £3,154.5s.8d.[71] The rent books of Robert French of Monivea record a total income of £867 in 1749; by 1774, rental income stood at £2,060.[72] The rent rolls for Castle Bellew, the estate of Sir Patrick Bellew, reflect similar increases. By comparing a list of the rents from 1746–47; a calculation of rents in 1775 by Michael Bellew, serving as Sir Patrick's agent; and a rental book for 1784 kept by Michael, it is possible to trace increases for five specific pieces of property that appear in all three reckonings:

	1747	1784
Carrownaboe	£47. 0. 0	£72. 0. 0
Lower Clonoran	£58.11. 6	£128
Tenants of Lissmoyle	£26	£76.16
Killoscobe	£11. 5	£46
Carrownacreggy – 2 pts	£23.11	£64.10
	£166. 7. 6	£315. 6. 0

The rental book for 1784 lists the total rental of Castle Bellew farms as £1629.10s.11d., and Michael Bellew also noted estimated rental increases from 1–45s., commenting 'the above rises may be reasonably expected according to the past times'.[73] From the 1780s onward, rents would go even higher, first, from the competition for land prompted by population growth, and then, from the upward spiral of corn prices resulting from the wars with France. For example, the half-yearly rental of the Mahon estates in Galway in 1788 was £915. 4s. 2d.; by 1823, it was £2,584. 11s. 11½d.[74]

Even if the war-time inflation at the end of the century is discounted, rental increases for the period previous could easily be taken as evidence of landlord rapacity. Yet, these rent increases were part of a general trend in the period; English rents appear to have risen at corresponding rates. Moreover, prices of agricultural products increased throughout the period as well.[75] Perhaps a more important point to be considered is what lordlords did with their expanded incomes. If Irish landlords had earlier been hampered in their efforts at agricultural improvement and land reclamation because of a shortage of the initial capital required, as has been suggested, an increase in rent was one way of attacking the problem.[76] There is considerable evidence that at least some landowners in Galway used the income from their expanded rent rolls to engage in such activities on their estates. Another factor that enabled them to do so was a trend toward granting shorter leases, permitting a more direct role in land management and the local economy.[77]

IMPROVING THE LAND

One important area of improvement in Galway was bog reclamation. Because of the moist climate and low relief of the land, drainage is often poor, resulting in the formation of peat bogs; indeed, the topography has been described as a mosaic of grassland and bog. Reclamation of these boggy areas was a prime concern, since the peat often lay on potentially fertile soil.[78] Arthur Young recorded with approval the procedures employed by Robert French of Monivea and Frederick Trench of Woodlawn: After an arduous process of draining and trenching, the surface was covered with limestone gravel; coats of manure or marle were then applied, and potatoes planted or cereals or grass seed sown. (French's efforts in reclaiming a bog 20-30 feet deep would win him a gold medal from the Dublin Society.) The expense ranged from £4-6 per acre.[79]

Deposits of raised or lowland bog (referred to as 'red bog') were common on the Bellew lands as well. Surveys of different parts of the estate list boggy portions as a matter of course. One for a section known as Gorteen records five acres of bog out of the total acreage of nineteen. Reclamation, through their own and their tenants' efforts, was a concern of Michael and Christopher Dillon Bellew. The family papers contain 'modes for reclaiming bog', sent to Michael Bellew by an unknown correspondent, in which the following procedure used by a Mr Sands of Kilecavan in Westmeath was recommended: If the bog had tussocks, they were to be pared and levelled for plowing, then burned with the surface when it was plowed up. If the ash was sparse and white, according to the account, the bog wouldn't produce rape or turnips, but a good crop of rye. The rye stubble, turned and burned the year following, would then produce an excellent crop of rape or turnips. By burning the stubble every year and repeating crops of rye or rape, the farmer would produce 'as rich a surface as you please'.

Some of Michael Bellew's tenants were instructed, as conditions of their leases, to drain their lands and gravel bog areas. For example, a lease of 1787 to Gilbert Dowling directed him to level the land and manure it with limestone gravel under penalty of £10; in exchange, Bellew would pay him 20s. per improved acre. His son Christopher Dillon continued the improving tradition into the nineteenth century: the family papers contain records of his payments, often substantial, for the ploughing, burning, levelling, and sowing of bog areas and constructing drains. These efforts were noticed and praised by Hely Dutton in his survey of Galway for the Royal Dublin Society:

> Mr Bellew of Mount Bellew, has made an admirable improvement of 20 acres of cut-away bog, which, from not being worth 5 shillings an acre,

is now [1817] under a crop of oats, after a fine crop of rape: he is continuing his bog improvements with great spirit.[80]

In addition to bog reclamation, the improving landlord often encouraged
industries on his estates. He was urged to do so by numerous publications
advocating not only agricultural progress but the improvement of conditions
for tenants as well. Samuel Madden, one of the founders of the Dublin Society,
stated in *Reflections and Resolutions Proper for the Gentlemen of Ireland, as
to their Conduct for the Service of their County* (1738) that the best means of
accomplishing the latter was the establishment of 'manufactures' on estates.[81]

The 'manufacture' best suited for the purpose was deemed to be the linen
industry. English legislation of the late seventeenth and early eighteenth century had provided an impetus for its development in Ireland, permitting the
import of hemp, flax, and their manufactured products into England duty-free,
and the direct export of coarse white and brown linen to the colonies. By the
1720s, manufacturing had progressed significantly in Ulster, and the Irish linen
industry experienced a rapid growth country-wide from the 1730s.[82] Spinning
and weaving in rural areas in particular was regarded as an excellent supplement to agricultural income for the cottier or small tenant. The Irish parliament
established the Linen Board in 1711 to regulate the industry, disseminate information concerning manufacturing techniques, and, significantly, offer subsidies for development. From 1724, £2,000 was granted annually for the encouragement of the industry outside Ulster.[83]

Linen manufacture in Galway on a significant scale began in the 1750s
with the spinning of yarn, and the increase in demand led to weaving as well in
the following decades. By 1770, sales of linen and yarn at markets in the county
either to factors or for local consumption amounted to £40,000; the total of
sales realized was actually higher, since a considerable amount of cloth woven
outside Ulster was sent to Dublin, where it was sold on the account of local
entrepreneurs, including landlords, who had organized its production.[84]

The gentry could promote manufacturing in a variety of ways, as shown by
the activities of the Frenches of Monivea and the Bellews of Mount Bellew.
Robert French started a spinning school on his estate in 1746 and provided
flax for his tenants. In 1749, eight weavers and their families were brought to
Monivea and a bleach green and mill were constructed. To ensure its success,
French apprenticed a local man in Ulster to learn the trade and its management; he also hired experienced men from Belfast to build mills and oversee
bleaching. By 1776, there were 276 weavers' houses, 96 looms, and 370 wheels
on the French estate.[85]

Both Michael Bellew and Sir Patrick Bellew made attempts to encourage linen manufacturing on their estates, with varying degrees of success. In 1763, shipments of flaxseed, some eight hogsheads, were delivered to Michael Bellew by his Galway merchant brother-in-law Andrew French; shipments appear to have continued at least through 1766. He also considered bringing weavers to his lands; however, in 1766, French informed him of a great 'damp on linen', worrying that it was 'not as good a business as you and I were inclined to believe', and advised him to wait 'before you build houses for weavers'.[86]

Sir Patrick also attempted to establish linen manufactures by granting favourable terms in his leases, but seems to have been thwarted by the reluctance of his tenants. In a letter of February 1775 to Michael Bellew, he referred to correspondence from one of them, a Mr Bodkin, and spoke of 'getting him the money for the looms which I have done, I hope effectively', by writing to the secretary of the Linen Board. He planned to give Bodkin as long a term of the lands as he requested, because 'he is the only person who has complied with his agreement in regard to the linen business and I will give him every encouragement in my power'.[87] Sir Patrick's difficulties in encouraging his tenantry in the linen industry may have been due in part to the economic climate of the period; the 1770s was the only decade of the century in which it did not expand. A depression in England caused a severe slump in Irish sales from 1776; by 1777–78, it had led to the under-employment of rural weavers.[88]

It is not clear whether Michael Bellew followed his brother-in-law's advice and retrenched his efforts in the late 1760s, but after the recovery of the industry in the 1780s, he carried on a correspondence with his merchant brother Patrick in Dublin concerning flaxseed prices. Following his purchase of Sir Patrick Bellew's lands in Galway, he continued to grant favourable peppercorn (that is, nominal) rents to weavers in the market town of Newtown Bellew,[89] and Christopher Dillon Bellew corresponded with the Linen Board through 1824.[90]

Unfortunately, the linen industry was not to be a lasting rural 'improvement' in Galway. The post-Napoleonic War recessions hit hardest in the areas in which spinning and weaving had only recently been established, and the spread of power-spinning in the northeast led to the concentration of the industry in Ulster. The west was simply unable to compete economically. By 1817, Hely Dutton, compiling his statistical survey, described a country industry in decline.[91]

LANDLORDS AND TENANTS

Although this study is concerned primarily with the effects of the penal laws on the Bellews as Catholic gentry and their ownership and maintenance of their lands, a discussion of rentals – their terms and their increases – and estate improvements prompts consideration of another issue: the relations between the Bellews as landlords and their tenants.

In the system of farm rentals in areas of both pasturage and agricultural areas, in which the former predominated, categorization of 'farmers' was not clear-cut, and there was no simple correlation betwen size of farm and kind of tenant. The largest farms, from several hundred to a thousand or more acres, were stock farms, rented by graziers who often sublet to smaller tenants. Yet, these graziers could also farm directly a portion of their lands and style themselves as 'gentlemen farmers' as well.[92] Small farmers rented plots from 30-100 acres, but areas of 200 or more could also be rented by 'small' farmers in partnership. The small farmer, whether he rented from a grazier[93] or head landlord, could benefit from the increase in grain prices in the second half of the century, and might supplement his income with linen spinning or weaving. At the bottom of the scale were the cottiers, renting a few acres in exchange for labour or cash, subsisting on what crops could be grown on their plots. For this group, rising rents could make existence marginal.

Conditions for the poorer classes varied not only within the county but even from estate to estate. Arthur Young's well-known description of the cabins of the poor rural classes ('the most miserable looking hovels that can well be conceived') and his observations in Galway of those who had simply a house and garden, whose diet consisted of potatoes and oatmeal, must be balanced against the conditions of those living around Monivea and Woodlawn, who had cows, several pigs and a complement of poultry. Poverty in eighteenth-century Ireland was a relative condition; observers who expected the worst in Connacht often to their surprise found just as bad or worse elsewhere. Despite the poor conditions he observed in 1776, Young concluded that in areas of Galway, 'circumstances are much improved in 20 years'.[94]

The Bellew papers provide glimpses of the relationship between landlord and smaller tenant – a relationship that was a reversal of the usual one in eighteenth-century Ireland, where Catholic tenants encountered a landlord class not always familiar with the Irish language and culture, of relatively recent origin, and of a different religion. The eighteenth-century rent rolls are only partial, for particular pieces of land in random years, often indicating only the rent received without enumerating the acreage. However, some general observations can be made.[95] By the 1770s and 80s, the lands were generally let for 10 to 20*s* per acre; unimproved or 'mountain' acres were rented at only 3–4*s*. These figures correspond to Young's rental estimates for Galway and are similar to those rents charged by the Bellews' neighbours. They also reflect the rise in land values and rentals after 1750. Many of the leases were to neighbours of the lesser gentry and graziers, often one and the same groups. The rental of 485 acres of the Castle Bellew estate in 1787 to Daniel Geraghty and 'his undertenants' would seem to indicate a grazier who sublet. Other rentals were to small farmers, individually and in partnership; acreages ranged from 40-60, and a few from 100-150. It is difficult to discern any pattern in the length of leases: they ranged from 1 year to 12, and from 1–2 lives. There were also rentals of smaller amounts of land, 1–10 acres, and of conacres – land rented seasonally to cottiers or labourers for one or two crops, most frequently including potatoes.

The Bellews were treated by their smaller tenants, as were all Irish landlords, with subservient respect; yet, they could also be approached with what tenants considered legitimate grievances. Both aspects of this relationship are illustrated in an undated 'humble petition of the tenants of Culleturly and Shipe' to Michael Bellew:

> [they] humbly showeth that they are these eight years past groan under the weight of a heavy landlords rent and several under hard [dearths?] two tedious to be related here ... now being striped of the most part of our worldly substance and having no other resource but to apply to your honour [we] do hope youell charratably inspect into our miserable situation and encourage us to live in some degree like Christians. Enable us to improve your own land and as we have a strong inclination to live under you and have your protection in the country we live in. Your compliance to this sorrowful situation will make your tenants happy, and will forever pray [for you] and your family ...

The petition was composed by the tenants with the help of an Edmond Kelly who attested its validity, and Bellew's response is written underneath: 'the different tenants shall have their lands this year at the rents they hitherto paid as the season is so far advanced with this condition, that they sufficiently gravel three acres of the mountains [unimproved land] ...'

Those tenants who were hard-working and willing to improve the lands they rented appear to have been treated fairly, or at least listened to, as good estate economy would dictate. Another example is given in a letter of 1781 from Sir Patrick Bellew to Michael Bellew, to whom he had granted a power of attorney to make leases of his property in Galway:[96]

> Cassidy writes me that he thinks the tenants of Patch and Lismoyle are sorry they did not take their holdings at my offer, if so (and that you can

bring it about without courting them) you may let them know that you
have a power of signing leases for them ... they are industrious people
and I would not wish to part them. I would give them also this year at the
old rent.

Yet, as the tone of Patrick Bellew's letter indicates, the land was ultimately
at his disposal; shrewd, if not sharp, dealing and estate economy were paramount. The landlord's power as ultimate arbiter and judge over his tenants is
seen clearly in another petition. In 1768, John Kenney and his wife, a peasant
family in dire circumstances, enlisted the aid of a C. Abbott, who wrote to
Michael Bellew that

> they have been so unfortunate as to disoblige you, by harbouring some
> tinkers who you suspected had stolen some of the lead off one of your
> [turrets?] in consequence of which you have applied to my son Thomas
> to turn her [the wife] off. She has importuned me to intercede with you to
> let her remain in her cabin till next November to save her crop, as her
> husband threatens to leave her and the children to beg if turned off at
> May. I assure you, Sir, I would not interfere in this business, but from a
> belief that they would not dare to misbehave during that time, however
> you are a better judge, and if you think it safe to let them remain during
> that time, please to acquaint me, and Thomas will certainly discharge
> them this May if you think it requisite.

Bellew's response to the Kenneys' plea is not known.

In all respects, Catholic landlords were faced by the same problems with
tenants as their Protestant counterparts. Chief among these, as might be expected, was difficulty in collecting rents, a prominent theme in the Bellew
correspondence. Sometimes, drastic means were resorted to: Sir Patrick Bellew
in 1762 wrote of taking back a farm from a tenant named Fitzgerald to whom
'I have given no lease nor will if ever without a covenant of paying double rent
if one half year is not paid when the other becomes due'.[97] Another problem
resulted when tenants, unable to meet their rent, simply ran away. In 1787,
those on part of the Clonoran properties did so, leaving behind a debt of over
£100, only a small portion of which was recouped by the sale of their crops.
Repeated failures to pay rents often led to legal action and ejectments, but
serving the latter was not always easy. In 1788, Michael Bellew learned from a
correspondent of difficulties in Westmeath: 'the last man that was sent was so
frightened and terrified that he did not serve above 2 or 3 of the tenantry, and
then run off ...'[98]

In any examination of landlord-tenant relationships, it is, of course, difficult to assess the attitudes of the latter, simply because they are not well-docu-
mented. However, one manifestation of tenant discontent would be participation in or support of secret societies and their activities to force change. Of
course, acts of violence directed at landlords were rare; small farmers who
refused to go along with the societies' demands and the hated tithe-proctor
were the usual targets of coercion. Nonetheless, outbreaks of rural violence
were frequently an indication of dissatisfaction with aspects of the land sys-
tems – increases in rents, high rents for conacre plots, distraints and evictions.

In comparison to other areas in eighteenth-century Ireland, Galway could
be considered as peaceful for much of the century. There was an outbreak of
cattle and sheep houghing (maiming) and slaughter in 1711, that spread to
Mayo, Clare, and parts of Roscommon, most likely the result of the growth of
pasture at the expense of tillage.[99] This, however, was short-lived, ending in
1713. Moreover, Whiteboyism did not spread from the south to the west in the
1760s and 70s, perhaps because one of its major grievances, the tithe on potatoes, was simply not an issue in Connacht, where they were not subject to the
tithe. There were disturbances in Galway during the Rightboy movement of
1785–88, but they were not widespread. The area around Gort in the extreme
south was affected early on the movement; however, its proximity to Clare,
where Rightboy activities was more pronounced, may have been a contributing factor. Not until early 1787, were there disturbances to the north, from
Tuam to the outskirts of the city of Galway; yet eastern Galway remained
calm. It has been proposed that conversion from pasture to tillage, under the
stimulus of rising demand for grain at home and in Britain and the export
bounties afforded by Foster's Corn Law, was a major factor in the outbreak of
the movement. Tithes now payable on grain became a grievance for small farmers, who, seeing their bounties effectively cancelled out, were attracted by a
movement that demanded a reduction in tithes.[100] If this is the case, the Rightboy
activities in central Galway and their absence to the east might be explained. In
contrast to the areas to the west, where land was not as well-suited to grazing
and thus conversion to tillage more attractive, pasturage remained paramount
in the east. Not much conversion appears to have taken place; both Hely Dutton
and Edward Wakefield, compiling their surveys and statistics in the early nineteenth century, at a time when tillage would have been most attractive, remark
on the secondary role of arable farming in the rural economy.[101] Although
small farmers and tenants may well have been concerned about evictions,
distraints, and the general increase in rents (all issues raised by the Rightboys),
this concern did not manifest itself in Righboyism. In the crisis decade of the
1790s, Galway experienced disturbances linked to Defenderism, but the po-

litical and sectarian aspects of that movement differentiate it from more typical forms of eighteenth-century agarian protest. Galway's relative calm for much of the century serves as a reminder that agrarian protest in Ireland was often localized and the result of specific grievances; moreover, such protest was usually directed against the abuses of the land system rather than the system itself.[102]

Another factor in the generally amicable landlord-tenant relations in eighteenth-century Galway may have been the better possibility for communication on a variety of levels. Most of the proprietors, especially the Catholics, were not absentee landlords, but resided on their estates. Residence was no guarantee of better estate management, but at least resident landlords might be more immediately cognizant of conditions and problems. Moreover, in Galway and much of the west, many of the gentry understood and spoke Irish.[103] The Bellews may have been among their number – there were both Irish dictionaries and grammars in their library. Being able to discuss problems and grievances in a common language does not necessarily guarantee their alleviation, but these landlords must have been perceived by their tenants as slightly less alien.

Nevertheless, a review of the Bellews' dealings with their tenants – in matters concerning leases, amounts of rent, indeed, in control over their lives – indicates that the Catholic tenants on the Mount Bellew estates were treated in the same way by these Catholic landlords as they would have been by Protestant. A shared religion made absolutely no difference. In this respect, as in many others, the Bellews were very much members of their class.

LIVING ON THE LAND

The marked increase in landlord incomes from the mid-eighteenth century onward was reflected in not only estate improvement but also in the building of country houses as well. The seat of an Irish gentry family was a mark of their social status and influence in their county and Galway had an impressive number; in 1812, Edward Wakefield noted 'more gentlemen's seats than in any other district of Ireland'.[104] Among them was Mount Bellew house, to which Michael Bellew and his son Christopher Dillon devoted considerable energy and money in the eighteenth century.

The family papers provide no information concerning the origins of the house – whether it dated from the late seventeenth or early eighteenth centuries or whether any earlier buildings were near or on the site. Christopher, the third son of John Bellew of Willistown, was generally referred to as 'of Mount Bellew', yet this may have been simply an estate designation for there is some

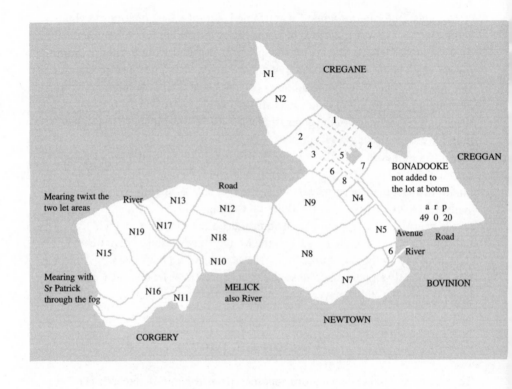

Figure 3: Part of Lands of Mount Bellew in 1767 and Part of Michael Bellew's Estate after Folio, 1767.F.76 (21)

indication that the family may have resided in Moylough for the late seventeenth and part of the eighteenth centuries. Moreover, Michael Bellew's father Christopher, in marriage articles of 1742 for which he served as a trustee, is designated as 'of Kelly's Grove'. Nonetheless, he is also referred to as 'of Mount Bellew' in 1748, and Andrew French in a letter to Michael Bellew mentions a Mount Bellew house existing in 1700.[105]

Whatever its origin, Michael Bellew appears to have either built or renovated the house which stood at Mount Bellew for the second half of the eighteenth century. His brother-in-law wrote in April of 1767 that 'you are now employed in finishing your house ...'[106] and the first, albeit primitive, representation of Mount Bellew house is of the mid-eighteenth century. An estate map of 1767 (Figure 3) shows a square house block, with two canted bays forming a three-sided entrance, with a considerable portion of surrounding desmesne subdivided into various parks and a nursery/wood.[107] The housepark was some 34 acres; there was a nursery of 7 acres, a pigeon park of 4, a park near the house itself of 19, and a miller's garden of an acre. The house park was further subdivided into cow yards, 3 paddocks, orchards, a kitchen garden, and a pond park added to the lawn. The entire desmesne was some 100 acres.

Legend
Part of lands of Mount Bellew, also part of Michael Bellew's estate, 20 May, 1767; Owen Flanagan, surveyor

N 1	reclaimable bog	N 9	Cregannacask-cow park
N 2	nursery or wood	N10	Shracoore meadow
N 3	house park	N11	bottom by Corgery and Melick
N 4	pigeon park	N12	east side of big park
N 5	Cloghaneboy Park	N13,18	Monaghan park
N 6	miller's garden	N14	the mountain to gravel
N 7	bottom set to Newtown tenants	N15	red bog
N 8	Teanamore bottom	N16	red bog

arable and pasture exclusive of bogs and mountain – 198 acres, 21 perches

Subdivision of house park N 3	A	R	P
No. 1 West Bonadooke park	9	2	-
No. 2 the cow island	5	0	0
No. 3 3 paddocks	3	3	0
No. 4 pond park added to lawn	7	2	0
No. 5 the old orchard	1	2	38
No. 6 the new orchard, cow yards	2	0	16
No. 7 the old paddock added by lawn	2	0	0
No. 8 the kitchen garden park	2	2	-
	34	1	-

Provisions for the nursery and orchards reflect the increasing interest in gardening and planting in the eighteenth century. Country gentlemen in Ireland often purchased seeds for their gardens from merchants in Dublin;[108] in the 1770s, Michael Bellew dealt with a Mr Phelan of Christchurch Lane. Besides ordering hayseed and thorn-quicks (young thorn plants for hedging), he also bought asparagus plants for the garden and fruit trees – plum, apricot, and cherry – for planting along 15 perches of walls. Phelan provided extensive advice on preparation, bedding, and soils, advising 'you'll probably stare at all this trouble, but if you consider a diamond won't shine unless it is worked with great labor and industry', so it was with gardening.

The grounds also included stands of trees. Defoliation – from war, the destruction of trees for charcoal as well as timber, and the depredations of peasants concerned less with forests than tillable land – was widespread in this period. Despite government efforts in the early eighteenth century to compel planting on estates, success in this area came about more from the initiative of individuals influenced by the improving spirit. By 1749, Lord Orrery remarked that 'every gentleman in Ireland is become a planter', and by the second half of the century, the Dublin Society was offering premiums for planting.[109] Judging from Michael Bellew's orders from Phelan for Dutch elder (particularly well-suited to moist, boggy soil), mountain ash and birch (brought from county Wicklow to Dublin for sale), Mount Bellew was among those estates in county Galway with areas of woods by the end of the eighteenth century, if not before.

Timber could also be a source of revenue from already-standing woods. Sir Patrick Bellew contracted with a local farmer in 1774 to permit the felling of oak and ash trees in the Wood of Doon to the southwest of Mount Bellew. Patrick Coghlan was to pay £700 over four years in consideration of the timber; Bellew would lay out one contiguous acre for a lumber yard which Coghlan could use for an additional two and a half years. An element of conservation for the future use of the wood was introduced in a clause directing Coghlan 'not to permit any beast to trespass, graze, damage young shoots' under penalty of £100. Similar use of – and profit from – the Wood would continue after Michael Bellew's purchase of Sir Patrick's estate.[110] Generally, plantings around a desmesne tended to be small and served primarily as a screen.[111] However, Michael Bellew's son Christopher Dillon would expand his father's plantings to include larch, oak, Norway spruce and the relatively new hardwood, beech. On his tour of Galway in 1817, Hely Dutton noted the trees on the estate, one ash in particular called 'Cromwell's tree', which tradition held had been planted while he was subduing Ireland.[112] There was also a small nursery at MountBellew Bridge, the estate village.

References to the interior of the eighteenth-century house at Mount Bellew are scant, although account books from 1769 indicate the existence of a library, a glazier being paid £1.2s. 9d. for work there; and five hearths, if the 10s. paid in hearth money was an honest reckoning. Payments of 13s.16½d. were made for plastering chimneys and £4 for the carriage of a chimney piece from Dublin.

Expenses of country life in Ireland were generally lower than in England. Servants' wages in particular were estimated at some 30 per cent less; as a result, the Irish gentry often had more household servants than their counterparts in England.[113] The Bellews appear to have had a full complement of household help. Cash and wage books from 1769 to 1775 record a variety of payments to cooks, kitchen help, grooms, and housemaids. The wages paid them illustrate the lower pay scale; indeed, wages in the west of Ireland appear to have been even lower than those paid in the north, although some of these servants may have received keep in lieu of full money wages, a common practice.[114] On occasion, the Bellews were asked to supply servants for their relatives. Christopher Bellew, a Dublin merchant cousin of Christopher Dillon Bellew, wrote in 1793 that he needed a 'pretty smart ... little boy or servant very much'. He suggested that his cousin 'might get me one from your land ... whose parents you know', and added, 'as you know, his parents will thank you'. The boy was to be bound for seven years, receiving board and £20 at the end of his term; in case of misconduct, Christopher Bellew asserted that he could 'discharge him without giving him a shilling'.[115]

Accounts from 1778–1781 also show payments to the variety of help required for the upkeep, and display, of the estate and house of a fairly well-to-do gentry family: £4–5 yearly for gardeners; £5 a year with a suit of clothes for a butler in charge of plate and furniture, 'if he behaves careful and honest', and £3 yearly and buckskin breeches for a postillion, who was also to take care of the horses and stable. By the end of the century, the account books reflect an increasingly prosperous lifestyle: gardeners and planters hired at £10 a year and a coachman at 6 guineas with 2 guineas for yearly boots and breeches. The latter was to 'find himself in everything else but livery', which 'he is to wear when he is ordered only'.

Account books also provide some idea of the stable the postillion was to oversee. In the late 1770s, a list of 'stable furniture' included, besides the expected variety of bits, snaffles, and harnesses, horsechairs and pillions for the women and a post-chaise. There is also an earlier inventory, from 1767, of the horses owned by the Bellews – 2 car horses and 8 riding and carriage horses valued at over £100. In 1776, Arthur Young considered the numbers of horses kept by the Irish gentry an extravagance and, as illustration, supplied a table of country lords and gentry showing sizes of desmesnes and, among other statistics, the number of horses they kept.[116] In 1767, the Bellews' stable was comparable to those of gentry of their means; by the time of Young's tour, it had probably expanded further as four sons reached riding age.

What, if any, construction at Mount Bellew house beyond that mentioned in 1767 was undertaken by Michael Bellew is not clear from the family papers and accounts.[117] On the desmesne itself, besides the planting referred to earlier, he began the construction of an artificial lake in 1790, using the waters of the River Shivan, which lay between the desmesne and the road from Ballinasloe to the western part of the county. His cousin Christopher Kelly Bellew supplied advice as to the shaping of the water: '... the larger the scale it is done upon, the better I think will be the effect that a natural correspondence between the water on each side will have on the eye of the passenger'.[118] Michael Bellew also built a new chapel in 1793, replacing an older one which was permitted to fall into decay.

After Michael Bellew's death, Mount Bellew house was to undergo considerable renovation and expansion in the early nineteenth century under the direction of his son Christopher Dillon. The years immediately preceding and following the Union saw a rapid increase in country house building in Ireland,[119] and one of the most influential and popular architects of the period was the Irish-born Richard Morrison. He both built and renovated along modified neo-classical lines a number of country houses in county Galway, including Castlegar, for Ross Mahon, and St Clerans, for John Burke; and it is to him that the renovation of Mount Bellew is attributed.[120]

Whether Morrison supervised construction or whether a local architect worked from his designs is not clear. Some earlier specifications for the renovation of the central house block are from 'Dominick Madden, Arch.'. Madden was an architect of some local repute who completed the chapel at Mount Bellew and was later to construct, in Gothic style, the Roman Catholic cathedral at Tuam.[121] Nonetheless, a 'Morrison' oversaw extensive stone-cutting, which employed 30 masons from 1806–8 for both the central block and the new wings, and the interior design of the center was in typical Morrison style, particularly the free-standing internal columns, a trademark which also appears in St Clerans and Castlegar.

The starting point for Morrison's renovation, judging from nineteenth-century prints of the completed house, was a three-story Georgian block. The new center block retained the old three-sided entrance front, but a porch with two Ionic columns surmounted by a large urn was added, and perhaps a Venetian window in the first story. Two single-story pedimented wings were joined to the center by two links, which were three bays (or windows) in width.

The interior of the house was also impressive. A long hall of 63' was divided by screens of Ionic columns; it led by way of anterooms, each 24' by 17', to a large gallery of 32' by 26' on one side and a dining room of 34' by 21' on the other. If Madden's specifications were followed, additional rooms included two nurseries, dressing rooms, a reading room, bedrooms, a library, and a barrack room. (The latter was an Irish convention indicative of the well-attested hospitality of the gentry; it was a large guest-chamber furnished with a number of beds to accomodate unexpected or overflow visitors to a country house.)[122] The furnishings were lavish and expensive; bills from Lewis and Anthony Morgan of Dublin for the years 1810 to 1812 show that well over £1,000 had been spent up to July of 1811. The listing of the furniture purchased reflects the neo-Classical influence, with a few touches of Gothic, the popular competing style of the period: there were mahogany and rose-wood sofa tables; 'Grecian' chairs for the parlor and a 'Grecian sofa with carved scrolls'; large and small sofas covered in blue velvet with matching curtains; as well as cabinets, one inlaid with ivory at a cost of £60. Besides mahogany dining tables and sideboards, the dining room was also furnished with mahogany sofas with white calico coverings, 60 yards of Brussels carpet, and drapes with printed 'allegoric borders'. The library, an important room in Christopher Dillon Bellew's household, as will be demonstrated shortly, had mahogany doors, bookcases, and ladders; a large table in 'Gothic style', blue calico curtains, and brass fixtures.

The desmesne too had been enhanced by Michael Bellew's artificial lake. To provide access to the eastern approach to the house, an iron bridge was constructed. The results were enthusiastically described by J.P. Neale in 1820 in his *Views of the Seats of Noblemen and Gentlemen in England, Wales, Scotland, and Ireland*:

> ... the House stands on a gentle swell, nearly half a mile to the South; between it and the road, runs the Shivan, spreading to a considerable expanse, as it proceeds eastward ... the varied outline it then assumes, its wooded islands, and lucid waters bathing the opposite acclivity form together a scene of no ordinary interest and beauty ... As the river advances, it opens to an external lake, shewing to the traveller, by openings judiciously made, the Mansion on his right ... while on his left, he is forcibly struck with the Church, its Tower, and Pinnacles ...

Before concluding this survey of the Bellews as landowners, one final topic should be explored, that of their participation in the intellectual and cultural life of the eighteenth century. Contemporary accounts stress the relative lack of culture in country life and portray a gentry concerned primarily with drinking, hunting, gambling, and duelling. This gentry lifestyle was considered to be particularly prevalent in the west. Connacht provided such spectacular figures of this type as Robert 'Fighting' Fitzgerald and 'Hairtrigger' Dick Martin, and the Galway Blazers, described as the 'most sanguinary fox-club in Connaught – a gang who would literally devastate the country, if it did not please heaven to thin their numbers annually by broken necks and accidents from pistol bullets'.[123]

The Bellews also experienced the wilder – and violent – side of Connacht life through the misadventures of their close relatives. Dominick Bellew of Mount Kelly was notorious for his bad temper and apparently profligate lifestyle. His dilatory rent payments on lands leased from Sir Patrick Bellew are a constant theme in the latter's letters to Michael Bellew through the 1770s and early 1780s. By 1786, part of his lands had been vested in trustees, including Michael Bellew, for the payment of his debts.[124] One of Dominick's sons, Christopher Kelly Bellew, rented some of the lands in order to satisfy the debts and touched off a volcanic response from his father, which he described in letters of May and September of 1786 to his cousin Michael Bellew: 'He asked me how I dare set his lands and that he should not have it'. A stream of invective followed and 'it concluded by throwing a dish of tea in my face and running into the room for his gun'. Fortunately, a relative intervened, 'whom he laid upon with his fists'. Kelly Bellew resolved to break off relations and commented it 'must end at Ballinasloe Fair', presumably a reference to at least some money being realized from the sale of cattle there.

The reference was a tragically ironic one, for attempted homicide at Mount Kelly in May 1786 would be followed by the real event in Ballinasloe in October. A second son of Dominick, Patrick, was murdered there by a gang of conspirators, some of whom included his own Mount Kelly servant and a stable-helper, intent on stealing the money received for the sale of cattle at the Fair. Lured into a stable near the River Suck by his stableboy Patrick Greaghan, Patrick was robbed and stabbed to death and his body dumped on the riverbank. When his father Dominick offered a substantial reward for the capture of his son's killers, one of the conspirators, a servant at his house, attempted to poison the old man – along with his houseguests at dinner – in an attempt to get him off their trail. The act of desperation was of no avail: Dominick Bellew and his dinner guests survived; the gang was arrested, convicted, and ultimately hanged in the town of Galway.[125]

Slightly less sanguinary events are also attested in the Bellew correspondence. Duelling, although on the decline by the end of the century, was still engaged in. As late as 1790, Edmond Taaffe, Michael Bellew's brother-in-law, could report sarcastically on his return from Castlebar, county Mayo that it was 'very peaceable while I was there. Harry Bingham was very near killing Hugh O'Donell, Jonathan Bingham and Denis Browne fought the same day. No shot took place. I hope that day's work will put an end to duelling'.[126]

Apart from its reputation for violence, Connacht was also regarded as distinctly lacking in culture. The Irish playwright Richard Cumberland's description of the intellectual life of Lord Eyre of Eyrecourt in southeast county Galway reinforced the stereotype: Lord Eyre, a friend and neighbour of Cumberland's father, who was the Protestant bishop of Clonfert, had never been out of Ireland. 'He lived in an enviable independence as to reading, and of course he had no books'.[127] As late as 1812, Edward Wakefield in *An Account of Ireland, Statistical and Political* spoke of the 'circumscribed knowledge' of the country gentleman: 'libraries are not common ... by some families they are purchased on their first commencing housekeeping as a part of the furniture, and the choice of the volumes depends greatly on the elegance of the type and binding'. Such impressions of the west as Cumberland's and Maxwell's appear to have been shared by Irishmen in the other provinces, where, even into the early nineteenth century, Connacht was thought to be 'far behind them in civilization'.[128]

Nonetheless, Arthur Young, while condemning the profligate and wasteful lives of many of the country gentlemen, noted a welcome change in lifestyle exhibited by many he had visited on his Irish tour in 1776: 'there are great numbers of them who are as liberal in all their ideas as any people in Europe ... a man may go into a vast variety of families, which he will find actuated by ... the most liberal urbanity'.[129] Young mentioned such Galway families as the Frenches of Monivea[130] and the Trenches of Woodlawn as among these; he might well have included the Bellews (at least the Mount Bellew branch), for they too provide a contrast to the stereotypical wild and ignorant country gentleman of the west.

Michael Bellew's plans for his house included a library, referred to earlier, and his accounts with a Dublin merchant, John Blake, record payments for newspapers. His son Christopher Dillon was to indulge his bibliophilic interests in an impressive – and expensive – way. The library he amassed was regarded as one of the finest private collections in the west of Ireland.[131] Hely Dutton made use of its resources when compiling his statistical survey in 1817, referring to 'Mr Bellew's extensive and choice library'.[132] Indeed, a remarkable proportion of the family papers from the early nineteenth century consists of his book orders, although he had already made major purchases from the prominent Dublin book seller John Archer in the 1790s.[133]

An 1812 catalogue of the library, which records the volumes, their size, and the date and place of purchase, runs to 92 full pages, with approximately

30 entries per page. It is an interesting reflection of the literary tastes of the educated and cultured Irish country gentleman of the period.

His collection of the classics – Greek and Roman authors in the original and in translation – is of particular interest. Besides the authors and works expected in an eighteenth-century classical library (Herodotus, Plato, Sophocles, Plutarch, Virgil, Horace, Tacitus, and, of course, 'Tully's *Offices*'), there are some which indicate Bellew's considerable skill and discernment as a collector. Among these are the works of Sallust and, in particular, of Ammianus Marcellinus, which were not printed in the British Isles until well after 1816; a 1772 edition of Xenophon; and an extremely rare 1588 edition of Apuleius' *Opera Omnia*, published in Leiden.[134]

The library also included authors of the European and English Renaissance – Dante, Bocaccio, Rabelais, Cervantes, and Thomas More. 'Modern' classics ranged from the works of authors of the Enlightenment and the English Augustan Age – Bayle, Smollett, Goldsmith, Johnson, Pope, and Swift – to those of the Romantic period – Scott, Burns, Goethe, and Walpole's *Castle of Otranto*. (Works of a less literary nature are also represented by such titles as *Tales of Terror*, *Anecdotes of a Convent*, and *The Chinese Spy*.) Reference books included grammars in a variety of languages and an 18-volume set of the *Encyclopedia Brittanica*.

Besides literature, the interests of a country gentleman are seen in Bellew's collection of Blackstone's *Commentaries*, *Davey's Agricultural Chemistry*. and *The Farmer's Calendar*, as well as numerous books on gardening.

The library also contained works on 'Gaelic antiquities', a Gaelic-English dictionary, and an Irish grammar, indicative of both the Irish-speaking area in which Bellew lived and the growing interest in Irish antiquities and the serious study of the Irish language. Also holding a place of prominence were works on more recent Irish history and in particular the place of Catholics, including Bellew's own family, in that history. Written from both Protestant and Catholic points of view, they included Carte's *Life of Ormonde*, Curry's *History of the Civil Wars in Ireland*, O'Conor's *History of Irish Catholics*, and McNiven's *Pieces of Irish History*. Indeed, Bellew's interests were truly catholic; along with a number of priests' memoirs, his library contained a copy of Wesley's hymns.

Ultimately, Christopher Dillon Bellew's library would contain nearly 3,800 titles[135], but his cultural interests also extended beyond literature to the arts – music, paintings, and prints – and the sciences. His purchases of sheet music from W. Power of the Music Warehouse at Westmorland Street, Dublin included Mozart's sacred music, selections from Hume's Musical Circulating Library for harp and pianoforte, as well as two small books of Irish melodies (although his interest in Gaelic airs seems not to have been wide-ranging; he returned 'Scots Songs').

His art dealer in Dublin was William Allen, from whom he apparently made regular purchases; in 1808, Bellew sent 'a box of pictures from Allen' to Mount Bellew with careful instructions for its opening.[136] The family papers also contain several notices of Dublin art sales in which he appears to have been interested. In 1809, Allen, just back from England, informed Bellew that he had 'picked up very fine specimens of the ... Masters' of which he wished him to 'have the refusal as I think some of them would be beautiful additions to your collection'.[137] They included paintings by Murillo, of interest to collectors at the beginning of the nineteenth century as Napoleon's campaigns released a number of works from Spanish royal collections onto the open market, and Neysmith and LaPort, contemporary landscape watercolourists. If Allen's offerings were indeed ones he thought consonant with Bellew's tastes, the latter were rather eclectic for the age, for Allen mentions paintings by Fra Angelica and Ruysdael. It was considered unfashionable to collect the Italian works of the thirteenth and early fourteenth centuries, and while Rembrandt was always popular with collectors, Flemish and Dutch art of the seventeenth century was not in as great a demand.[138] In regard to the latter school of painting, there is also a vague reference in his correspondence with Allen to a portrait of a 'Jewish rabi' Bellew acquired which had once been in the collection of Lord Mountcashel; this was probably of the seventeenth century.[139]

Besides a collection of cabinet pictures mentioned by Neale in his *Views*, Bellew had also purchased 'Boydell's Prints'. These were from a series of paintings on Shakespearean subjects by such artists as Henry Fuseli, Benjamin West, George Romney, Gavin Hamilton, and James Barry. Commissioned by London printer and engraver John Boydell for his Shakespeare Gallery beginning in 1796, they were then printed in a collection completed in 1805.[140] They were a notable addition to the extensive collection of prints Neale also refers to, 'including those of all the Royal Cabinets of Europe: the famous one of the Louvre, Le Muse [*sic*] Francais, not excepted ...'[141]

Finally, indicative of the fashionable scientific curiosity of the late eighteenth century, Bellew paid a rather substantial sum, close to £70, for the following 'scientific' miscellany, most likely for electrical experimentation among other purposes: a microscope, an 'electrical machine', a large camera, bell apparatus, spiral tubes, brass conductors, and an 'electrical cannon'.

As this review of his literary, artistic, and scientific interests has shown, Christopher Dillon Bellew was obviously a well-educated man of some discernment and familiar with the culture and prevalent tastes of his time. The more interesting point perhaps is how a member of the Catholic landed class

acquired such a background, for Bellew received his education during a period
in which the penal laws severely limited such opprtunities for a Catholic in
Ireland. Those who wished to acquire a classical education or who were attracted to that other tradition of employment for young members of gentry
families, military service, were obliged to reside on the continent. The following chapter will discuss the experience of these Irishmen – soldiers and students – abroad.

'We Must Part Our Native Lands':
Military Service and Education

A notable part of the experience of the Irish Catholic gentry in the eighteenth century was the emigration of large numbers of their class who felt that, as a result of the restrictions placed upon them, opportunities for advancement, wealth, education, and glory lay elsewhere. The Irish Catholic gentry abroad included significant numbers of merchants, soldiers, clerics, and students scattered over Europe, and in smaller numbers, planters and traders in the West Indies.

Even though some of the provisions of the penal laws were only nominally in force from mid-century, galling restrictions remained: the barring of Catholics from professions, the denial of a Catholic education, the exclusion from positions in government, and most important, the need for circumspection or outright subterfuge in land dealings and ownership. Life overseas – in one of the Catholic countries on the continent or in the less restrictive atmosphere of the West Indies – was appealing to many gentry families.

At one time, even Michael Bellew of Mount Bellew seems to have considered settling abroad in France, home to so many Irish Catholics. A brother-in-law, Andrew French of Rahoon, had spent a period of time there for his health, and sympathized with Bellew's consideration of emigration: 'You say you have some thoughts of settling your family in this kingdom – to preserve the religion of our posterity is what every good Catholic might endeavour to do'. However, his report on conditions in France, particularly on landholding, must have been discouraging:

> There's many difficulties and risks in purchasing lands here, every district have usages and customs, generally they go at 25 years purchase, subject to a land tax, capitation or poll tax, and many other kinds of duties, each vary every year ... in corn countries you must give the land to laborers at halves, if at a rent, you must be answerable for the casualties of the crop and expect rent in proportion, in short you can't depend on having a certain income any year and will be always subject to the knavery of bailiffs as few or no gentlemen live always on their estates.

French saw the only hope for his class in the relaxation of restrictions by the Irish government: '... I hope God will incline the hearts of our rulers, to mitigate the Penal Laws, and thereby make us useful subjects, and not compel us to the dreadful necessity to emigrate from our beloved country'.[1]

Michael Bellew did not go abroad, but his sons, relatives, and members of fellow Galway Catholic gentry families did, and their experiences reflect the diversity of reasons for extended sojourns, or in some cases, permanent residence, outside Ireland. Bellews were merchants in France and Spain; would-be planters in the West Indies; students, both lay and clerical, in France and the Low Countries; and officers in the French and Hapsburg Imperial armies.

There is an important distinction to be made, however, among these temporary or permanent emigrants. Those who wished to serve in the armed forces or receive a secular or priestly education were obliged, because of the penal laws, to reside on the continent. Those who lived abroad as traders or merchants, careers open to Catholics in Ireland with few penal restrictions, chose to do so. The following chapter will discuss members from the first of these groups, the gentry who lived on the continent as soldiers and students, both lay and religious. Those who emigrated to the West Indies, to trade and/or purchase plantations, will be discussed, along with the second group, merchants and traders, in Chapter 4, which deals with gentry mercantile connections.

MILITARY SERVICE

A substantial number of gentry émigrés in the eighteenth century served as soldiers and regimental officers in almost all the armies of Catholic Europe. Although careers of this sort dated at least from the sixteenth century, 1690 and the exchange of three regiments of James II's Irish army for 6,000 of Louis XIV's French troops marked the start of a large-scale exodus from Ireland. These troops were augmented after the surrender of Limerick in 1691; the treaty allowed James's Irish to pass freely into French service, and some 14,000 chose to do so.[2] Among this number was Richard Bellew, second son of Lord Bellew of Duleek. During the War of the Two Kings, he was captain of a troop of dragoons in the regiment of the earl of Limerick. After the death of the regimental commander at Aughrim, Bellew succeeded to the command and, under the terms of the treaty, brought his regiment, known as the King of England's Dismounted Dragoons, to France in 1691.[3]

These departures were the beginning of the 'flight of the wild geese', that emigration to Europe from 1690 to the third quarter of the eighteenth century, 'which was to draw off from Ireland almost all that was best among the remaining gentry of Gaelic and Old English blood'.[4] The circumstances of the Jacobite defeat, intensified by the barring of Catholics from the British forces, would result in Catholic officers of Gaelic origin – O'Donnells, Macquires, O'Neills – as well as those of Old English descent – Butlers, Plunketts, Dillons, Taaffes – serving foreign masters for most of the subsequent century.

The best known of the Irish soldiers abroad were in France. The famous Irish Brigade descended from the three regiments (Mountcashel's, Clare's, and Dillon's) transferred to France in 1690 which became part of the French army, though the Brigade was treated as a foreign unit whose members drew higher pay.[5] Thousands of Irish, clad in their red coats, took part in many of the French campaigns of the eighteenth century, including the spectacular French victory at Fontenoy in 1745, where Irish troops played a significant role in breaking the English ranks. Irish gentry and aristocratic families furnished their officers, some of whom achieved the highest military rank. Lord Clare became a Marshal of France; the Dillons were found in the upper echelons of the army; and Lally of Tollendal, who was at Dettingen and Fontenoy and commanded French troops in India during the Seven Years War, was the son of a Galway country gentleman. Indeed, Galway itself was illuminated in celebration of his success at Bergen-op-Zoom in 1747.[6] Other Galway natives who served France included Count Patrick Darcy of Kiltulla, a captain in Condé's regiment, aide-de-camp to Marshal Saxe at Fontenoy, and a colonel in Fitz-James's Irish Horse in the Seven Years War; Richard Kirwan, son of Patrick Kirwan of Cregg and Mary Martin of Dangan, a well-known member of Dillon's regiment; and Isidore Lynch, son of Isidore Lynch of Lynch Grove, who fought with the French expeditionary force in America and in 1783 was a colonel of Walsh's 2nd Regiment.[7] Members of various Bellew families were also in the Irish Brigade in the eighteenth century: Luke Bellew was a lieutenant in Rothe's Regiment of Foot in 1761, a Captain Bellew served in Berwick's Regiment from 1767 to 1769, another Bellew was a captain and chevalier of St Louis in Walsh's Regiment in 1787, and Lieutenant Michael Bellew was in Dillon's Regiment at the time of its disbandment in 1791.[8]

A second group of Irish soldiers, the Jacobite troops from Limerick, were permitted to retain the organization and uniforms of James's army and served only as French auxiliaries. These troops were used in the suppression of the Camisards in 1694 and in the Flemish campaigns of the War of the League of Augsburg. With the conclusion of the war in 1697, nearly all of the units of the original Jacobite army were disbanded; a few were incorporated into the Irish Brigade, the rest simply dismissed. This began a second dispersal of Irish soldiers, which led to enlistments in the armies of southern and eastern Europe.[9]

In Spain, the regiments of Irlanda, Hibernia, Limerick, and Ultonia constituted still another Bourbon Irish Brigade. One regiment, that of Limerick, was sent into Spanish service in Naples, where it became the Regimento del Rey.[10] The Irish in the employ of Spain in the eighteenth century came from regiments of King James' disbanded army, and like the Irish Brigade in France, fought in their distinctive red coats. The numbers of the Irish rank and file in the Spanish army dwindled during the course of the century – emigration dropped off, recruitment of Spanish nationals increased, and costly campaigns such as Campo Santo in Italy in the War of the Austrian Succession decimated the Irish ranks – but the Irish gentry still furnished the Brigade's officers. The family of Macdonnell gained great distinction in the service of Spain; General Reynaldo Macdonnell was the founder of the Hibernia regiment, his brother Alexandro was a lieutenant-general, and his son Daniel was an acting brigadier-general and colonel of the Irlanda regiment. Other Irish generals included O'Mahoney, O'Gara, O'Kelly, O'Neill, and Guillermo de Lacy, the colonel of the Ultonia regiment.[11]

Among those Irishmen who also established successful naval careers in Spain was a Galway native, Edward Lynch. A relative of the Bellews through his sister's marriage to Michael Bellew's younger brother Patrick, Lynch was a lieutenant and later captain in the Spanish navy. In 1768, he also became a Knight of the Order of St James; his sponsors included Captains Macdonnel, Kelly, and Savage, all Irishmen in Spanish service.[12]

In the east, several Irishmen achieved high rank in the army of Russia, a country whose religion was Orthodox, but whose need for competent officers of any religion was great. Peter Lacy, a member of a county Limerick family, became a Russian field marshal, entering the Russian army after the dissolution of the French Jacobite units. He assisted Peter the Great in the re-organization of the military and campaigned against the Poles, Swedes, and Turks. Another Limerick Irishman, of the Browne family (and also Lacy's son-in-law), was a field marshal and a governor of Riga.[13]

While the great majority of Irish troops were in the service of the Bourbons, in France and Spain, significant numbers of Irish Catholics found employment in the Imperial Hapsburg forces. The tradition of Irish service to the Austrian Hapsburgs was not wholly a result of the Jacobite defeat, an event of major significance in filling the ranks of Bourbon armies. Taaffes and Butlers were in the Imperial army before the end of the seventeenth century, and, although the father of Field Marshal Maximilian Browne had served in James' army, his great-uncle had been in the Hapsburg service a generation before. In 1689, several Irish regiments that had been raised by Tyrconnell were disbanded for want of arms and entered into the armies of central and eastern Europe, and after James' defeat a year later, increasing numbers of Irishmen filled the Hapsburg officer ranks. Some, like Maximilian Browne's father, whose regiment in the French army had been disbanded, owed their appointments to the recommendation of the duke of Marlborough, who preferred the exiled Irish officers in the employ of Austria, then an ally, rather than with the French enemy.[14] By the third quarter of the eighteenth century, the Irish families of Browne, Macquire, Lacy, Nugent, and Plunkett had all contributed prominent generals who participated in campaigns against the Bourbons, Prussians, and Turks. The O'Donnells of Leitrim and Mayo had three members in Austrian service: all achieved the rank of general and became counts of the Holy Roman Empire. Field Marshal Franz Moritz Lacy not only participated in Austrian campaigns from the War of the Austrian Succession of 1740–48 to the Austro-Turkish War of 1788–90, but also held the presidency of the *Hofkriegsrat* (the Imperial War Council), and, with Joseph II, continued the re-organization of the military begun under Maria Theresa.[15]

However, there were never as many Irish rank-and-file with the Hapsburgs as with the Bourbons; thus, there were never any Austrian Irish Brigades. Moreover, Austrian military organization militated against the establishment of an Irish tradition of service within a particular regiment. Each regiment had two colonels: a colonel proprietor, to whom the *Hofkriegsrat* granted ownership, and a colonel commandant, installed by the colonel proprietor, who was responsible for its day-to-day operation. If an Irishman was appointed colonel of a regiment, other Irish could, and did, gather under him, but with the end of his tenure, the appointment of the proprietorship went back to the *Hofkriegsrat*, and another colonel proprietor, not necessarily an Irishman, would replace him. There would no longer be any particular incentive for other Irish to join the regiment, and with normal rates of attrition, the Irish contingent would shrink and any continuity of membership be broken.

Nonetheless, for Irish Catholic gentry seeking positions of command, there were definite attractions in Imperial service. The first, common to employment in any of the Catholic continental armies, was expressed in a petition to Maria Theresa and Francis I by Nicholas Taaffe:

> Because he was afraid that his descendants pressed by the Penal Laws would not resist the temptation of becoming Protestants ... He therefore took refuge to a Catholic country where his ancestors were well-known by the military services they had rendered at different intervals to the House of Austria. He had abandoned his relations and his estate and the rank and liberty he had in his country to prevent his descendants from deserting a religion to which their Imperial Majesties so fervently adhered ...[16]

Moreover, the Austrian army, more multinational and polyglot than any other in Europe, stressed loyalty to the sovereign over national origin, and had a long tradition of employing capable foreigners.[17] The Irish were particularly welcomed and soon established a reputation for bravery, if not discipline. The Emperor Francis stated, 'The more Irish in the Austrian service the better; our troops will always be disciplined; an Irish coward is an uncommon character; and what the natives of Ireland dislike from principle, they generally perform through a desire of glory'.[18]

Perhaps one of the strongest appeals of Imperial service was its attitude toward appointments and promotions, a slightly different one than that encountered in the Bourbon armies. The selling of positions and commands was officially frowned upon in the Austrian army. Although reality often fell short of the ideal, the purchase of military place was regarded as corruption rather than standard practice, and officials at least tried to limit it: advancement could proceed by only one rank at a time, and the rights of others were to be protected. Likewise, although promotions, to be awarded solely for seniority or excellent service, were often helped along by cash and gifts presented to colonel proprietors, frequent periods of war afforded opportunities to advance if an officer was capable, but lacking in funds. Despite the drawbacks mentioned earlier, for an Irishman of ability but little patrimony, opportunities for advancement were, or could be, slightly more favourable in the Imperial army.

Because of the official attitude toward the sale of military positions, Irish generals, colonel proprietors, and high officers might have felt less constraint in both recruiting and preferring their generally less wealthy countrymen. An Irish officer writing to a relative in Ireland whose son had expressed an interest in the Austrian army, recommended as 'the best means' going through General D'Alton.[19] With his protection, and the boy's conduct and good behaviour, he could rise in the service.[20] As for the advantages of Irish connections in securing position and preferment, the entourage of Field Marshal Browne in mid-century included his sons Philip and Joseph, his cousin Major O'Neillan, his adjutant-general Colonel Thomas Plunkett, Major Franz Lacy, General Macquire, cavalry general O'Donnell, and Colonel MacEligot.[21] Nevertheless, such preferment was dependent on at least a modicum of ability and good behaviour (as the officer's letter indicates), particularly in the lower echelons of service. In 1788, the death in battle of an Irishman whose 'breakfast daily was a quart of brandy' and who was 'continually drunk and in bad company' was regarded by a fellow Irish officer and relative with sorrow but resignation. Because of his behaviour, this particular inebriate had had little hope of promotion in his military career – 'his Proprietor couldn't advance him'.[22]

Thus, clusters of Irishmen could be found in regiments and staffs, and close ties existed between them. However, because of the factors mentioned previously – the smaller number of Irish in Imperial service and the organization of the Austrian regiment – the history of the Irish in the Hapsburg army is reflected more in the careers of individual officers than in regimental tradition. All told, the Irish supplied the Imperial army with thirteen field marshals, dozens of generals, and hundreds of junior officers. In this regard, the correspondence of John Bellew, a relative of Michael Bellew of Mount Bellew, provides an interesting view of the life and experiences of one such Irish junior officer in Imperial service in the last quarter of the eighteenth century.[23]

John Bellew was a captain in the Imperial cavalry and served with several cuirassier regiments. His letters to his relatives in Ireland, written from 1778 to 1792, span the reigns of three Austrian monarchs, Maria Theresa, Joseph II, and Leopold II, and his billettings and activities reflect Imperial foreign and domestic policy in this time period and, not incidentally, the importance of the army in both.

Eighteenth-century Imperial attempts at expanding power and territory in the West, that is, in Germany, had been blocked first by the resistance of the German princes, backed by France, and then by the rise of Prussia, after the Seven Years War a rival for influence and power within the Holy Roman Empire.[24] Austrian plans to add Bavaria to the Hapsburg dominions on the death of its Elector in 1777 were met by Prussian resistance. In the resulting War of the Bavarian Succession, John Bellew's cavalry regiment, one of sixteen, was stationed in Bohemia from 1778–79, part of the total of 200,000 Austrian troops facing the Prussians in Bohemia and Moravia.[25]

Frustrated by the Prussian check in the West, Imperial policy turned eastward in an attempt to build an alliance that would isolate Prussia and support future ventures in Germany, and an alliance with Russia was concluded in 1781. Unfortunately, this also led to involvement in the Empress Catherine's aggressive policy toward the Ottoman Empire and further campaigns against the Austrians' traditional foe in the East, the Turks. In 1783, John Bellew was in 'Patch in Tolmeinser' (Pacs in Tolna) in southern Hungary as a part of the Austrian force mobilized along the Danube to support Catherine's suppression of a revolt in the Crimea; from 1788 through 1790, he was on the border regions of Serbia and the Banat (a Magyar administrative region) of Temesvar, participating in the joint Austro-Russian war with the Ottomans.

After the conclusion of Austrian participation in the Turkish war, hastened by Imperial concern with internal turmoil in Hungary and the Austrian Netherlands and the situation in France, 1792 found Bellew and his unit in Mantua, one of the Empire's Italian possessions, preparing to embark for Sardinia as a part of the European forces opposing Revolutionary France.

Bellew's personal participation in military actions was of a varied nature. It was limited in the War of the Bavarian Succession, derisively dubbed the Potato War by the Prussians, the Plum Riot by the Austrians, names given according to the type of forage sought by each side after the initial confrontation degenerated into a series of what Bellew accurately termed 'many skirmishes' and a war of attrition.[26] Likewise, the mobilization of 1783 did not lead to more active support of the Russians against the Turks, although Bellew stated optimistically that if they didn't 'agree in their preliminaries, we march straight to Belgrade'. However, five years later, he was to participate actively in operations around Belgrade. In 1787, the Turks declared war on Russia, and this time, to fulfill treaty obligations (and seize the opportunity lost in 1783 to acquire Turkish territory), the Empire entered the war against the Ottomans.[27]

Imperial encounters with the Turks were marked by a ferocity beyond even that associated with eighteenth-century warfare in western Europe. The beheading of Christian prisoners was commonplace, and Austrian troops entering Belgrade during the Turkish campaigns of 1737–39 were appalled to find the Grand Vizier's tent adorned with pieces of an Imperial general.[28] John Bellew, with the western Austrian army in Bosnia, was to witness this aspect of war with the Turks some fifty years later. He described 'what a shocking inhumane prospect' it was 'to see a field covered with dead bodies, without heads' and characterized the enemy as having 'no manner of humanity'. An eighteenth-century Bavarian officer remarked of the Turks:

> It becomes impossible for an army which once shows its back to them, to save itself by flight or in any other way. They are most expert in the use of the sabre ... and such is their skill in its use that, should their opponents give way before them, they produce an incredible carnage in the shortest possible time.[29]

Bellew's 'friend and relative' Pat Bellew was killed and beheaded at such a retreat from Mohidye, a key border fortress taken by the Turks during an offensive into southern Hungary in 1788. John Bellew credited his 32-pound wrought-iron cuirass and the heavy iron cavalry helmet, designed specifically for protection against Turkish scimitars, with saving him from such a fate.[30]

In November 1789, he wrote from Hungary of his major action in the war, his participation in the final Austrian assault against Belgrade, which fell in October after a month-long siege. He described to Michael Bellew the final taking of the citadel following a 48-hour bombardment and attack, in which the man and horse in front of and behind him were killed by cannon fire. He reported the deaths of two fellow Irish officers – the son of General Plunkett, 'who you knew for many years in Ireland with Sir Pat Bellew, killed during the siege', and the son of a Mr Reilly of Ballinlash, 'killed by Fuxan [Fokshani in Moldavia] under Prince Coburg' in July – and the survival of a kinsman, Sir Patrick Bellew's son John, who had been with him in Belgrade.

The army also participated in peacetime Imperial domestic affairs. From the early to mid-1780s, Bellew was in various camps in northern Hungary, the usual station for cavalry units because of the inexpensive provisions.[31] In 1785–87, he was with the troops in the Trans-Danubian county of Győr who assisted in conducting Imperial land surveys and kept order among the peasantry. Here as well, he encountered military action of a sort.

In 1784, Joseph II had ordered a census of Hungary, which was to register property, households, and dwellings, including those of the nobility. The nobles, whose property had traditionally been tax-exempt, feared, correctly, that the census was the first step toward their eventual taxation in an attempt to increase state revenue. In several Hungarian counties, the military had to be used to enforce registration.[32]

As well, the peasantry had to be kept in order; the government feared they too would cause problems, 'as they imagined they would lose some of their meadows and plowing lands' as a result of the survey. The peasants may have been afraid that the census would uncover landholdings beyond the maximum specified in the Urbarial regulations of Maria Theresa; if this was the case, the excess could be confiscated by their landlords. In any event, peasant unrest was a problem the government could not ignore; there had been a number of minor peasant revolts and insurrections in Hungary in the 1750s and 60s and a major one in Transylvania in 1784, which had been put down by the nobles and the army. Exploitation by their lords, heavy taxation and duties, the *robot* or forced labor, and the heavy tithe were at the root of these revolts. Poor leadership and lack of adequate weapons ensured their suppression.

John Bellew, stationed at 'Pallas Gyarmath' (Győrmat) in the county of Győr, experienced one of these peasant insurrections with its typical result. In 1784, serfs on the estates of the Batthyánys in Vas, a county contiguous to Győr, had revolted; in 1787, in Győr itself, trouble arose. Bellew was sent to a town where the peasants had rebelled against their landlord. The troops took twelve of the ring-leaders prisoner, then found themselves set upon by the remaining peasants who assaulted them with 'scythes, pitchforks, hatchets, sticks, and stones'. Bellew was attacked by a peasant with a scythe, but parried the blow, which struck his horse instead. With perhaps forgiveable bravado, he concluded: 'he received the reward due to his bravery. I immediately discharged a brace of balls through his brains so that he and my horse lay together'.

Besides providing descriptions of his participation in Imperial military campaigns and domestic peacekeeping, John Bellew's letters portray eighteenth-century military life in general and Imperial service in particular. In a letter of 1783, he responded to Michael Bellew's request for advice in regard to one of his son's entering a military career. He outlined a plan of action for this prospective Irish Imperial officer: he would spend one year at least in the 'college at Vienna'[33] to learn German, then (a familiar theme) he would be placed through Irish connections in a regiment of infantry, 'which we can easily do through Tom D'Alton, the priest. He can write to his brother the general'. Interestingly, Bellew recommended the infantry over the more glamorous cavalry, primarily for economic reasons. An officer would receive the same pay, but be spared the expense of housing a servant and maintaining a horse.[34] He estimated that with a supplement of £50 a year to his infantry pay, an officer could live 'well and genteel'. He concluded that for him, the military life was both a pleasing and disagreeable one. He boasted, 'I have had the honour to dine three times with the Emperor' and he enjoyed his military companions, but regretted his continual lack of money. The expenses of maintaining a horse and equipage, his uniform, and a servant, as well as general appearances – he asked Michael Bellew to send him his deceased father's seal with the family arms and gold chain, 'very necessary for me here' – appear as constant themes in his correspondence. In addition, the dangers of service are stressed; besides the obvious ones of death or wounds in battle, poor health was another. As a result of his Turkish campaigns in territory Maria Theresa considered 'a lot of barren mountains and feverish swamps', he complained that 'the heat, the bad climate, bad water, and many other inconveniences has wrecked my constitution entirely'.[35]

Bellew's correspondence also provides the basis for an examination of the Irish in foreign service within a larger and more significant context: the process of assimilation as well as the attempt to preserve Irish identity. Irish officers in Imperial service considered themselves loyal and faithful supporters of the Hapsburgs, not mercenaries. (Nor did they consider themselves disloyal to Britain, normally an Austrian ally: Generals Richard and James D'Alton erected an obelisk on their Westmeath estate in the 1780s that honored Maria Theresa, Joseph II, and George III.)[36] The references to Austria in Bellew's correspondence as 'our country' demonstrate well that the Irish generally served their adoptive country faithfully. Their assimilation was evidenced in a variety of ways. Gaelic and Anglo-Norman names underwent a Germanic transformation; Brownes changed their names to Brouns, and O'Nolans to O'Neillans, or in one case, Neulau. Many Irish officers attached the Germanic *von* to their place of origin, resulting in such hybrid names as Johann Sigismund Macquire von Inniskillen, or Kavanaugh von Ballybrack. In cases of a family's long-term service, languages changed as well. While Field Marshal Maximilian Browne spoke English well, albeit with a brogue, his spelling became Germanicized, and his son Philip was unable to speak English at all.[37]

Nonetheless, there remained strong ties to, and an abiding interest in, Ireland and things Irish. When Philip Browne was considering marriage in 1763, his first inquiry was to the eligibility of one of Lord Kenmare's daughters. Some officers in the first generation of Irish service to the Empire preferred to use Gaelic with their compatriots, and thus a distinctive sense of Irishness continued. There were gatherings and reunions of Irish officers on St Patrick's Day; a notable one occurred on 17 March 1766 in Vienna when the Spanish ambassador, a Count Mahoney, invited prominent Irishmen to a fête. The military contingent included Count Lacy, president of the *Hofkriegsrat*; six generals; four Chiefs of the Grand Cross; two governors; several Knights Military; six staff officers; and four privy councillors. In response, the state officials and the entire Imperial court wore Celtic crosses to honor the Irish element in their army and nation.[38] Communication with other Irish in Europe and with the mother country was maintained through relatives, newly-arrived Irish officers, or through the good offices of the House of the Irish Franciscans in the 'Street of the Irish' in Prague.[39]

This continuing tie to Ireland is reflected in John Bellew's correspondence as well. Besides, as we have seen, his reports to Michael Bellew of Irish casualties, he also mentioned the fellow Irish with whom he associated: his relatives, John and Matthew Bellew, sons of Sir Patrick, and members of local families, 'Garrett Kelly and young O'Kelly of Ballinlass'.[40] Moreover, his knowledge of events in Ireland, both national and local, was impressive, considering that most of his camps were in Hungary. In 1783, he read that a Mr Fitzgerald was hanged in county Mayo and asked, 'was that one of Capt. Fitzgerald's family and what was his crime? Likewise, the Whiteboys, if they are so desperate as the newspaper says that they burn and murder in every place they come ...'[41] He was always eager for news of home, begged to be remembered to local friends, and fretted over the health of his relatives: when he heard of the illness of Michael Bellew's wife, 'cousin Jenny', he replied that he was in quarters in a Hungarian town with a religious order and would get 'Mass read for her recovery, and that from every friar in the convent'.

In summary, while it appears clear that gentry émigrés preserved their Irish identities, it is equally clear that their emigration was a loss to Ireland. It is impossible to calculate this loss in quantitative terms; in qualitative terms, it was enormous, since it included many members of an industrious class whose enterprise and intelligence were put to the service of foreign countries rather than their own. This was obvious to enlightened contemporary observers. Arthur

Young, of all the eighteenth-century improvers the one to whom this waste would have been most abhorrent, perhaps stated this view best:

> Think of the loss to Ireland of so many Catholics of small property re-sorting to the armies of France, Spain, Sardinia, and Austria, for employ-ment! Can it be imagined, that they would be so ready to leave their own country, if they could stay in it with any prospect of promotion, success in industry, or even liberal protection? It is known that they would not; and that under a different system, instead of adding strength to the en-emies of this Empire, they would be among the foremost to enrich and defend it.[42]

EDUCATION

The provisions of the penal laws concerning Irish Catholic education, in the words of Lecky, 'amounted simply to universal, unqualified, and unlimited proscription'.[43] Any Catholic teaching school, publicly or in a private house, was considered and prosecuted as a 'Popish regular', and a reward of £10 was offered for the discovery of a Catholic schoolmaster. Catholics were not only forbidden to have schools of their own in Ireland, but also proscribed from sending their children to be educated abroad under penalty of outlawry and forfeiture of property; the penal fine was £100, to be awarded to the discov-erer.

Nevertheless, these laws prohibiting Catholic education were contravened or disregarded by the aristocracy and gentry. They continued to provide their children with a primary or preparatory education by employing tutors and schoolmasters in their private homes and also supported schoolmasters for their localities.[44] For example, a report to the government in 1731 enumerated thirty-two schools 'taught by Papists' in the diocese of Tuam and its compilers went on to comment that 'many Papists keep tutors in their houses' who taught not only their children but those of the neighbourhood.[45] In a household ledger kept by Michael Bellew in the late 1760s and early 1770s, when his first two sons were under ten years of age, entries include the following payments:

> April 1, 1769 – 'pd Kelly the schoolmaster ... £0.6.6'
> August 3, 1769 – 'pd James Kelly the schoolmaster ... £0.16.3'
> December 16, 1770 – 'pd JK schoolmaster in full to this day ... £1.8.10½'
> May of 1771 – 'pd John Gavan schoolmaster in full ... £1.2.9'

For a higher classical secondary or university education, however, eighteenth-century Irish Catholic gentry families able to afford the expense sent their children to the continent, particularly to France.[46] There, seminaries had been established as a part of the Catholic Reformation to supply the educational training of priests for the English and Irish missions. With the increasing demand from the seventeenth century onward for the education of the children of the Catholic aristocracy and gentry, these existing seminaries developed humanities and philosophy courses for the laity. The development of the English College at Douai in this manner has been characterized as a 'growth downwards';[47] moreover, new schools, such as the Jesuit institution at St Omers and the Benedictine school of St Gregory's in Douai, began specializing in the lay education of Catholic youth, specifically in the humanities.[48]

There was a tradition of Bellew family attendance, of both the Louth and Galway branches, at these humanities schools in France and the Low Countries from the second quarter of the eighteenth century to the French Revolution. Bellews attended St Omers, and the English College and the Benedictine school of St Gregory's, both in Douai. Their progress, as well as that of their relatives and friends, can be charted through school records and family correspondence.

The course of study at these schools, whether run by the Jesuits, Benedictines, or the regular clergy, was much the same. This similarity can be attributed to not only some derivation from the highly successful Jesuit *Ratio Studiorum*, but the common scholastic medieval tradition from which it was derived, a tradition reflected in the pre-Reformation grammar schools as well.[49] Classes, themes, and studies were all integrated around the study of Latin,[50] and the levels of the different schools in the course of studies were determined according to proficiency and the degree of difficulty of the authors studied. The humanities course began with Rudiments, also referred to as Little or Low Figures, in which the first elements of Latin were taught in three divisions, depending upon the students' preparatory education. Students then progressed, year by year, through Grammar, Syntax, and Poets, to the final and highest humanities school, Rhetoric. The boys worked up from the basics of Latin, with stories adapted from Cicero and the Bible, to the verbatim texts of Caesar, Cicero, Sallust, Vergil, Horace, Seneca, Juvenal, and Terence. Similarly, although with a lesser emphasis, pupils also mastered the rudiments of Greek and progressed to the study of the Greek New Testament and such authors and poets as Homer, Hesiod, Demosthenes, and Xenophon. This was the standard, rigorous Jesuit classical curriculum. In addition, depending on the school, works of history and geography were recommended. The schools also offered instruction in French, an understandable supplement considering their location;

English literature and arithmetic were introduced at the English College of Douai after the mid-eighteenth century, although not without considerable discussion.

A student could spend from five to seven years in the course of study, depending on his placement in, or out of, Rudiments; the majority spent two years in the lowest school. The average age at entry was 13–14, although school records show beginners as young as 10–12; the age at completion was 18–19.[51]

The daily routine of these schools began at 5 a.m. and ended at 9 p.m. There were approximately four hours of classes, two in the morning and two in the afternoon, and three to four hours of study periods, broken by breakfast, dinner, and supper meals. Interspersed were times for chapel, prayer, and private meditation, with Sundays given over to Mass and devotions. The students, garbed in black cassocks, were also regarded as active boys and young men by the school authorities, and provision was made for recreation and play – bowls, handball, and football – and the keeping of pets. Dramatics were usually a part of the curriculum, and excursions to country houses owned by the schools were made during holidays and the summer months. The standard rate, or pension, for attending these schools was a £25 minimum; supplementary allowances could be provided by a boy's family.

The English College at Douai, founded and run by English secular clergy, attracted many sons of the Catholic aristocracy and gentry.[52] The majority were from England; the traditional Catholic family names – Aston, Blundell, Howard, Jerningham, Kendal, Petre, Tichbourne, and Weld – appear in the school records and presidents' diaries that provide a great part of our knowledge of the school in the eighteenth century. Irish Catholic family names – Dalton, Plunkett, and Brown – appear as well and those of Irish boys from Spain, Portugal, Bordeaux, Rouen, and the West Indies. The five sons of Sir Edward Bellew, third baronet of county Louth, all attended the English College. The eldest, John, who succeeded to the baronetcy in 1741, began there in 1734 as a Grammarian, arriving with the Dillon family, who also brought their sons Thomas and John. He left in 1739, having completed his final year in Rhetoric. John was followed by Patrick, the future fifth baronet, in 1739; Michael in 1740; William in 1745, listed under the second and third Classes of Rudiments in 1747; and the youngest, Francis, entered under Novitii in 1749, and the first class of Rudiments in 1740.[53]

The school records and diaries of Douai during this period, besides showing the progress and comings and goings of the students, also reflect the more sober side of eighteenth-century communal school life. In 1750, an epidemic, which judging from the contemporary description (a 'variolarum morbo' [a pox-like disease] with 'exulcerato guttere' [inflamed throat]) might well have been strep throat, swept through the College. Entries for November and December of that year mention the illness and record that William Bellew, along with William Jerningham, was sent to Cambrai for recovery. William's younger brother Francis was not so fortunate: afflicted with the same disease, he died at Douai in November.[54]

The sons of Michael Bellew of county Galway followed a different course of education in the humanities. The eldest, Christopher Dillon Bellew, began his humanities studies with the Jesuits at St Omers College.[55] Established in 1593 by the English Jesuit Robert Persons, it soon became the largest of the institutions providing a lay education, establishing an enviable reputation with the aristocracy and gentry as the 'English Catholic classical school par excellence'.[56] Eighteenth-century Irish Catholic youths were educated there as well: Plunketts from Ireland and Austria, including the sons of Thomas Plunkett, baron of the Holy Roman Empire; the son of Henry, 11th viscount Dillon; and Lynches from the West Indies, among others.[57]

At Christopher's arrival in 1773, the college was in Bruges. In 1762, the Jesuits had been expelled from their original school in St Omers in France by a decree of the Parlement in Paris. The masters, taking most of their students with them, re-established the school in 'the House of Flowers', in the High Street of Bruges. Since Christopher's age on admission was only 12, he may well have been entered in the St Omers preparatory school.[58] At any rate, his stay in Bruges was short; the Jesuit order itself was suppressed in 1773, and the students dispersed. The Jesuits moved to Liege where, under the protection of the Prince-Bishop Mgr. Wilbruck, they continued the school as the English Academy; Henry Dillon, son of the 11th viscount, followed them there, as did many of the former Bruges students. Others were sent to different continental schools. Christopher, along with an Irish classmate, Patrick Fallon from Cloone near Athlone, who had also arrived at Bruges in 1773, was sent to the English College at Douai, where his Louth relatives had been educated.[59] Their entry, along with twelve others from Bruges, is recorded in the Prefect of Studies' Book ('Patric. Fallon, Christoph. Bellew venere Octobris 21 [arrived on October 21] ab ... Collegio Brugensi dissoluto' [from the dissolved college at Bruges]) and the diary of Henry Tichbourne Blount, president of the College ('Arrived ... Messrs. Patt. Fallon, Christr. Bellew, Edm. Hearn, Hy. Hearn. For Low Figures, Irish youths').[60]

However, Michael Bellew was apparently displeased with both the English College's discipline and his son's performance there; Christopher's stay was as short as it had been at Bruges. A letter of 14 November from H.T. Blount, president of the College, to Michael Bellew reported that Christopher was being sent to another college. He defended the boy against his father's charges of idleness and inattention, and told of his low spirits, being 'complained of and severely reproached by a parent'. Nonetheless, Blount's diary for November records that, 'On the 16th Master Christr. Bellew left the College, and went by his father's order, to pursue his studies at the English monks'.[61]

The new college he was sent to – that of 'the English monks' – was the Benedictine school of St Gregory's, also at Douai. In the early seventeenth century, the Benedictines earlier expelled from England had been united in monasteries, one at Douai. By 1622, they were running a school there, which, along with St Omers and the English College, met the educational needs of lay Catholic youths in the humanities. In 1626, according to an informer, 'they have many scholars which are beneficial to them, and many gentleman's sons'; the latter paid pensions for their education and board and lived within the precincts of the monastery. By the eighteenth century, the enrollment was from 50–60 students.[62] The course of study was similar to that at St Omers and the English College; nevertheless, the new school must have been more satisfactory to the Bellews – both father and peripatetic son – since Christopher appears to have completed the humanities course at St Gregory's, and the second son Luke was sent there in the 1780s, as were the sons, Henry and Christopher, of Michael Bellew's brother-in-law Edmond Taaffe.[63]

Another educational option for gentry sons pursuing courses in the humanities was that of the Irish Colleges on the continent. All were primarily concerned with the theological training of priests for the Irish mission, but most provided humanities courses for both future clerics and lay youths.[64] The two youngest Bellew sons educated abroad, Harry and Patrick, attended the Irish College at Douai for a time, and there are references to their attendance in their elder brother Luke's letters from Douai to his brother Christopher in Ireland. Michael Bellew's brother Patrick, a merchant, visited them at Douai in 1786 and reported on their progress; he, however, was not pleased, expecting more from their schooling, and sent severe letters to the prior. Luke mentioned his uncle's visit and defended the College, pointing out that his brothers were, after all, 'schoolboys, not polished gentlemen', and in response to his elder brother's inquiries, supplied information about the school. There were approximately 30 boys there, and the teaching, cleanliness, and neatness were 'on the best footing'. Nevertheless, his uncle was thinking of having them removed to a French house. Patrick Bellew's displeasure carried more weight; in 1786, Harry and Patrick left the College to continue their studies elsewhere.[65]

Nor was the education of Michael Bellew's daughter Mary neglected. In an undated letter to his brother, Luke Bellew suggested sending his sister to a school run by the Ursulines in Lille which was attended by 'young ladies from

London' and other parts of England. There she could learn French and 'pick up a better accent from the English'. His suggestion also reveals something of what was considered a proper curriculum for young ladies of gentry families: 18 guineas a year would provide room and board and instruction in French, arithmetic, writing, music, and dancing. This education was, of course, designed to enhance daughters for the marriage market. Whether Mary ever attended the school is not clear from the family correspondence – there is also mention of the possibility of her being sent to a school in Hampstead, or perhaps Liege.[66]

After completing a humanities course, several options for further educational or career training on the continent were available for gentry youths, and the experiences of the Bellew sons reflect them. For those wishing to continue their studies, philosophy courses were available at many of the continental schools. A need for such courses was evident from the seventeenth century forward, not only as a preliminary for theological training for future priests who found such instruction difficult to obtain at home, but also as a partial substitute for the English and Irish university degrees denied the sons of the Catholic aristocracy and gentry. As a consequence, and as a part of the growth downward mentioned earlier, two-year courses in philosophy were offered at schools run by Jesuits, Benedictines, and secular clergy.[67]

The philosophy course at the English College at Douai serves as a general model of such studies.[68] First-year students, called Logici or 'Low Philosophers', studied logic, metaphysics, and general philosophical problems. The second-year group, Physici, or 'High Philosophers', studied Natural Philosophy which, reflecting the overlap of philosophy and natural science, dealt with problems of physical science as well. The course at Douai was based on Aristotle's *Physics*, and the 1689 constitution required that the philosophy professors cover

> the usual ground of universal philosophy, i.e. the 5 universals, the categories, argumentation, and the other sections usually assigned to Logic; the various matters contained in the eight books of 'Physics' – the earth and the sky, coming to be and passing away, the soul, metaphysics, the ultimate purpose of man and other matters pertaining to ethics.[69]

Lectures in Latin were written down by the students and served as reference books.

The best students participated in public 'defensions' before other students and professors. These took place three times during the two-year course; students defended theses in logic and metaphysics in the spring of their first year, and theses taken from the whole range of Universal Philosophy during their final year. Michael Bellew, the third son of Sir William, completed the philosophy course at Douai. He is recorded among a group of students defending 'theses philosophiae Rationalis' in June of 1746, and 'theses Philosophiae naturalis' in February 1747, and is listed under 'Philosophi 2 anni' in December 1747.[70]

Christopher Dillon Bellew also completed one of these philosophy courses. From 1779 to 1781, he was in the Collège Académique a l'Abbaye Royale de Saint Vaast. This was a Benedictine college in Douai, often referred to as the College of St Vedast,[71] which was closely connected with the Benedictine abbey of St Vaast at Arras. The abbot there had provided the expelled English Benedictines with a house in Douai in 1608, from which the monks had established the school of St Gregory's, referred to earlier. In 1619, he stipulated that they provide professors of theology and philosophy for his own college, which he had founded in Douai in 1611 for the education of his monks. Students at St Gregory's were often sent to Benedictine colleges for further education, and the humanities school must have provided a natural conduit for philosophical studies at the Collège Académique.[72] This appears to have been the case with Christopher. In 1779, five years after his entry into St Gregory's, long enough to have completed the humanities course there, he appears in the printed *Catalogue des Écoliers* of the Collège Académique among those 'étudians en Philosophie', with the note 'né en Irlande en 1762'. His classmates included seven Irishmen, five priests among them, and two members of the English Catholic Throckmorton family, Francis and William. The Bellew papers also contain copies of the Latin certificates presented to Christopher at Douai in August of 1781, attesting his attendance and completion of the two-year course and his successful defense of his thesis in Universal Philosophy. The certificates were signed by Dom Hiliare Weugue, 'philosophio professor omnibus', along with Dom Vigor Lorquin, 'religieux de Saint Vaast'.

Before completing this review of the gentry's association with the humanities and philosophical schools, one additional aspect of attendance abroad should be noted. In the earlier days of the penal code, aliases were commonly used by the students, usually the maiden name of the mother or the name of a relative. This practice has been assumed to have died out in the course of the eighteenth century. Yet, at Douai the future Lord Kenmare went by the name of Taylor in 1738, the Plunketts used the names Robinson in 1744 and Wollascot in 1772, and the Bellews of Louth often were entered as Thompsons in records from 1738. The Prefect of Studies Book from 1750 to 1794 shows that more than 5 per cent, 47 out of 850 of those who began studies there during this period, used aliases.[73] At St Omers the practice was also common; in 1773, Henry

Dillon used both Harrison and Taylor.[74] By 1789, the practice had virtually died out, at least at Douai. However, the Bellews of Galway continued to employ aliases. Christopher used the name Kelly at the English College in 1774, and at St Vaast in 1781, he called himself Taaffe; both of these aliases were taken from relatives' names. In the 1780s, the younger Bellew sons, Henry and Patrick, also used Taaffe while at St Gregory's.[75] Perhaps this was just ingrained habit, a holdover from an earlier period when at least the letter of the law regarding Catholic education abroad (if not its actual enforcement) was savage. Nevertheless, Sir Patrick and perhaps Michael Bellew were members of the Catholic Committee during this period, and Sir Patrick was particularly active in Catholic affairs. They may well have wished not to draw undue attention to the Bellews' education abroad, even in a period when it was common practice.

A scion of the Irish Catholic gentry might also direct his education toward entering the priesthood, another vocation with necessarily close associations with the continent. The Catholic church in Ireland had survived the government's effort in the late seventeenth and early eighteenth centuries to destroy it: the banishing of bishops, regulars, and those exercising any form of ecclesiastical jurisdiction, the registration of the secular clergy to identify them and restrict their movements, and the prohibition of any new Catholic clergy, secular or regular, from entering Ireland after 1704. The hope that the registered diocesan clergy would, in due course, die out with no replacement of their numbers (since theoretically no ordinations by the bishops would be possible and new clergy would be barred from entering the island) had died unfulfilled. From 1707, Catholic bishops had been appointed to fill vacant seats, a process largely completed by 1750, and they carried on ordinations of new priests. Only when France threatened the Hanoverian monarchy in the first half of the century was there notable repression; otherwise, the clergy in Ireland remained relatively unmolested. By 1760, the penal laws of the early century directed against them were seldom enforced.[76]

Nevertheless, the training of new priests posed a potential problem, since the laws against the institution of Catholic schools in Ireland, whether lay or clerical, remained. This was resolved through the traditional tie to the continent. From the early seventeenth century, Irish Colleges had been established in France, Spain, Portugal, the Low Countries, and Rome, some 30 in all, to supply priests for the Irish mission; the majority of the Irish clergy was trained in these colleges.

The methods of circumventing the statutes prohibiting religious education abroad were numerous. Even in the harsh days of the late seventeenth and early eighteenth centuries, there was a regular exchange of priests between

Ireland and the continent. To evade government spies and informers, students often passed themselves off as merchants or apprentices to the various Irish trading houses in Europe. There was also the option, especially for those young men of the south and west, of availing themselves of passage on smugglers' boats, so hard to detect along the rugged coastline. Similarly, priests returning to Ireland were smuggled in; for those who chose to re-enter at the port cities, bribes to officials could be offered. Moreover, priests of the eighteenth century did not wear a distinctive clerical dress; consequently, their identification was difficult. In the more lenient period after mid-century, this traffic became even easier.[77]

The majority of the eighteenth-century Irish clergy was educated in France, the greatest number at the Irish College of Paris, where enrollment increased from 90 in 1739 to 180 in 1787. But other Irish institutions in France – the Irish Colleges of Nantes, Toulouse, Bordeaux, Lille, Tournai, and Douai, among others – also provided priests for the Irish mission.[78] The second Bellew son, Luke, chose this religious vocation while in France. He apparently wanted to stay with the English Benedictines from whom he had acquired his humanities schooling at St Gregory's, but encountered the opposition of the bishop of Arras ('every person in his diocese intended for the Irish mission shall study at the Irish college') and entered the institution at Douai in 1786. There was a Bellew family precedent of sorts for this choice: Dominick Bellew of the Louth branch had studied at the Irish College of Bordeaux and the Pastoral College at Louvain earlier in the century, and, at the time of Luke's decision to enter the priesthood, was bishop of Killala.[79] The colleges attended by the Bellews were relatively small. The total number of students at Bordeaux in the eighteenth century never exceeded 30 to 40; the enrollment at Douai and Louvain appears to have been even smaller.[80]

Luke Bellew's decision was not greeted with approval by his eldest brother. Christopher's reaction, as reflected in his younger brother's letters, is an interesting example of the almost schizophrenic attitude of Catholic gentry families concerning an education abroad: torn between wishing to provide their sons – or brothers – with a Catholic education, yet worrying over a too-close association with, and the undue influence of, the religious who provided that education.[81] Luke countered his brother's accusation of 'inducements thrown out by churchmen in order to possess the minds of young people in favour of the Ecclesiastical Estate'. On the contrary, he argued, not only was his choice one resulting from conviction, the ecclesiastical estate was not a materially attractive one. The monks bewailed the misery of those, including clerics, who lived in the world, and the priests of the Irish College were ill-provided for, a reminder that they were 'not yet quite in heaven'.

In a later letter, he responded to comments by his elder brother, apparently still not reconciled to his choice, concerning the prevailing complaint of the Irish clergy as 'vulgar and sottish'. These opinions might have been just concerning other Irish colleges, but not his seminary. He admitted to disorder, mismanagement, and drunkenness at Douai before his entry, but not after the installation of Abbé Dillon as president; under the new regime, 'no more than a pint of beer out of meals' was permitted. He further reassured his brother that most of his time was spent with Dillon, apart from the other students, and he still spent a portion of his time with the English monks.

Seminary students from gentry families could, of course, be supported in their studies from family resources; such was the case with Luke Bellew. His diet and lodging cost 25 guineas; clothing and the expense of theological studies were extra. His letters home constantly stress the need for more money: first, an additional four guineas every four months, and later some 45 guineas beyond what his father was sending. He requested quick payment of his pension as well: as a result of earlier students leaving town without paying their debts, no credit beyond a month was available in Douai. His pleas for additional money were supported by the argument that his financial difficulties 'would be greater still in French seminaries'. At one point, he considered staying with the English Benedictines where the pension was less.[82]

Students at the Irish colleges run by the secular clergy, which included those at Bordeaux, Douai, and the Pastoral College at Louvain, usually entered before being ordained. They studied philosophy and theology at the facilities of the college itself, or attended lectures at universities in their localities or at Jesuit institutions. At the Irish College of Douai, prospective priests attended the University of Douai, and the Irish College of Louvain was also in close association with the University; at Bordeaux, students attended lectures at the Jesuit College of La Madeleine. The course of study could occupy a minimum of five years or a maximum of seven to eight, depending on the requirements of the individual college. The curriculum at Douai was six years: two were spent in philosophical studies, three at theology, and a final year was devoted to the study of pastoral theology. Besides attending to studies and lectures, considerable time was given over, as expected, to the religious life. At Bordeaux, there was daily Mass, prayers and meditations, reading of Scriptures, and recitation of the rosary and divine office. On Sundays, the juniors recited the office of the Blessed Virgin and assisted at the sermon, High Mass, and Vespers in the public church.[83]

One final theme in Luke Bellew's letters from Douai is of note. He was very much interested in the ecclesiastical careers of Bishop Bellew and Edward Dillon, the president of his college, who was also a relative. As a member of a gentry family of some prominence in both the east and west of Ireland, he was also interested in what influence might be provided on their behalf. With regard to Dominick Bellew, in 1787 he asked of the bishop why he wasn't 'in the ranks for some vacant see', presumably one more prestigious than Killala. He joked that he thought Bellew would succeed Dr Carpenter (the archbishop of Dublin from 1770 to 1786); instead the post went to a 'Dominican friar', but added, 'friars are good beggars and begging at Rome will go a great way'.

The 'Dominican friar' referred to was Carpenter's successor, John Thomas Troy, a member of the Dominican order. The reference is not without a certain irony. Bishop Bellew's ecclesiastical career is a good illustration of the rivalry between the Irish secular clergy and the regulars, as well as the machinations within the Congregation of Propaganda, responsible for the selection of Irish bishops after the death of James Stuart in 1766. Bellew had been the Roman agent of James Butler, archbishop of Cashel, before his appointment as parish priest of Dundalk in 1772 and his later translation to Killala in 1779. According to the Rev. Valentine Bodkin, Warden of Galway and successor to Bellew as Butler's Roman agent, Dominick Bellew had opposed Troy's promotion in 1786 and 'thus made for himself a mortal enemy in Dr Troy and the whole tribe of Dominicans who have blown up the other regulars against him. This is a thing that frequently happens in our Church, and woe be to him who incurs the indignation of the regulars, who are both formidable and numerous in our Church, and who, with the spirit of a monk ... persecute their rivals'. In 1788, Bodkin had written to Rome in support of Bellew's translation to the vacant see of Tuam, but the bishop of Ossory, John Dunne, opposed Bellew, as did Cardinal Stefano Borgia, since 1770 secretary *a secretis* to the Congregation of Propaganda. Bellew had offended Borgia during his stay at Rome in 1770 (he had apparently joined with Cardinals Albani and Rezzonico in an attempt to lessen Borgia's influence with Pius vi), and the Cardinal, perhaps in consequence, had supported Troy's promotion in 1786. Dominick Bellew died in 1812, still bishop of Killala.[84]

Edward Dillon, the president of Luke's college was, as noted earlier, a fellow Galwayman and relative; he was a cousin of Michael Bellew's. Born in 1739 at Caltra, Ballinasloe, he was sent to France for his education, entered a clerical career, and became superior of the Irish college in the 1780s, succeeding Luke McKiernan, of whose administration Luke Bellew had complained.[85] In an undated letter of 1786, Luke mentioned the death of the bishop of Clonfert, Andrew Donellan, and subsequent efforts to 'get Mr Dillon a mitre'. He begged Christopher to throw his influence for Dillon as well as that of his uncle Edmond Taaffe, then serving as a land agent for Lord Dillon; Dillon might then prevail with his brother, the Archbishop of Narbonne,[86] to use his good offices in the abbé's behalf. He also had the assistance of Michael Bellew's brother Patrick in his quest for preferment. The latter wrote his brother in 1787 that

> Abbe Dillon at Paris has wrote his brother Col by my desire to send me a proper letter of introduction to Lord Dillon. If I receive same ere end of this month (sooner the better) I will wait on his Lordship to procure his recommending our abbe to the Archbishop of Narbonne, being a pity that for want thereof poor Jack has been without a good church living these many years back, and otherwise very bare of means.[87]

As for Luke Bellew, his only stated ecclesiastical ambition was to succeed 'Father Harry' in the parishes of Mount Bellew and Moylough, although 'without doing as much honour to your claret'.

The two youngest Bellew sons educated in France pursued still different paths. After their removal from Douai, both went to Paris, Harry to study 'physick', along with the son of James Lynch of Loughrea. Medicine was one of the few professions open to Catholics in Ireland,[88] and many Irishmen went to foreign universities for their medical studies, particularly to France, to study at the famous school at Montpellier as well as the University of Paris. Some returned to Ireland to set up successful practices; others remained on the continent serving as doctors in the continental armies and navies, joining medical faculties, and becoming physicians to kings of France and Spain, as well as to the Stuart court-in-exile.[89]

Harry stayed at lodgings in the rue St Dominique in the faubourg St Jacques, where he was to be given the same allowance as Lynch's son, and to be 'totally governed by Cousin Jack Dillon', who was 'very discreet, well-behaved, as becomes a good clergyman', since Harry's past behaviour had been a topic of family concern. (His ecclesiastical chaperone notwithstanding, Harry seems to have relapsed; Luke Bellew would later report that he was spending much time 'at the Regiment'.)[90] In 1786, he spent part of his vacation at Versailles with a Lady Annelly 'who has apartments there'; she was a friend of another Bellew relative, 'Mrs O'Shee', Sir Patrick Bellew's daughter who lived in France. She was the second (and apparently much younger) wife of Count Robert O'Shee. Born in Ireland in 1736, O'Shee entered French military service as a cadet in Bulkeley's Irish Regiment in 1752, participating in campaigns of the Seven Years War and achieving the rank of captain; he entered Dillon's Regiment in 1775. Sir Patrick Bellew reported to Michael Bellew in 1773 on a visit by his son-in-law, 'who has provided a very good place at court for Mrs Shee which will make them independent for life, but he has some money yet to pay for it'.[91]

Patrick, after his initial removal to Paris, vacillated as to future plans. His uncle Patrick pushed him toward his occupation, trade. In a letter to his brother Michael, he described his attempts to place his nephew with 'several manufacturers in France and Flanders that are under no small obligation to my house'. For an unspecified sum of money, Patrick was to stay with them for six months to a year, learning goods and merchandizing and becoming fluent in French. This plan was unsuccessful – 'these folks are so tenacious of giving smallest insights of their business, nor choosing to be any way troubled with beginners' – so his uncle sent him to a pension in Rouen 'to get complete in the French, also figures and a good hand whereof he stands in great need as [it] was not intelligible when [he] left Douay'. There, he would also improve in getting 'polished for the world and fitted for a counting house'. In the meantime, friends would keep an eye on him.[92]

Patrick, however, had other thoughts. In a letter to his eldest brother Christopher from his pension at Rouen, he described himself as being torn between what he really wanted, a vocation in the church, and his father's wish for an eventual apprenticeship with his merchant uncle. He hoped, after one or two years, if his inclinations were the same, to be allowed to pursue them. Luke Bellew, apparently in his younger brother's confidence, also wrote to Christopher of Patrick's desire to become a priest, despite his 'former neglect of the sacraments', of which his parents were aware. Patrick was afraid to approach his father directly (the implication seems to have been that one priest in the immediate family was enough); nevertheless, he wanted his permission 'for his going through a course of theology with me here at Douay'.

The exact point of resolution of this family conflict is unclear from the correspondence, although the process was exhaustive: at one point, reference is made to Patrick's returning to Ireland, despite the friction between son and family, to follow 'the farming business' under Christopher. However, in February of 1787, Patrick was back in Paris at a seminary or college (both terms are used, with no indication as to lay or clerical studies), where he was extremely happy, 'as great a point gained as if he already enjoyed the advantages which might possibly have accrued to him, had he embraced the proposals held out to him by my uncle', according to Luke Bellew. Whatever his final decision, he was to try to further himself through use of Irish connections; Luke recommended trying to get Patrick introduced to Count Walsh, the son of an Irish émigré with influence and 'high favour' at court.[93]

For the greater part of the eighteenth century, the schools, colleges, and seminaries of Europe provided an educational haven for Catholic lay and clerical students. The less fortunate aspect of this experience lay in the attraction of the continent to those forced there for a Catholic education. Despite the large numbers of students, priests, and doctors who returned to Ireland, others stayed in Europe to practice the medical profession, establish banking or commercial houses, join the faculties of educational institutions, or minister in the churches of France and Spain. Like those of their gentry counterparts in military service, the talents of these Irishmen were lost to their native country. This situation, however, was soon changed, as the close of the century marked the end of an era of close ties and associations with the continent. Two factors – one domestic, one foreign, and both interrelated – were instrumental. They removed, first, the necessity and, secondly and even more important, the attraction of temporary or permanent residence abroad.

First, the last quarter of the century brought the dismantling of the penal structure, opening those careers and endeavours formerly denied to Catholics and repealing the restrictions that had prompted their emigration. Legislation in 1778 allowed Catholics to lease land for 999 years; in 1782, all restrictions on landownership and purchase were repealed. As a further part of the relief in 1782, Catholics were given permission to teach, after obtaining a license from the local bishop, and they began establishing their own schools for the instruction of both lay and clerical students. Nevertheless, the law still forbade Catholic universities, colleges, or endowed schools. In 1793, Catholics were at last authorized to endow their own colleges and universities and could also obtain degrees at Trinity. The final barrier to Catholic religious education was overcome in 1795 with the establishment of Maynooth, a college specifically instituted for the education of the Catholic clergy; colleges could now be established and endowed for the education of Roman Catholics only.[94] Further, the relief act of 1793 permitted a Catholic to hold a commission in the army and the newly formed Irish militia.

The lifting of many of these final restrictions in the 1790s was directly related to the second of these factors: the upheaval in Europe caused by the outbreak of revolution in France. For those members of gentry families who still chose military service or education abroad, or for those in the midst of such service or studies, this second event was decisive; it completely disrupted the lives of the Irish in France and, ultimately, the Low Countries.

The Irish Brigade, which had served the Bourbon monarchs faithfully throughout the century, was disbanded and no longer existed as a separate and distinct unit within the French army. Despite the gradual reduction of the Irish rank-and-file since mid-century, the Brigade's officers were all Irish.[95] Some chose to stay in France and serve the revolutionary regime; others joined the royalist forces or the armies of other continental countries. Of those who remained in France, however, many fell under suspicion because of their former associations with the Bourbons; an extreme example was the fate of a member of a prominent Mayo and Roscommon family. Lieutenant-General Count Arthur Richard Dillon, the son of Henry, 11th viscount Dillon, was colonel of the famous Dillon Regiment and played a leading role in the revolutionary French army's victory at Valmy in 1792. However, he was suspected of aristocratic, hence traitorous, leanings; arrested in 1794 and brought before the Revolutionary Tribunal which found him guilty of plotting to restore the monarchy, he was guillotined 14 April 1794.[96]

The fate of a Bellew relative, Count Robert O'Shee, the son-in-law of Sir Patrick Bellew, who also remained in French service after the Revolution, was less drastic. He was commander of the National Guard at the time of the fall of the Bastille, and in 1792 was *chef de bataillon* in the 87th Regiment, formerly Dillon's Regiment, participating in the Ardennes campaign. In 1796, he was commandant on half-pay at the École Militaire; however, his reputation was not a good one. In the preparations for the Hoche expedition to Ireland, Carnot, chief director of the war effort for the Committee of Public Safety, suggested to the Minister of War that Richard O'Shee, a relative, be sent along. However, he cautioned against confusing Richard O'Shee with Robert, since the latter's character was in question and his reputation in Paris not of the highest order. Michael Bellew's cousin, Christopher Kelly Bellew, in Paris in 1802, mentioned O'Shee in a letter to Christopher Dillon Bellew. Contrasting the 'scenes of blood and horror' of the Revolution with the 'peace, order, and regularity' under the Napoleonic regime, he reported the only discontent being among Irishmen: 'your old friend Bob Shee...was Count Shee before the revolution, but now *citizen* and a violent Republican'. However, he 'made two million in assignats, but behold, they were good for nothing'. Shee died in Paris on 5 December, 1806, aged 70.[97]

Some former officers of the Irish Brigade returned to Britain and accepted George III's invitation to join the newly formed English Irish Brigade; however, the history of this organization was a short one. Only part of the brigade's proposed six regiments were raised; a few were sent to Canada and some to the West Indies, where the oppressive climate and tropical disease decimated their ranks. Within two years, the Irish Brigade in the service of England ceased to exist.[98]

For Captain John Bellew of the Hapsburg Imperial army, the war against revolutionary France may have been his last campaign. His final letter to Ireland that is included in the Bellew papers was sent from Mantua in 1792. Christopher Kelly Bellew, travelling on the continent in the brief period of peace from 1802-1803 was unable to locate him through contacts in France –

'of our cousin poor John Bellew I can get no accounting' – nor were his inquiries in Vienna in 1803 any more successful.[99]

In general, the long tradition of the Irish Catholic gentry's military service abroad came to an end with the French Revolution; not only did it disrupt the traditional Irish military ties but now, as mentioned, Catholics were free to enter British service. In the nineteenth century, Bellews continued to serve in the military, holding officer rank both in the militia and the regular army. Indeed, Lieutenant William Bellew, of the 2nd Batallion, Royal Regiment, serving in the same theater of war as his relative John Bellew some sixty years before, died of wounds received in an attack near Sebastopol during the Crimean War. But now the Bellews served Britain.[100]

The French Revolution also brought the end of the educational institutions that had been attended by the sons of the gentry. As early as 1791, the Taaffe sons were considering departure from Douai and removal to a Catholic school in Staffordshire.[101] In the next year, significant numbers of students began leaving the English College at Douai. With the outbreak of war between Britain and France in 1793, the institution was suppressed by the French authorities and professors and students arrested. Some managed to escape confinement; the rest were eventually sent back to England.[102] Nonetheless, the best-known of these humanities schools in France, the English College and St Gregory's among them, were re-established in England, albeit under different names, to continue their educational tradition.

The Irish Colleges were not so fortunate. Considered as English institutions by the French, but as French institutions by the English, they received no share of the eventual compensation made to the English colleges by the restored Bourbons.[103] With only a few exceptions, the Irish clerical colleges were confiscated, and their revenues and property lost. Of the colleges attended by Dominick Bellew, Bordeaux was closed in 1793 and its rector Martin Glynn eventually guillotined; the Pastoral College at Louvain remained in operation until 1795, when it was closed by the French on their occupation of Flanders. The Irish College at Douai managed to receive an exemption for its Irish priests from the civil oath demanded of the French clergy, but it too was finally closed in 1793. Edward Dillon returned to Ireland unharmed and finally received his mitre, becoming bishop of Kilmacduagh and, in 1798, archbishop of Tuam.[104]

The younger Bellew sons, Luke and Harry, were among those Irish students whose residence in France was ended by the Revolution. Luke Bellew was among the 30 priests and students still remaining at the Irish College of Douai at the time of its suppression. His fate, as well as that of Harry, also in France, was a constant source of concern to the family in Ireland. Harry managed to send a letter to his eldest brother Christopher in Ireland explaining their predicament: 'I have been in prison since the siege of Ypres in the town of Arras ... I don't know what has become of Luke. I have not seen him since the week precedent to the siege ...' Both brothers survived through the aid of their fellow Irish, an Englishman, and an American. The American, a Mr Fenwick, gave Harry money and attempted to free him from prison, and the president of the Irish seminary of Lille loaned both brothers some 600 livres each. In 1796, John Smith of Ostend lent Harry 401 florins, 12 styvers 'out of compassion' for his board, clothing, and passage back to Ireland.[105] Luke Bellew, on the other hand, stayed at Douai. Imprisoned a number of times, he appears to have sought refuge with the Irish Franciscans at the College of St Anthony's at Louvain, where he stayed for over a year before returning to Douai. He was made responsible for the affairs of the College in Dillon's absence, acting as virtual president, and took an active role in what would ultimately become the futile attempts to reconstitute not only his institution but others in France.[106]

For gentry clerical students, as well as lay, the educational future lay in Ireland with the establishment and endowment of Catholic colleges and seminaries. Both the Irish government and the Catholic hierarchy were in agreement as to the dangers of continued education in Jacobin France. In 1794, the Irish bishops no longer wished to send prospective priests abroad, to be exposed to 'the contagion of sedition and infidelity; nor their country to the danger of thus introducing the pernicious maxims of a licentious philosophy'.[107] This shared attitude, together with the absolute necessity of providing an establishment for those clerical students no longer able to be educated on the continent, paved the way for the foundation of Maynooth in 1795.

This discussion of the Catholic gentry soldiers and students abroad would not be complete without one final comment. If there is a dominant theme – both stated and unstated – running through the correspondence of the Bellew family members in France and Austria, which is also reflected in the experiences of many others of their class in Europe, it is that of the divided nature of Irish residence overseas. On the one hand, there was strong involvement in the affairs of the countries in which they lived, and the establishment of ties, emotional as well as residential. Assimilation of continental life-styles must also have been common, perhaps accompanied by fears of losing a wholly Irish identity.

Yet countering all of this was the maintenance of strong relationships with fellow Irish on the continent and the use of Irish connections for financial aid, influence, and assistance. There was also an intense thirst for news of Ireland no matter how long the separation – as evidenced by John Bellew's pleas for correspondence – or how young the age at departure – as shown in one of Luke Bellew's letters from Douai. Expressing his concern over his mother's 'sickly constitution', he assured her of his strong affection despite 'the early age at which we left Ireland'. He urged everyone to write to him, 'not excepting Nanny Duffy in her homely cottage where I have spent so many happy days'.

The divided nature of enforced residence abroad is common to all exiles, as is the pain of separation from a native country, whether permanent or for lengthy periods of time. The words of Andrew French in 1767 might well have served for all of the Irish exiles of the eighteenth century. Commenting on the birth of Michael Bellew's sons, who were to be 'refined and polished' in France and Spain, he lamented, 'God help us Papists. We must part our native lands, or bear with daily insults.'[108]

'The Trade of Ireland Is All in the Hands of the Papists': Commerce and Trade

In contrast with penal restrictions in other areas, those specifically governing Catholic participation in trade and commerce were relatively few. Catholics were forbidden to sell or manufacture firearms and prohibited from employing more than two apprentices. However, this second restriction appears to have been largely disregarded. Catholics had also been excluded from the corporate franchise by statute law in 1727 and from full participation in corporate guilds by local by-laws; they could be at best 'quarter brothers', paying a fee known as quarterage for the maintenance of guild activities and the ensurance of some economic privileges.

The commercial aspect of the penal code appears to have had little delete-rious effect on Catholic business enterprise.[1] Urban by-laws and impositions were sometimes an obstacle to Catholic merchants, but these could be circum-vented or, in the case of quarterage, resisted successfully. Restrictions on the purchase and leasing of urban property remained, however, and Catholics could not enjoy the ready access to the patronage and influence available to guild and corporate members. In general, the proscriptions were no doubt vexatious, but hardly crippling to those Catholic merchants with sufficient resources.

Questions which still have not been satisfactorily resolved, however, are how many Catholic merchants had sufficient resources to succeed, from which social groups they came, and whether their numbers and wealth were growing over the course of the eighteenth century. Certainly Catholic control of trade was a recurrent theme in correspondence and pamphlets: in 1718, Archbishop King wrote that the Catholics 'had engrossed almost all the trade of the king-dom'; a pamphleteer of 1739 complained that they had 'captured most of the commerce and current coin' of Ireland; and Lord Wilmington stated in 1757 that 'the trade of Ireland is all in the hands of the Papists ...'[2] Yet, it has been argued that such contemporary observations must be assessed with great care, since they were used in support of both continued penal restrictions (Catholics were becoming too powerful) and relaxation (Catholics should be awarded civil rights because of their enterprise and wealth). Moreover, it is difficult to see a rapid proportional expansion of Catholic representation in the mercantile community. It may well be, as David Dickson has suggested, that the general economic expansion of the eighteenth century was a tide that lifted both Catholic and Protestant mercantile boats;[3] Protestant paranoia may have focused intensively on the former.

As to the composition of the more successful segment of the Catholic merchant class trading and dealing on a larger scale, speculation is on slightly firmer ground. A sizeable component was certainly that of younger sons and brothers of the remaining Catholic gentry who found trade and commercial enterprise an attractive prospect. Historians have disagreed, however, on the nature of the relationship between the penal laws and landed families' entry into trade. Maureen Wall saw the decline in Catholic landholding as responsible for an increased Catholic commercial presence in cities and towns; however, L.M. Cullen and David Dickson posit a different connection: the loss of capital accompanying the loss of land meant that only those merchants who came from families who had survived forfeiture had the resources to succeed in wholesale trade.[4]

Certainly the town and county of Galway serve as good examples to support the latter argument. There, Catholics were notably successful in keeping their estates, and trade was a useful outlet for those younger sons, with little prospect of land, who did not go into the church or the military. Moreover, this career choice was not limited to just the merchants of the town of Galway who had acquired estates; county gentry families with no previous involvement in trade could provide for younger sons in a similar manner. The Bellews of Mount Bellew provide a particularly good illustration of this gentry participation in both foreign trade and commerce within Ireland.

In the eighteenth century, they joined a trading network already established by the merchant-landowners of Galway, one that linked the west of Ireland, Dublin, London, the Continent, and the West Indies. Two of Michael Bellew's younger brothers, Luke and Patrick, were merchants in France and Spain; a third, Francis, went to the West Indies. Patrick left his business in Spain and returned to Ireland where he continued foreign trade and also set up as a flour factor in Dublin. His son Christopher continued the family business there, maintaining dealings with his father's former house in Cadiz, remaining active in the inland flour trade, and expanding into the provisions trade with England. The landed Michael Bellew, himself brother-in-law to a Galway merchant, had flour mills in eastern Galway – an enterprise carried on in close association with his nephew Christopher in Dublin. Both aspects of this gentry mercantile connection, foreign and domestic, will be examined, drawing upon the experiences and careers of Galway families in general and those of the Bellews in particular.

FOREIGN TRADE

The town of Galway's continental trade dated back to the fourteenth century,[5] and many of the families of the 'Tribes', the Blakes and Lynches in particular, acquired conspicious wealth from this overseas commerce. From the sixteenth century onward, Galway ships carried butter, beef, tallow, leather, and especially tanned hides to Continental ports, and the greatest import-export trade centered on France and Spain. In the early seventeenth century, St Malo imported most of the hides from Galway, but hides and leather were also sent to a profitable Iberian market which included Lisbon and Seville.[6] The opening of the New World provided yet another outlet for the livestock products of the county's agrarian economy.

Return cargoes included salt from France and Spain, iron from Spain, and quantities of condiments and spices – pepper, ginger, saffron, and cloves. The biggest item of import, however, was wine. French wines had been imported from the thirteenth and fourteenth centuries, and continued to be, but in the first half of the fifteenth century, Spanish wines were introduced. They gained great popularity and soon became Galway's major import, not only bringing great profits to the town's merchants who distributed them but cementing an already strong Spanish connection. In 1611, the customs of the town were estimated at £20,000, and in 1614 one Galway merchant, Sir Valentine Blake, was bringing in cargoes on two of his ships, one from Cadiz, estimated at £3,000.[7] By the mid-seventeenth century, Galway was regarded as second only to Dublin for its riches.

However, Galway's zenith as a port had been reached. The Cromwellian and Williamite conquests brought disruption of trade and the dislocation of Catholic merchants. In 1655, the Cromwellian government ordered the expulsion of Catholics from not only town government but trade. However, attempts at plantation – by luring settlers from London, Holland, even America, then settling debts with Gloucester and Liverpool with grants of Galway property – were fruitless. Even though, with the Restoration, Catholics were permitted to regain trading privileges, the economic blows of the Interregnum – disruption of trade with the Continent, the expulsion of Catholic merchants, even an outbreak of the plague in 1649 – had been damaging.[8] Eighteenth-century political turmoil and religious discrimination also affected the Catholic mercantile community. An act in 1709 required Catholics in the town to enter into a bond for security and attempted to restrict further Catholic settlement in Galway. In 1708, a Jacobite invasion scare prompted the temporary expulsion of the Catholic inhabitants and the imprisonment of a number of the merchants and gentry,[9] and in 1715, Catholics were again expelled for a time. In 1717, the Protestants of Galway petitioned the Irish parliament, complaining of Catholic influence in the town, and a bill was passed to strengthen the Protestant interest. Moreover, the Protestant corporation appears to have been lacking in initiative and efficiency, neglecting the harbor's quays and facilities and imposing injurious taxation and regulations on trade.[10] Despite these disruptions, corporation attempts at control, and government scrutiny, however, Catholic merchants still monopolized Galway's trade.

More important in the decline of Galway as a port were changes in the patterns of both domestic and overseas Irish trade, which began with the Restoration. First, with the growth in the volume of trade came a much greater concentration in Dublin. The Irish capital rapidly grew to claim the major portion of the commodities trade, both domestic and foreign, and could furnish foreign exchange facilities for merchants in smaller towns. The era of smaller ports, each serving its own particular area, was ending, and Galway, among others, experienced decline with the 'growing activity of Dublin merchants as buyers and sellers in what had once been Galway's exclusive hinterland'.[11] As one example of this development, Spain, as previously mentioned, was an important seventeenth-century market for Galway hides; by the eighteenth century, more than 90 per cent of Irish hides exported were sent there. However, by this time, it was Dublin which was the center of the tanning trade: in 1772, of 65,643 hides exported, 63,358 were sent to Spain; Dublin supplied 56,353 of these.[12] Similarly, even Galway's lucrative wine trade, healthy through the 1720s and 30s, was moribund after mid-century, unable to withstand the competition of the Dublin importers.[13]

At the same time, there was a change in the kind of livestock products exported, which also had its effects on Galway. Along with other regulations on Irish trade imposed by the English parliament, Irish live cattle and sheep, and beef and pork, were excluded from what had been their primary market, Britain, in the Cattle Act of 1667; subsequent acts included mutton, lamb, butter, and cheese among items prohibited from Irish export to England. Although Irish trade may well already have been moving away from live cattle as a result of economic changes brought about in the crisis years of the 1640s and 1650s,[14] livestock products now required new outlets. These were developed through a provisions trade in salted beef, pork, and butter, which augmented an already established trade with the British West Indies in hides and tobacco, but concentrated on what had formerly been a secondary market, Europe.

At first, these products were shipped directly to the major continental importers, France and Spain, for domestic consumption. With the development of European dairying, the domestic need within these countries dwindled, but another arose – that of the French and Spanish colonies of the West Indies. Irish beef, pork, and butter were relatively cheap and, since they were salted, could survive the lengthy trans-Atlantic passage. Some of these products were shipped to the West Indies direct from Ireland, but much was shipped to European markets for re-export to French and Spanish colonial possessions. Besides providing for colonial consumption, Irish beef and butter also augmented the supplies of the ships engaged in Atlantic trade.[15]

Galway had already been exporting these products to Europe on a small scale from the sixteenth century, but the rapid expansion in the volume of the provisions trade[16] had much the same effect as that mentioned earlier in the case of Dublin with tanned hides and wine: the concentration of the trade in one major port – in this instance, Cork. Better-situated than its rival southern ports of Youghal, Kinsale, and Waterford and able to draw on the grazing areas of the southwest, Cork rapidly became the center of the lucrative provisions trade.[17] Although, as will be seen later, Galway shared to some extent in the trade in the seventeenth century,[18] by the eighteenth, it had lost most of it to its neighbour to the south. In 1761 and 1762, only two ships sailed from Galway with provisions cargoes, one of beef and one of butter.[19]

By the end of the seventeenth century, Galway merchants had responded to these changed conditions, and the growing complexities of marketing and credit they brought, by settling in the Continental ports with which they traded.[20] Resident merchant communities in French ports also contributed to a two-way traffic – of both merchants and goods – between the home country and the West Indies, where Galwaymen were already well-established. Galway interests in the West Indies in turn resulted in the placement of family members in London, the center of colonial finance. Galway itself, although a port in decline, remained an important regional financial center; merchants there could provide bills of exchange (even though they were increasingly for Dublin or London rather than overseas) and banking services for the gentry. Yet, recognizing the growing importance of Dublin as the major agricultural commodities market, Galway houses had established branches there as well by the early eighteenth century. This was the complex network of merchant houses and families of which the Bellews would become part. An examination of their activities begins with one of the first areas of Galway mercantile expansion in the seventeenth century, the West Indies.

GALWAY GENTRY-MERCHANT FAMILIES IN THE
BRITISH WEST INDIES

Galway families had been in the West Indies as early as the 1630s; however, it was not until the second half of the seventeenth century that discernible communities of Galwaymen emerge, particularly in the eastern Caribbean colonies.[21]

Those who arrived in Barbados and the Leewards joined an already significant Irish population there, comprised mostly of those serving, or who had served, as indentured servants. In 1667–68, William Stapleton, governor and captain-general of the Leewards, conducted a census that provides perhaps the best idea of the Irish portion of the Leewards population, since English and Irish colonists were counted separately. Proportionately, 69 percent (1,869 of 2,682) of the white inhabitants of Montserrat were Irish; on Antigua, 26 percent (610 of 2,308); on Nevis, 23 percent, (800 of 3,521); and on St Kitts, 10 percent, (187 of 1,897).[22]

Galwaymen participated in the still-active trade between the West Indies and Galway in tobacco, hides, and provisions and used mercantile capital as a base for establishing plantations. The emigration of members of the Blake family is a good example of this trend.[23] John Blake, who was mayor of Galway in 1646, was transplanted to Mullaghmore under Cromwell. While his eldest son Thomas stayed in county Galway as a merchant, eventually succeeding his father in the family estate, his second and third sons emigrated to Montserrat in 1668, where they purchased an estate and became part of an Irish community that also included members of the Galway Darcy and Bodkin families. The eldest brother, Henry, stayed in Montserrat, while John became a merchant in Barbados.

Like many of those who went to the West Indies, Henry Blake hoped to make enough money through his plantation and trade to repair his finances and eventually return to Ireland: 'my living here was to recruit my great losses whereby I should be enabled to pay my debts at home'. He participated in trade in tobacco, then the major cash crop, sending shipments to Galway from 1673 to 75, but this was not always as profitable as he had hoped. His father informed him in 1675 from Mullaghmore that 'tobacco is very plentiful in this country and in no request', and in 1676, his merchant brother in Barbados was also 'cruelly troubled in mind of the bad market of tobacco'.

Henry provided trading information to his family and relatives in Galway as well, writing his merchant cousin Patrick Brown Fitz-James that there were 'glorious looks for such leather as yours are', and in 1675, John Blake advised his Galway merchant brother Thomas, 'If you could at any time send hither 10 or 20 barrels or more of good beef, and finding freight at a moderate rate, you may expect thereby reasonable profit'. By 1676, Henry Blake had made sufficient profits to return home, and purchased the Renvyle estate in county Galway in 1678. He sold his share of the Montserrat 'plantation and negers' to his brother John for 106,899 lbs. of sugar (the lack of currency in the West Indies in this period frequently made payment in kind necessary for land purchases and payment of debts and salaries).[24] John then moved from Barbados to Montserrat, where he died in 1692. Other Galway families remained on the island as well. By the end of the seventeenth century, sugar had replaced tobacco as the most profitable crop; a 1729 survey of the island lists Darcys, Skerretts, and Dalys with sugar plantations of 200-380 acres with hundreds of slaves to work them.[25]

From 1680 through 1706, other Galway merchant-landowning families made their way to the Leewards. Kirwans, Lynches, Skerrets, Frenches, and Brownes established themselves in Antigua. By this time, as mentioned above, sugar had replaced tobacco as the major West Indian cash crop; it required larger investments of capital for the purchase of slaves, sugar works, and the larger quantities of flat land its cultivation demanded. Using mercantile capital as a base, the Lynch family acquired a 693-acre estate with 253 slaves; the Brownes and Skerretts 500-acre estates, and the Kirwans a 700-acre estate. Moreover, significant changes in trade patterns had occurred. By 1696, as a part of mercantilistic trade legislation, the direct export of sugar to Ireland was prohibited; it was shipped to England, then re-exported. Whereas the Brownes, arriving in Antigua sometime before 1680, had their mercantile base primarily on the island, the Kirwans and Skerretts, later arrivals, had younger sons or family members in London, marketing sugar, purchasing plantation supplies, and generally overseeing shipping and other financial arrangements.[26] (This was part of a general pattern among other Galway families in the islands: Blakes, Lynches, and Frenches were among those who established London houses based on colonial trade.)[27]

Despite their acquisition of lands and settlement in the West Indies, Antigua families, like the Blakes, still maintained personal as well as financial ties to Ireland: Patrick Browne in 1705 wished to send his children to Galway for their education, and a member of the French family resident on the island left a legacy for the benefit of the poor of his native city.[28]

This brief review of the settlement of Galway families in the Leewards from the second half of the seventeenth century to the early eighteenth reveals both continuity and change. Throughout the period, mercantile capital continued to be extremely important as a base in purchasing and establishing plantations, thus making the division between merchant and planter a permeable one. Yet, a re-orientation of mercantile patterns had occurred. Both tobacco, the earliest cash crop and one dwindling in importance, and sugar, which succeeded it, now were sent to and marketed in England. While the economic impact of these restrictions on Irish merchants may not have been all that damaging,[29] they were part of a pattern. By the eighteenth century, as mentioned earlier, the provisions trade, once an important part of Galway commerce, was now centered in Cork. These changes resulted in the declining importance of Galway as a source of capital; indeed, the place of origin of these merchant-planters was now on the periphery of the Atlantic trade network, both geographic and financial, a factor reflected in the next wave of West Indian settlement.

This next wave would be to the Windward Islands of the eastern Caribbean. In 1763, at the end of the Seven Years War, Britain acquired Grenada and the Grenadines from France; and Tobago, St Vincent, and Dominica, islands whose possession had formerly been disputed between Britain and France – all referred to as the 'ceded islands'. These new acquisitions were initially regarded with enthusiasm by prospective investors and both established and would-be sugar planters: First, the profitability of sugar had increased rapidly by the mid-eighteenth century, ushering in the 'silver age of sugar', in which prices were 50 percent above the level of the 1730s.[30] Second, large landowners had increased their holdings in the already-developed British islands, monopolizing arable land and shutting out the smaller planters and more recent arrivals. The ceded islands held the promise of rich sugar estates for these two groups, as well as for established planters whose estates were becoming soil-depleted, and numbers of them arrived in the new acquisitions.[31] Galway families too, would be among those who attempted to seize new opportunities for plantations and fortunes offered by the spoils of war. But for those who chose to go to Dominica, including a younger brother of Michael Bellew, hopes for Montserrat or Antigua-style riches would not materialize.

The island of Dominica, lying some 30 miles equidistant from the French possessions of Guadaloupe and Martinique, was, some 250 years after its sighting by Columbus on his second voyage, still relatively virgin territory. The native Caribs had fought off attempts at European settlement with notable success during the sixteenth and most of the seventeenth centuries. In 1660, after a series of sporadic attempts at settlement, the French and English agreed to leave the island to the Caribs, a state of affairs ratified in 1748 in the Treaty of Aix-la-Chapelle, which provided for its neutralization. Nonetheless, from the seventeenth century, there was illicit and steady French settlement along the coast. Settlers from Martinique and Guadaloupe set up small to medium-sized estates, worked by relatively few black slaves; they joined French missionaries, the Jesuits in particular. At the time of British acquisition, however, there were fewer than 8,000 inhabitants: 1,718 Europeans, mostly French; 5,872 slaves; 500 free men of color; and 60 Carib families.[32] The early crops on the island included tobacco, spices, and some cacao and cotton; the French introduced coffee plants, which became the major crop. There were a few sugar plantations, but the French did not place the same emphasis on monoculture as the newly-arrived British, who began planning sugar cultivation in earnest.

Plans for settlement of the ceded islands called for surveying and the dividing of lands into parishes, allotments for plantations, lots for poor settlers, and areas for fortifications. Crown commissioners were empowered to sell lots of no more than 500 acres; moreover, no one person was permitted to purchase more than one lot of uncleared land in his own name or in another's name in trust for him.[33] On Dominica, however, because of its location between two French islands, speedy settlement was considered paramount; thus, sales of land were limited to 300 acres, to promote greater numbers of settlers. There was another reason for this limitation, one of which prospective buyers were as yet unaware, to be mentioned shortly. French settlers also had to be dealt with, since most of the available cleared land belonged to them: they were allowed to take leases on lands in their possession at the time of the surrender of the island to the British.[34] The Caribs, whose numbers had steadily dwindled, were eventually given a kind of reserve on the windward side of the island. Land sales commenced in 1765, and by 1773, 95,134 acres had been purchased from the Crown and from those Frenchmen who had left the island.[35] Forty-one sugar plantations were recorded in 1773, 6 of whose works were powered by water, 15 by wind, and 20 by cattle mills.[36]

The survey map of Dominica was drawn by John Byres, an Ordinance engineer. From 1764 to 1776, Byres surveyed all of the ceded islands except Grenada, and a list of allotments, their size, and the original owners and/or subsequent purchasers accompanied each of his maps.[37] Byres' lists do not distinguish between absentee owners and resident proprietors, and some of the land was certainly bought for speculation with no intention of residence. Nonetheless, by examining both map and land allotments, it is possible to sketch an anatomy of purchasers of land in Dominica, one in which Galway families figure.[38]

There were about 500 landholders, with approximately twice that number of leaseholders. Among the names, approximately 37 are recognizably Irish. Four were leaseholders, perhaps among those who had been unable to establish themselves in the older islands. Ten owned between 100–199 acres; 12 between 200–199; 3 between 300–399; and approximately 10 owned over 400 acres, 5–6 in partnerships, 3–4 as sole owners. Among them are to be found the Galway names of Browne, French, Lynch, and Bellew. The first three may well have come from the Irish community on Antigua, for the island has one of the driest climates in the Leewards, and Antiguans were among those purchasing heavily in Dominica, where rainfall was abundant.[39] Robert Browne, in partnership with Charles O'Hara, had 557 acres in the parish of St David; William French 232 in the parish of St Andrew; Ulysses and Marcus Lynch, 265 and 200 in the parish of St Paul; Francis Bellew 190 and Michael Bellew 227 in the parish of St Andrew. A John Kirwan, possibly from Montserrat, also appears in the deed registers for the parish of St Andrew in 1769.[40]

The acreage held by these Irishmen certainly compares favourably with that of other landowners. It also represented substantial investment; in the initial sales of land, cleared lands sold for about £8–£10 sterling, with the highest lot at £45; uncleared lands, judging from the equivalent sales on St Vincent's, perhaps one-fifth as much.[41] Yet, by the end of the eighteenth, and the beginning of the nineteenth century, few Irish were left. Six of the thirty-seven sold out sometime before 1772; I have been able to confirm the deaths of at least three by 1778. The same toll can be observed among the Galway families. Some undoubtedly sold their lands; Ulysses and Marcus Lynch disposed of their 440 acres to James Symth and Thomas Campbell by 1776. Francis Bellew may have died on the island in 1773. By the early nineteenth century, Galway names have almost disappeared, save for a lone reference to the baptism of slaves on a Kirwan estate near Portsmouth (the second-largest town) in the period 1821–23.[42] Why had settlement and investment in Dominica been so disappointing?

The primary reason can be summed up in the words of a modern geographer: 'Of all the British Ceded Islands, Dominica presented the greatest environmental hindrances to rapid development'.[43] One of the biggest obstacles to establishing successful plantations was simple topography, a factor noted as early as 1763 in the report of the Board of Trade to the Privy Council. The report describes an island with 300,000 acres of potentially fertile land, 'well-watered with no less than 83 rivers and rivulets sufficient for sugar mills'. The report goes on to note, however, 'the country is so remarkably mountainous and hilly, that it is less adapted to sugar plantations than the other islands', one of the reasons, previously referred to, for restricting the permissible size of acreage to be sold.[44]

Dominica is one of the most rugged islands in the Lesser Antilles. The Windward chain of islands are the tops of a submerged volcanic mountain range; volcanic cones on Dominica result in a range of mountains some 4,000–5,000 feet high and little coastal plain. There are, as noted by the Board, rivers and streams in abundance, but they are also prone to damaging flooding. Rainfall is heavy, resulting in forests dense and lush, but difficult to clear, and the potential for damaging soil erosion. The soil itself is moderately fertile in spots, but less so than on neighbouring islands.

The rugged nature of the island made transportation – of both people and crops – difficult. Thomas Atwood, chief justice on the island and the author of a 1791 tract designed to promote settlement, lamented that 'the very bad state of the public roads is a great disadvantage to the island, as some of them are perfectly dangerous to travel'. The coastal roads were 'in general dug on the sides of mountains of stupendous heights above the rivers or sea'; roads in the interior were 'very steep of ascent' and narrow, 'so that a person's head turns giddy on casting a view to the bottom as he passes along'. The heavy rains also resulted in frequent wash-outs.[45] These obstacles might have been surmounted by adequate sea frontages for loading, but Dominica has few sandy beaches. There are a few around the capital of Roseau, but the most extensive are in the north, on the leeward side of the island; those on the windward side are less attractive because of heavy surf.[46]

Other factors doomed the hopes of quick fortunes in sugar. Atwood presents a depressing list of mistakes made by the newcomers: 'a rage prevailed in the new settlers for having extensive estates ... they flattered themselves that ... in the course of a few years, their fortunes would be made ...' What they had not reckoned on was the amount of time needed to clear forests, make roads, and transport materials for buildings and sugar works before any cane could be planted, let alone harvested and produced into sugar.[47] Slaves, who were to perform all these tasks, had become increasingly expensive; a male slave who might have been bought for £40 in 1764, cost £60 by 1770.[48] Moreover, those either bought by the new settlers or brought with them from other islands were frequently ill-suited to the heavy labour necessary to establish plantations. Many former domestic slaves or recent arrivals from Africa, who were not 'seasoned', either died or ran away. Those who escaped into the thick forests joined another group, slaves bought from the Jesuits who had rebelled against the harsher treatment they received from their new masters. Setting up their own camps and provisions grounds, these 'maroons' sometimes raided plantations, and were encouraged by the French during periods of war with Britain; they would not be wholly suppressed until 1815.[49] Lastly, according to Atwood, the restrictions on acreage were also flouted, to the ultimate detriment of development: 'Others from a unpardonable greediness, purchased, in the names of their acquaintances or families, several lots of land, each containing the number of acres limited in the grants; by which means, persons who would have been more fit settlers, were deprived of them; and large quantities of land thus purchased are now in the same state (in woods) as they were, when first sold at the Commissioners sales.'[50]

Some failed planters and investors were no doubt casualties of the wave of speculation touched off by new possibilities for sugar in the ceded island. In 1771, for example, it was reported that a Dominican plantation that sold for £500 in 1763, was sold in 1765 for £5,000; 3 years later, for £15,000. Succumbing to the temptation to buy on credit, many met with financial distress or ruin.[51]

The experience of Francis Bellew displays in microcosm the general failure of hopes for quick fortune. When his eldest brother Michael succeeded to the family lands in Galway, he embarked on a mercantile career. Francis began in Cork, then emigrated to St Kitts, the provisions trade a likely link. Sometime after 1765, he purchased lands in Dominica – a lot of 190 acres in the parish of St Andrew on the windward side of the island. A near-by plot of 227 acres was registered to Michael Bellew. If this was his eldest brother, which appears very likely, it was no doubt a circumvention of the restrictions on purchase of the kind mentioned by Atwood, since there is no indication, at least in the family papers, that Michael ever went to the West Indies.[52]

The purchases might well initially have been for speculation, since there is evidence that Francis remained on St Kitts through 1771: Francis Bellew 'of the island of St Christopher' appointed John Kealy and John Shea of Cork as his attorneys for the recovery of money from Dominica in 1770 (an ominous note), and in 1771, he shipped via Cork a hogshead of rum from St Kitts to Michael Bellew and one to his uncle in county Galway. Yet, at some point after that date, he may have gone to Dominica. His residence, however, if such it was, was brief. He died sometime before March of 1773. The family papers contain a copy of the power of attorney Michael Bellew, as his brother's heir and executor, granted to Abraham Shaw, Francis Magarret (two merchants) and Jeffrey Keating in Dominica on 6 March 1773, 'for matters relating to the estate and effects of Francis Bellew, Esq., late of aforesaid island deceased'.[53] The appraisal of the estate, dated 22 September 1774, is also contained in the family papers: it consisted of 49 acres leasehold @ £40 an acre, 23 acres in fee simple @ £50 an acre, 7 acres in woods @ £10 an acre, 12 'able slaves' @ £66 and 4 'sickly slaves' @ £10. Estate structures listed were 'Buildings, an old French house, a frame for a house of 40 feet square and six Negroe houses'. The total value was £4262 or £2521.16s.4d. sterling.[54] What had happened to the rest of the property? Byres' list, which shows land transactions at least through 1771, does not indicate the sale of Bellew lands, and the Bellew name does not appear in the fragmentary register of deeds for St Andrew's parish.

Had Bellew over-extended himself? As mentioned above, this frequently happened to those who speculated in properties in the ceded islands. Had he unloaded most of his property (perhaps the 'recovery of money from Dominica' in 1770 was in regard to sales) and entertained thoughts of trying his hand in establishing a plantation on what was left? Or had he been hoping to find someone to lease or buy it? Unfortunately, the family papers are silent on the matter.[55]

Given what is known of conditions on Dominica, however, informed suppositions about the land itself and its potential for development are possible: the location of the lands in St Andrew's parish was, simply put, not particularly promising. Successful sugar plantations were established on the windward side of the island, but the Bellew acreage would have presented problems. Although well-watered, lying between two rivers, clearance of forest would have had to have been extensive, and the distance to the coast was at least two or more miles. Furthermore, the terrain is rough and steep.

Whatever the specific reasons for Bellew's failure to make money out of Dominica, he was not alone. The letter book of Charles Winstone, a Dominican merchant and 'attorney', that is, manager of absentee estates, tells similiar stories of deaths, over-extended planters, the difficulties of establishing sugar plantations, and the take-over of estates by creditors.[56] Sugar plantations were not a total loss on Dominica; sugar was certainly produced there, but never in the quantities hoped for. (Of the four ceded islands, Dominica usually ranked third in sugar exports.)[57]

For would-be planters and investors from Galway, Dominica was a sore disappointment. Although concentration on sugar as a main crop would have been difficult in any case, they faced another major problem. The amounts of capital and credit needed to overcome environmental obstacles and successfully exploit Dominica were probably beyond their means. A Galway mercantile base, while adequate in the seventeenth century, was inadequate by the eighteenth, and if these Galwaymen had any sources from contacts in Britain or on the Continent, they too appear to have been insufficient. By the last quarter of the eighteenth century, developmental capital for the island came from London, Bristol, and Scotland. Here were the non-Irish mercantile houses, agents, and absentee landlords with whom important Dominican merchants, planters, and attorneys dealt. Those who made money from Dominica did so because of their previous wealth and connections – East India Company associates among the former, and Scottish planters and land investors who benefited from association with Lord Bute (prime minister at the time of the acquisition of the ceded islands) among the latter.[58] These were the sort of financial and political connections the Irish, at least on Dominica, could not hope to match. For the members of the Bellew family who resided in the two Continental countries that attracted the majority of Irish gentry-merchant families, financial ventures would be far more successful.

GALWAY GENTRY-MERCHANT FAMILIES IN FRANCE

The strong Irish link with France, so pronounced in education and military service, is reflected in the commercial sphere as well, and Galway families were among those who emigrated there in the seventeenth and eighteenth centuries to become resident traders and merchants. They served primarily as agents for the profitable Franco-Irish trade, receiving shipments of salt beef, butter, hides, and tallow, most of which were sent to the French plantations of the West Indies, and exporting French wines and brandies.[59]

La Rochelle and St Malo, the two leading French ports for Irish trade after the mid-seventeenth century, were the first to attract Galway families. A Galway branch of the Butler family, related to that of Ormond, settled in the Atlantic port of La Rochelle; they were followed by members of the Bodkin family, with whom they intermarried. The port of St Malo in Brittany included in its Irish merchant community representatives of the Kirwan, Browne, Darcy, and Lynch families. St Malo was also, between 1680 and 1730, a privateer headquarters; Thomas Darcy was in one of their squadrons, as were several of the Lynches, profiting from these commands as well as trade.

By the end of the seventeenth century, however, with the expansion and redirection of trade referred to earlier, La Rochelle and St Malo lost their prominence. Nantes became the major importer of Irish beef and butter, and thus more important in colonial trade, while Bordeaux became the center of a growing wine trade. The Joyce family began the Galway merchant community in Nantes in the early eighteenth century, followed by the Frenches, Brownes, Kirwans, Lynches, and Darcys. Among the large Irish contingent in Bordeaux, Galway Lynches appear in 1699, Quins by the early eighteenth century. Prompted by the increased profitability in wine, Kirwans and Frenches established themselves by the second quarter of the century, followed by Blakes, Bodkins, Burkes, Darcys, and Joyces somewhat later.

The Irish mercantile community, particularly that of Nantes, exhibited much the same pattern of both assimilation and maintenance of ties with their native country as their soldier and student counterparts discussed in Chapter 3. Many entered the French nobility, married into French families, served as mayors and municipal officials in French cities, and built or acquired chateaux in the countryside. In 1756, when war with Britain brought a royal decree ordering the expulsion of British subjects, the Irish community in Nantes successfully petitioned the crown to remain, pointing out their long and varied services to France. Indeed, a precedent was established in 1784 regarding the legal status of the Irish in France. In that year, the Parlement of Paris, in connection with a case involving inheritance rights, ruled that Louis xiv had decreed that Irish

Catholics emigrating to France should be treated as French subjects and were not required to take out letters of naturalization. Yet, the emigrant Irish maintained strong marital ties with their fellows in France and their families and acquaintances in Ireland. The intermarriage among Galway families in all of their colonies in France, not to mention those with the Irish town from whence they had come, was both prolific and complex.

Just as complex were their commercial ties. Not only were relations maintained with branches of their families in other French ports but with family members in Spain as well. As Galwaymen, particularly those in Nantes, went out to the French Caribbean islands (and sometimes back again), another connection was forged. Blakes, Bodkins, Skerretts, Frenches, and Brownes were merchants and plantation owners in Saint Domingue, and Lynches settled in Martinique. Just as in the British West Indies, the need for representation in London prompted settlement of family members there as trade contacts. The complexity of these connections can be seen in a commercial transaction of 1762: John Blake, a merchant in Saint Domingue, consigned the proceeds from cotton sales to Thomas Blake in Bordeaux, who in turn was to forward them to Luke Blake, the brother of John, in London.[60] Another commercial connection was to Dublin: as Galway's trade in Bordeaux wine collapsed, members of the Lynch, French, Blake and Joyce families settled in Dublin to carry on the Bordeaux trade.

The prosperity of the Bordeaux colony is reflected in the letters of Michael Bellew's brother-in-law, Galway merchant Andrew French, written during his sojourn in France in 1766–67;[61] they mention many Irish families and acquaintances – Deanes, Redingtons, O'Farrells, and Naughtons – in residence in the Bordeaux-Toulouse area. French himself gave as his mailing address, 'care of messrs. Vall Quin Freres of Bordeaux', fellow Irish merchants (with Galway relatives and connections), prominent in that city.[62] He also reported on the activities of one of Michael Bellew's younger brothers, Luke, a Dublin merchant with links to the merchant community of Bordeaux. Luke Bellew, like others in the Bordeaux community, sought to take advantage of the boom in brandy by buying Cognac property.[63] According to Andrew French, he was 'much esteemed by his acquaintances and beloved by his corps, who are desirous to continue him with them. He will find it difficult to resign'. But in October of 1767, French informed Michael Bellew from Dublin that his brother had left for Cork (one of the Irish targets of Cognac brandy traders) 'and from what I can judge, he will make out a good establishment at Cognac'. Luke formed a partnership with a London brandy house, but it was short-lived; Luke Bellew 'of Choniack [Cognac], merchant' died in 1768.[64]

For those Irish merchants in France who continued to profit from their extensive commercial network into the last quarter of the eighteenth century, the Revolution brought unsettled conditions, although these varied from city to city. Unlike the Irish soldiers, students, and clerics, who found their institutions respectively transformed, closed, or made inhospitable, often forcing their emigration, the merchants could carry on their business activities with little interruption, at least until the outbreak of general European war, which disrupted and weakened their profitable ties to Britain and the West Indies. Political, as opposed to commercial, difficulties lay in whether their sympathies were perceived to be Royalist or Republican. Many accommodated themselves to the new regime without problem or incident; others were not so fortunate.

Of those Galway families whose history in revolutionary France is known, several encountered problems because of their loyalty to the Bourbons. In Bordeaux, Edward Kirwan, a member of the family of wine merchants, was briefly imprisoned as a Royalist sympathizer. This does not seem to have deterred his political activity, for soon after he was again in trouble with the government for having 'vilified the Constituted authorities' in his position as editor of a local newspaper. An entry in the town archives suggests that he eventually left France. John Baptiste Lynch was a lawyer and fervent royalist who had his property sequestered and was jailed until the death of Robespierre. He, however, made his peace with the Napoleonic regime, becoming mayor of Bordeaux in 1808. Whether the Galway families in Nantes, where the Reign of Terror was severe, were persecuted for royalist sympathies is not clear; however, other members of the Irish merchant community there were killed during the Terror – among them was Anne Shiel, a granddaughter of an Irish merchant who had been ennobled; she was one of the victims of the *noyades*, the infamous mass drownings.

GALWAY GENTRY-MERCHANT FAMILIES IN SPAIN

Another continental country in which Irish merchants established themselves, and one with an even stronger New World connection, was Spain. Irish-Spanish commercial relations had existed from the Middle Ages, with Galway, as mentioned previously, the most important port trading with the Iberian peninsula. Spanish merchants sailed to Galway as well, and the profitable reciprocal trade in wine, iron, hides, and provisions resulted in Spanish coins becoming a common circulating medium in Connacht.[65]

From the seventeenth century, Spain became a rich market for foreign imports, and Ireland exported fish, beef, butter, and textiles to the peninsula, importing iron, olive oil, fruits, nuts, and especially wine in turn.[66] By the seventeenth and eighteenth centuries, Irish merchants had established colonies in many of the Atlantic and Mediterranean Spanish ports. In the Mediterranean, George Moore of county Mayo became wealthy from the wine trade of Alicante, and Randell McDonnell of Dublin established a mercantile house in Cartagena.

Waterford families from the Irish colonies of St Malo and La Rochelle had control of much of the Anglo-Spanish trade, in contrast to those of Galway origin. Nonetheless, a few Galwaymen can be identified in mercantile activities in Atlantic ports: Lynches in Bilbao and Frenches in Saint-Sebastian around the mid-eighteenth century, both probably with links to the French family colonies through the wine trade.[67] In Barcelona, a Gregory French, who had settled there and married a Spanish woman, left a mid-century will identifying him as the son of Galway merchant Andrew French.[68]

Besides engaging in trade between Ireland and the Iberian peninsula, some Irish merchants also participated in the *carrera de Indias*, 'the Indies run'. With the founding of the rich Spanish colonial empire in the New World, Hapsburg economic policy dictated that one single Spanish port serve as the funnel for all Indies trade. In 1717, under the new Bourbon regime, Cadiz acquired this monopoly from Seville, the original base of the *Casa de Contratación*, and foreign merchants flocked to the Atlantic port to share in the profitable colonial trade. The kingdom of Spain was no more able to provide her New World possessions with necessary colonial supplies than her domestic market with sufficient raw materials and manufactured goods, and although Spanish law forbade the trade of foreigners with her colonies, sheer necessity led to toleration, and at times encouragement, of a foreign merchant community which served as import-export agents for the goods of other countries.[69]

From the sixteenth century onward, the Genoese, Flemings, and Germans, then the French, and in the seventeenth century, the British and Dutch, established mercantile houses first in Seville, and then Cadiz. It was possible to circumvent the Spanish restrictions on foreign trade with the New World in a number of ways – from employing Spanish merchants as *hombres de paja* (literally straw – or front – men) and trading under their name in exchange for providing them with a percentage of the value of the goods shipped, to engaging in outright fraud, by substituting foreign goods on ships in the harbour without registration with Spanish customs.[70] For those merchants who were Catholic and willing to establish residence in Spain, the evolution of government policy toward foreigners made licit trade possible.

From the reign of Philip II, merchants involved in transatlantic commerce were to be native Spaniards, but this was interpreted to mean sons of not only Spanish fathers, but sons of Catholic foreigners who had been living in Spain for ten years. After 1608, with twenty years' continual residence in Spain, a foreigner could apply for a decree of naturalization, enabling him to take part in New World trade. In the eighteenth century, despite the protests of the *consulado*, or merchant guild, of Cadiz, restrictions were eased still further.[71] The rights of Spanish-born sons of foreign residents to participate in the Indies trade were upheld, and in 1726 and 1728, a series of royal *cedulas* granted citizenship to any foreigner who gave proof of his willingness to apply himself to Spanish commerce or industry. Those who had resided in Spain for twenty years, ten of them in a fixed domicile; professed the Catholic faith; possessed more than 4,000 ducats in real or personal property; or married a citizen could be granted licenses to ship merchandise to the colonies and participate on equal footing with native Spaniards. By 1765, consulates and vice-consulates for foreign traders had been established in the major Spanish seaports.[72]

Cadiz, as might be expected, had the largest foreign community of any eighteenth-century Spanish city, which increased from 2,080 in 1714 to 8,544 in 1787. In 1773, foreigners comprised almost 15 per cent of Cadiz's metropolitan population of over 70,000. The number of merchants within this community rose steadily in the eighteenth century. At the end of the seventeenth century, there were 45 foreign commercial houses in Cadiz; by 1762, there were 153 registered foreign merchants, and by 1773, 386. The French, Italians, and English-Irish were the most numerous; they also reaped the major share of profits from trade.[73]

The Irish community in Cadiz was well-established and of a varied background; it attracted many Irishmen visiting the peninsula. In 1782, an Irish priest serving as a chaplain in the French navy, stopped at Cadiz, where, among other Irish clerics, he encountered Father Cummins, a Carmelite friar, and Dr O'Kelly, an Augustinian, both from Galway.[74] The governor of the city was General Alexander Count O'Reilly, former Inspector-General of Infantry and military governor of Madrid. Originally from Cavan, he was a favorite of another Irish Catholic in high office, Ricardo Wall, a Spanish minister of state and economic reformer.[75]

Irish merchants comprised a large part of this community. Some had served in English trading houses at the end of the seventeenth century. War between Spain and England in 1702 prompted the departure of many of the English Protestants from Spain for a time, but their Irish Catholic clerks were permitted to stay and carried on trade. New arrivals augmented their numbers through the first half of the century, and Irish names are conspicious in the municipal records which list the simple partnerships, or *societas*, which were prevalent in eighteenth-century Spanish trade.[76] These Irish traders were granted protection by the Spanish government throughout the diplomatic upheavals of the

period. In 1718, when Admiral Byng's sinking of the Spanish Mediterranean
fleet resulted in the breaking of relations between Spain and Britain, Cardinal
Alberoni ordered the seizure of the goods and vessels of British subjects in
Spanish ports. Nonetheless, Philip v ordered that Irish Catholics then residing
in Spain or any future arrivals remain unmolested.[77]

The activities of these Irish traders were often a source of concern to the
British government. In 1750, when a newly-appointed English consul was sent
to Cadiz, where the 'British' factory was by then predominantly Irish, he heartily
disapproved of the policies which had been developed under their administration. In the previous century, the merchants had voluntarily imposed on themselves a duty on goods and profits to provide a fund for the relief of distressed
British subjects in Cadiz. According to the consul Colebrook, the Irish had
been letting in the ships of their countrymen duty-free while charging some
English ships double. Of the money that was collected, much was unaccounted
for; the rest had been put to such purposes as outfitting a privateer in 1726 to
prey on English shipping and maintaining 'Irish officers in the Spanish service'. Colebrook wanted henceforth to control the fund and send a portion to
England to be invested so that the annual rate might eventually be lowered.
The Irish protested violently and appealed to the King of Spain, insisting that,
as naturalized Spaniards, they were exempt from any duty established by the
British parliament. The *Junta de Comercio* upheld this opinion, stating that
foreign law had no authority over Spanish subjects, and there the matter rested.[78]

The number of English and Irish merchants in Cadiz increased from thirty
in 1762 to forty-eight by 1773, and their trading houses brought in total profits
of 231,000 pesos in 1753–54 and 173,750 in 1762, second only to the French
among foreign merchants, and almost on a par with the Spanish. Of the thirty
houses registered in 1753–54 and 1762, twenty-one had profits between 1,00–
7,500 pesos, and two brought in a sizable income of 20–25,000 pesos. Of the
Irish contingent in these trading houses, twenty-seven Irish names appear in
records of 1776, divided among nineteen houses.[79]

Whether of seventeenth- or eighteenth-century origin, by the fourth quarter
of the 1700s, the Irish merchant community in Cadiz, though not large (a census of foreigners in 1773 lists 125 persons of Irish birth, 86 of Irish background)[80], was conspicuous in the eyes of visiting Britons. In 1774, Major
William Dalrymple, on leave from the British garrison at Gibraltar, toured Spain
(passing, it might be noted, as an officer in the Irish Brigade) and stopped at
Cadiz. While observing many French carrying on trade there, he also remarked
on the 'number of Irish Catholics'.[81] Among them was a member of the Bellew
family, Michael Bellew's brother Patrick. Listed in the 1773 census as 'Patricio
Bellew, 31' along with his son Christopher, age 7, he was a partner in the

House of Lynch and Bellew. His association was familial as well as commercial; while in Spain, he married Jane Lynch, sister of his partners Thomas and Henry (another Lynch brother-in-law was Sir Edward Lynch, a captain in the Royal Navy of Spain). The Lynches too were members of a Galway family who had emigrated to Spain in search of commercial profits; yet another Cadiz merchant, Bartholomew Costello, was a Bellew 'kinsman' and commercial contact as well.[82]

The House of Lynch and Bellew engaged in trade between Ireland and Spain, and the commodities involved reflect trading patterns in operation since at least the sixteenth century. Items shipped to Ireland from Spain included wine, fruit, and olive oil, provided through Spanish merchants; in 1789, Seville merchant Juan Gomez supplied three cargoes of fruit, 30 barrels of wine, and 30¼ casks of oil to the Cadiz house to be sent to Dublin in three ships. Butter appears to have been the main item of import; cargoes were brought in on joint account, primarily with the wealthy Dublin firm of Edward Byrne and Randell McDonnell. The latter also had a trading establishment in Cartagena and maintained other commercial contacts in Spain. This last commodity – butter – probably linked the House of Lynch and Bellew to the New World as well. Cadiz, with its trade monopoly, was the main Spanish market for Irish butter; agents from the various trading houses there arranged for the re-export of most of the Irish shipments to Spanish America.[83]

The firm of Lynch and Bellew appears to have enjoyed a certain degree of success in the favorable economic and trade conditions of the 1760s to 1780s; an estimate of the joint capital of the house in May, 1778, given to Bartholomew Costello by Thomas and Henry Lynch, put it at over 163,229 Spanish dollars, or approximately £32,000.[84] In any event, trade brought enough profit to enable Patrick Bellew to leave Spain sometime during the late 1770s or early 80s and establish himself in Dublin, where, while maintaining his partnership in the Spanish house, he began to enter other commercial areas as well.

Several factors besides a desire to return to his homeland or diversify his economic interests may have prompted Patrick Bellew's move. In 1778, as a part of Bourbon economic reforms designed to improve the Spanish economy, trade with Spanish America, with the exception of Vera Cruz, the port for New Spain, was thrown open to thirteen Spanish port cities. In 1789, Cadiz lost its monopoly of trade with New Spain (Mexico) as well, and the *Casa de Contratación* was abolished in 1790. While free trade was to have no immediate deleterious effect on Cadiz's prosperity,[85] its merchants were nonetheless apprehensive. In August of 1789, Thomas Lynch wrote to Michael Bellew that, 'our trade is everyday becoming more precarious'. Moreover, hostilities – actual or threatened – with Britain, whose naval supremacy could disrupt Spanish colonial trade, disturbed the equanimity of Cadiz merchants; war with England in 1779 as a result of Spanish support of the American rebels had previously had its effects on Spanish trade with her American possessions. For some Irish merchants in Cadiz, anxiety over these two factors – the end of the trade monopoly and threats of war with Great Britain – could well have reinforced a desire to return home if the opportunity presented itself; Patrick Bellew may have been among them.

For those Irishmen who remained – the Lynches and Bartholomew Costello among them – relative prosperity through the mid-1780s to the mid-1790s was punctuated by periods of alarm. The threat of renewed war with England in 1790 over rival Spanish and English claims to Nootka Sound (off Vancouver Island) worried Bartholomew Costello and also put a temporary damp on trade. Finally, the worst fears of the merchant community were realized: in 1797, war with Great Britain led to an English blockade of Cadiz and the seizure of those Spanish ships attempting to run it. Unable to supply the American colonies, the Spanish crown was forced, in 1797-99 and 1805–9, to allow Spanish subjects to mount trading expeditions to the New World from all Spanish ports and the ports of neutral powers as well. The complete shut-down of the port of Cadiz led to the loss of over one billion *reales* in trade in 1796–98, and an exodus of the foreign merchant community from its once-prosperous enclave ensued.[86]

Back in Ireland, Bellew kept up his continental connections. He continued to engage in Irish trade with the Lynches in Cadiz; the primary commodity again appears to have been butter, shipped on joint account with Byrne and McDonnell, although there is at least one reference to the export of linen as well. Other overseas commercial interests appear in his correspondence; as his previously-mentioned attempts to place his nephew Patrick with a continental commercial firm indicate, manufacturers and traders in France and Flanders were among them. However, his references to his commercial enterprises soon began to concentrate on Irish domestic trade, an area of extensive gentry involvement.

GENTRY PARTICIPATION IN DOMESTIC TRADE AND COMMERCE

Patrick Bellew's financial interests serve as a useful illustration of the avenues of trade available to an eighteenth-century Irish merchant. For example, in 1786 he mentioned a trip to the west of England to confer with 'some of our friends ere their sailing for Newfoundland'. The fisheries off Greenland and Newfoundland were controlled by England's West Country merchants and had been restricted to English fleets during the Restoration, but in 1704, they had been opened again to the Irish. In 1785, the Irish parliament placed a bounty on the export of fish which was extended to the catches of the Newfoundland fishing boats and provided a stimulus to the Irish fishing industry. Whether Patrick Bellew's 'friends in the fish business' were English or Irish, their fishing fleets would have been provisioned with beef, pork, and butter, much of it supplied by Irish merchants, who sold these commodities on commission to the West Country houses. Bellew may well have been attempting to develop further his business by becoming one of these factors.[87]

Bellew also began to develop trading connections within Ireland, extending to Galway. There is a brief reference in his correspondence with his brother to flaxseed shipment. In 1788, he sent 42 hogsheads and 5½ pecks from Dublin to Galway, and commented to Michael Bellew that 'having sent down said seed has opened an intercourse with buyers in your quarter which may prove beneficial in future'.[88] There is no further reference to such shipments in his letters to his brother, but this was an area of trade with which the Galway Bellews were already familiar. Andrew French, Michael Bellew's merchant brother-in-law, had been active in the import of flaxseed to Galway for some twenty years prior.

Flaxseed importation provides an interesting illustration of Irish trade with the American colonies, for Ireland was an important market for American flaxseed during this period.[89] Although importing supplies of seed to a land where it could easily be produced might seem wasteful, it was actually more efficient. The best-quality seed was obtained by pulling the flax plants before the seeds were fully ripe; by importing the quantities of seed necessary for the next year's crop, which would ordinarily have had to be taken from the total amount produced, the Irish growers could concentrate on the development of the mature plants which were then 'rotted', or soaked in water, for use in linen weaving.

Most American flaxseed was grown in Connecticut and New Jersey; after harvest in the fall, it was purchased by merchants in New York and Philadelphia for shipment to Ireland from November to January. The majority of the seed was sent on consignment to Irish merchants in Dublin and the ports of the north – Belfast, Newry, Coleraine, and Derry – although smaller quantities were also shipped to Cork and other ports. Although the prominent import centers indicate that the linen industry was concentrated in the northeast, efforts to develop spinning and weaving had also been made in Connacht, often on the initiative of local landowners.[90] By mid-eighteenth century, increasing amounts of yarn were being spun in the west, which were purchased by middlemen, then taken to Dublin and the northern centers of the linen industry.

Andrew French appears to have foreseen this development in the west. In 1776, Arthur Young recorded, in connection with his description of the growth of the linen industry in Galway, his meeting with 'Mr. Andrew French of Rathone [Rahoon] Galway' at Monivea. French told him he had brought in the first cargo of flaxseed, some 300 hogsheads, to Galway in 1760. Only 100 were sold then; there were only twenty looms in the town. Nonetheless, development of spinning and weaving appears to have been rapid. In 1763, French wrote to Michael Bellew that 'so many called for flaxseed, we had to write to Dublin for 20 hhds. of choice New York flaxseed which cost us £4.7 cash...' However, the vagaries of colonial trade were also noted; in March of 1766, French was informed not to expect flaxseed delivery from New York on time: '5 ships for this place [Galway] were delayed there the 30 December for want of stamp clearance'. If they sailed, they would be 'seized by the king's ships'. Despite these occasional, and probably minor, disruptions in the supply of seed to Galway, flax cultivation continued to increase. By 1776, Arthur Young was informed that 1500-2300 hogsheads were being imported yearly.[91]

While Patrick Bellew's dealings in flaxseed in 1788 appear to have been a minor element of his commercial interests, in that same year he embarked on what was to become the most important part of his domestic commerce – the inland flour trade.[92] In May, he reported to his brother that he had taken a house in Abbey Street, one of the 'best in Dublin, for good air being in the finest and widest part of said street'. Here he established himself as a flour factor. The location was thought to be particularly advantageous as Caldwell & Geale had their flour stores 'exactly in front whereof mine are, which situation I considered would be very useful as so much resorted to by the bakers'. He had acquired the business of Lamphier's mill, which he estimated would yield him £600 a year and perhaps more, as the mill was capable of grinding 15,00 barrels of wheat annually, and he hoped to procure other commissions that year which would bring in an additional £3–4,000 more. By June, he had filled his vaults and warehouses and acquired the business of three more mills in Wexford, Kilkenny, and King's County.

His friends and associations among 'both landed and trading gentlemen in different quarters of the kingdom' were expected to provide him a good share of the business, and his family connections in Galway counted for a great deal in this respect. In June 1788, he reported to Michael Bellew that, 'Mr. John Burke our kinsman tells me there are mills both at and near Galway whose business is well worth soliciting but that he knows not through what channel, which you probably may, and also inform me of all others you know in Connaught ...' Michael Bellew was quick to respond with the information his brother sought. The same month, Patrick expressed his appreciation for the information he received about the mills in Connaught and also enlisted the aid of his brother-in-law Edmond Taaffe in his quest for commercial contacts: 'It may prove useful if I knew the channels which might best secure me their business. You'll learn what [you] can at Galway assizes and I will trouble Ned Taaffe about Sligo quarter...No stone shall be left unturned by me to come at a good share of the business'. Still later in the year, he was pursuing the trade of a Mr. O'Connor of Ballimoe, whom 'Ned Taaffe promised to influence through Lynch of Clogher', and hoped that 'some of the rest of said gentry may accidentally fall also in his or your way'. Patrick Bellew died in July 1789, but his son Christopher, who had been employed by his father in the trade, continued as a flour factor, maintaining Patrick Bellew's Galway contacts. He informed his uncle in August 1789 that 'gentlemen in Galway continue to send me their flour and write me that they are perfectly satisfied with my management'.[93]

Patrick Bellew's establishment, and his son's continuance, in the inland flour trade was an adjunct to an area of business in which Michael Bellew had long been involved – flour milling. Although many of the gentry's commercial pursuits in Ireland were carried on by younger sons, the Bellews' mills in county Galway are an excellent example of the landed gentry's participation in domestic business and trade.

For the first half of the eighteenth century, flour millers in Ireland operated on a relatively small scale, supplying the needs of farmers and bakers in the immediate area of the mill on commission.[94] From mid-century, however, rising grain prices, the development of a profitable market for flour in Dublin, and parliamentary bounties placed on the inland carriage of grain and flour in 1758 provided the stimulus for the erection of new, larger mills and the expansion of older ones. These larger mills, with more efficient use of waterpower; improvements in the shelling, sifting, and grinding processes; and larger capacities for storage were able to accomodate both increased demand and the changes in marketing patterns. Mill owners now purchased grain from local farmers, processed and stored it, and sent their flour to factors to be sold in urban areas, particularly Dublin. The bounty on flour sent there was especially generous, exceeding the costs of transport, and making expanded milling operations in the provinces possible.

The effects of the bounty can be seen in two areas: First, the increasing number of counties that consigned flour shipments to the capital – in 1765–66, there were five; by 1769–70, there were fifteen. Second, the building of new mills in the provinces – this was particularly noteworthy in the western counties of Limerick, Roscommon, and Galway. During the period 1786–90, 21 of 26 mills in the county of Galway and eight of nine in the town were begun.

Much of the capital for this expansion was supplied by members of the landed gentry eager, in an age of improvement, to diversify their economic interests. Many landlords were already involved in milling through manorial rights that were often embodied in leases. For example, Michael Bellew's lease of lands to Andrew Berne, a farmer in the town of Mount Bellew Bridge, required that the tenant 'shall grind his or their corn at the mills of Mount Bellew or other corn mills of the said Michael Bellew, his heirs and assigns ... under penalty of 5s. each hundredweight for every hundredweight they grind at any other mill'. Prompted by the profitability of flour sales, landlords found it advantageous to involve themselves directly in the milling business. Such appears to have been the case with Michael Bellew, who began his flour milling enterprise in county Galway as early as the mid-1770s. In February of 1775, Sir Patrick Bellew wrote to him that he was 'glad our country mills have begun and I long to hear of our flour mills going. I think we shall stand at least as good a chance of being supplied with wheat as our rival Caulfield Byrne'. By November of the same year, a friend was wishing him well on his enterprise: 'good luck to the mills, say I, and to every undertaking of my friend Mick's'.[95] At least one flour mill was started up shortly after; a plaque on the side of it gave a brief family history and notes that Sir Patrick Bellew of Barmeath and Michael Bellew of Mount Bellew 'erected flour works in this building anno 1776'.[96]

The Bellew correspondence and account books give no indication of the amount of capital expended for the building (or refurbishing, since mills had been on the Bellew property since the seventeenth century) of the flour mills. However, judging from the amount recorded for the erection of other Irish mills during this period, such an undertaking required considerable sums of money, ranging from £1,000–7,000 for a moderate-sized mill.

The operation of the Bellew mills contained elements of both old and new patterns of organization and sales. Account books covering the period 1775–86 break down sales into three categories. The first two, those to local bakers and farmers and those to country gentlemen, are indicative of the extent of traditional milling operations; the third, that of 'Dublin sales', reflects the new marketing pattern, as well as the greater profit accruing to such expansion.

The accounts of local sales show the amounts sent to some of the larger purchasers and the kind of proceeds realized:

			£ s. d.
Aug.-Oct. 1775	Richard Gregory, Castlebar	50 cwt. or 25 bags	@ 40.16
Jan.-June 1776	"	74 cwt. or 48 bags	@ 122. 1. 1
Aug.-Jan. 1776	Charles Taaffe, Claremorris	27 cwt. or 13 bags	@ 22. 7. 8
June-Dec. 1776	"	10 bags	@ 16. 6
June-July 1778	Charles Bradley, Tuam	18 bags	@ 29. 7. 1

Local gentry, John Bodkin of Castletown and Caesar French of Fairhill, and family members, Edmund Taaffe of Woodfield and Dominick Bellew of Mount Kelly, received their grain and flour supplies from the Bellew mills. Supplies for Mount Bellew itself in the form of wheat, malt, and meal amounted to £18.0s.10d. from April 1775-January 1776 and £20.4s.8d. from January-April 1776. The area encompassed in these local sales ranged from the nearby towns of Newtown-Bellew, Tuam, and Loughrea to the more remote ones of Castlebar and Ballinrobe in Mayo and Athlone in Westmeath, as well as areas in Roscommon.

The Dublin shipments were sent to two flour factors in the capital. From 1775 to 1778, Michael Bellew dealt with John Blake of 37 Arran Quay. A member of the Galway family of Tower Hill, related to both the Bellews and the Lynches, Blake headed one of the most important and wealthy of the Dublin houses and carried on extensive business with the west of Ireland.[97] From 1778, his flour shipments were consigned to William Colville, another prominent Dublin merchant, who also served as the factor for the mill at Slane in Meath, the largest in Ireland.

It is in the account of these shipments that the largest sales and proceeds are reflected, as well as the advantage of the government bounty. Bounty rates were 3d. per mile for 5 cwt. of flour. Its application to county Galway and the procedure involved in receiving bounty on the Bellew mills' flour is described in the family correspondence: the bounty was sanctioned or certified by commerce officials, then bounty papers were made out before a justice in the county. The law allowed one day for transporting a shipment eight miles. The carriage route from the mills to Dublin was approximately 112 miles; thus, if bounty paper was sworn to on 23 April, Michael Bellew had until 17 May to ensure delivery to Dublin and receive the bounty.[98] From July through September of 1775, when the mills first began operating at full capacity, 1136 cwt. were sent to John Blake for £567.15s.0d. With the bounty of £224.6s.3d. from the amount shipped and the distance covered in transport, this shipment amounted to a total of £792.1s.3d.

From 1776 to 1778, the amounts of flour sent to Blake periodically were somewhat less, with corresponding proceeds. In 1779, the yearly shipment to William Colville broke down as follows:

		£ s. d.
April-June	198 cwt. or 99 bags	134. 0. 9
(the end of the winter stock)		
July-November	242 cwt. or 181 bags	173.16. 6
(the end of the summer stock)		

From this year through 1782, shipments and proceeds through Colville were, allowing for price fluctuations and variations in harvests during the period, roughly equivalent to these figures.

The profitability of this Dublin market in comparison to the Connacht market is readily apparent. In 1776, a particularly profitable year, the mill accounts show the following entries:

		£ s. d.
Jan. 28 –	By am't flour & bran sold at the mills as per day book Lib:1: to this date	133. 9. 9
"	By am't flour sold in Dublin as per account: nt. proceeds	636.10.11
June 31 –	By am't flour and bran sold in the mills as per day-book to this date	137.17. 8
"	By am't flour sold in Dublin as per account: nt. proceeds	532. 7. 6

The disproportionate proceeds from Dublin lessened in the late 1770s and early 1789s, which may be a reflection of the increased competition for the market created by the establishment of new mills countrywide during this period. Nonetheless, the advantage of the bounty and the larger shipments that could be accommodated by the Dublin factors continued to make 'Dublin sales' a profitable component of the mills' output.

The accounts also reflect something of the costs involved in flour milling, from employees' salaries to payments for both mill supplies and the grain milled. Payments to employees were not usually a major expenditure, since flour mills required few workmen; the large mill at Slane employed only 10–12 men. At the Bellew mills, from March 1775 to March 1777, John Drumgold, a miller, was paid £30 for one year's service during this period, less debits of £9.13s.1d. for absences, payments, and purchases. John Cornein and James Royan, millboys, received £6 each for a little less than one year's employment; Andrew Berne, a clerk, received £30. Nor were mill supplies particularly costly: from April 1775-April 1776, £58.1s.7d. was expended for sacks and bags; paper; materials, including 'tallow and twist thread'; as well as repairs, carriage, and payments to 'sundry workmen'.

The sums needed for grain purchases, however, were substantial, and attest the importance of the Dublin factor, who could advance money to the miller for the proceeds of the flour in his warehouses. The account book of the Bellew mills records the payments made for grain to be milled, starting from the beginning of operations –

		Bar.	St.	lb.	£	s.	d.
Nov. 1, 1775 –	am't wheat bought from commencement of the mills to this date	708.	8.	10	654.	7.10	
May 1, 1776 –	am't bought from 1 Nov. last to this date	616.	9.	12	460.	1.11	

and continuing through the decade –

	Bar.	St.	lb.	£	s.	d.
Nov. 1776	636.	15.	13	585.	17.	-
May 1777	764.	16.	6	687.	16.	8
Nov. 1777	641.	18.	10	687.	17.	6
May 1778	715.	13.	9	828.	13.	1
Nov. 1778	495.	19.	9	599.	2.	2
May 1779	537.	17.	10	474.	19.	2
Nov. 1779	549.	10.	9	501.	9.10	
May 1780	579.	11.	6	441.	9.	6

The Bellew mills were very much a family-oriented enterprise. Christopher Dillon, as eldest son and heir, took an active hand in their administration, and Michael Bellew's youngest son Francis also appears to have assumed a major role in their operation – his signature is on the mill account book, and references in the family letters indicate that he was responsible for overseeing the shipments to Dublin. As well, the Galway Bellews profited from the assistance of Michael Bellew's nephew Christopher in Dublin, who kept Christopher Dillon apprised as to the state of the market.[99] In October of 1791, he advised Frank to send more flour shipments there as good flour was then scarce. Later in the year, he recommended that Frank sell all of his flour in the country if it was possible to get a good price; it would not pay to send it to Dublin, since there was a great quantity on hand there. Again in 1791, he advised waiting to sell flour in the capital at 17s.6d. instead of the current price of 16s.6d. in Galway. He also kept an eye on its quality, once warning Christopher Dillon that the flour shipped from Galway was lumpy and had a bad smell, and, in 1791, commenting that the latest shipment was 'rather coarse'.

In 1795, this family commercial association entered a new phase when Christopher Bellew made plans to take a lease on the mills. In February, he described to Christopher Dillon his plans for their administration: two men were to oversee the mills and keep accounts; they were also to attend the country markets and purchase wheat. On 4 December, Michael Bellew formally leased the flour mills of Mount Bellew to 'Christopher Bellew of the City of Dublin, Esq.' for 21 years. The yearly rent was £440; £40 was to be expended by Michael Bellew or Christopher Dillon Bellew during the first year to keep up the banks and weirs of the mill streams and clear the weeds. After that, the £40 was to be paid to Michael Bellew for the expense of putting the mills in complete order.

Even after the transfer, the Galway Bellews still played an active role in the milling operations. Christopher Bellew in Dublin continued to rely on Christopher Dillon's assistance in Galway: directives to the millers and overseers were funnelled through him, and he was even asked to look for a replacement for a miller given to drink. Further, Christopher Dillon often raised money to stock the mills, and there is a reference to Michael Bellew keeping them supplied with money. Christopher Bellew's tenure at the mills was often rocky. At one point in 1803, in financial difficulties and unable to pay the rent, he surrendered the mills to Christopher Dillon, much to the latter's displeasure. However, he appears to have regained his financial footing, and in 1805 had 'upwards of £4,000 in the mill in corn, wheat, oats, and barley'.

The involvement of members of the Bellew family in eighteenth-century trade and commerce concluded with the mercantile career of Patrick Bellew's son Christopher. Born in Spain, he had accompanied his father on his return to Ireland and was employed by Patrick Bellew in the inland flour trade. After Patrick's death on 6 July 1789, one of the first steps taken by Michael Bellew, as his brother's executor, was to request from Lynch and Bellew in Cadiz immediate payment of £1,000 from his brother's Spanish assets to enable Christopher to continue the 'flour business here, which is established at some expence, and with which Kit is very conversant, as it is the only business he was applied to'. As previously mentioned, Christopher took immediate charge of his father's flour trade with success, maintaining Patrick Bellew's contacts in Galway and adding malt commissions in Kilkenny, Drogheda, Limerick, and Wexford.

The settling of Patrick Bellew's other business interests, those in and connected with Spain, was, however, to prove another, and more difficult, matter.[100] Immediately after Patrick's death, steps were taken to protect his Spanish assets; from Dublin, Michael Bellew granted a power of attorney to Bartholomew Costello, the Bellew kinsman and merchant in Cadiz. This was done to prevent the interference of the Spanish officers of justice with the mercantile house on the advice of Michael Bellew's 'friend Randall McDonnell, late of Cartagena, but now of this city'. Costello was also to determine if the laws of Spain would have any effect on Christopher's inheritance. This proved to be no problem, but the settling of accounts with his father's firm was to occasion much ill-feeling between the Bellews in Ireland and the Lynches in Spain.

The initial correspondence between Michael and Christopher Bellew and the Lynches was cordial; an invitation was issued to Christopher to join the Spanish house, but his uncles, as well as Bartholomew Costello, advised him to stay in Ireland where business prospects appeared better. When it came time to reckon the amount of Patrick Bellew's Spanish assets to be remitted to his son, however, difficulties arose. The Lynches argued that losses on cargoes of fruit incurred by Patrick in his Dublin business connections with the Spanish house should be subtracted from the total settlement on Christopher. In addition, payments of over £2,000 sent to Bellew from Cadiz from April-July of 1789 were to be immediately applied to the payment of sums due from Lynch and Bellew to Byrne and McDonnell for butter shipments. The final amount sent by the Lynches to Christopher, according to their account, was £7,003. The outcome of several years of correspondence between the Bellews, uncle and nephew; the Lynches; and Costello, who continued to serve as the Bellews' agent in Cadiz in an effort to untangle Patrick's accounts, was perhaps predictable: the Lynches considered financial affairs settled; Michael Bellew figured that the balance on his brother's account was £10,392.7s.2d. and that £3–4,000 more was due Christopher, and the Bellew family thought the charging of Patrick Bellew's Spanish estate with most of the firm's Irish trade losses unfair. It is impossible to judge from the Bellew correspondence the accuracy or fairness of these counter-claims; however, a passing reference in Costello's correspondence – 'Patt was not too informative about business dealings' – and comments about 'entanglements' and 'bad business dealings' suggest the Lynches may not have been quite as unfair in their accounting as the Bellews considered them.

Nevertheless, with legacies from his mother and his uncle Edward Lynch, the Spanish naval captain; the £7,003 remitted by the House of Lynch and Bellew; and Patrick Bellew's £7–8,000 in Irish interests, Christopher Bellew quickly established himself as a merchant in his own right at his father's firm in 42 Abbey Street.[101] He continued to carry on trade with the Lynches' house in Cadiz, although initial shipments of goods seem to have been regarded by both as a means of cancelling Patrick Bellew's outstanding debts: Christopher referred to the Lynches' desire that he 'procure consignments for them' and 'work it off in wine accounts and butter orders'. In the early 1790s, the commodities shipped to Dublin included port, wines, and mahogany. Christopher in turn sent butter to Spain; in 1795, he purchased 1,000 casks of butter for Cadiz, among other destinations. Trade with France is also indicated in his references to 'French wines' and claret. At least some of his wine imports found their way to Galway: wine and quarter-casks of port appear to have been supplied to his relatives at Mount Bellew at regular intervals.

Although Christopher Bellew continued many of the enterprises his father had begun, from 1792 forward there are references in his correspondence to another branch of overseas trade, which was to become more important than that with his continental connections, and is a reflection of a significant change in Irish foreign trade in general. The eighteenth-century provisions trade, dependent on the demands of the countries of the continent and subsequently their colonial possessions, represented an aberration in the normal patterns of Irish trade. England had traditionally been the main market for Irish agricultural and livestock products, and it was only the restrictive legislation of the second half of the seventeenth century that had diverted this trade to the continent; economic developments in the second half of the eighteenth century were to restore it to its more accustomed patterns.

The further development of European dairying and animal husbandry, the declining use of salt beef, and the competition for the provisions trade from North America resulted in a shrinking continental market. Exports of Irish butter, in particular, dropped in the 1780s; only Spain and Portugal continued to provide a significant market.[102] At the same time, there was an increasing demand from England for provisions, reflected in the suspension of the prohibition against the import of Irish cattle in 1758 and beef and butter in 1759. Ultimately, the legislation that had kept Irish provisions shut out from England was repealed in 1776. Between 1770 and 1800, Irish exports of beef to England quadrupled, those of butter doubled, and those of pork, including bacon, increased eight-fold. At the end of the eighteenth century, the reversion to traditional trade patterns was complete: England was the primary market for Irish beef, pork, and butter, and Anglo-Irish trade was the most important component of Irish foreign trade.

These economic developments and the long periods of war with France, which led to increasing prices for provisions[103] and the creation of a large army and navy to be supplied, made the English market extremely profitable, and Christopher Bellew was among those Irish merchants to develop it. From 1792 to 93, he wrote his uncle that the provisions business was heavy and that he was supplying the government with beef and pork; indeed, his dealings with the government were to continue through the turn of the century. In addition, English merchant correspondents were supplied with beef, bacon, oats, and butter. At least once, Bellew made his own arrangements for beef supplies: in August 1798, he informed Christopher Dillon that he had entered into a contract with Denis Browne of Westport, county Mayo for 4–500 head of cattle and planned to have the beef 'made up' for the provisions trade.

The pattern and structure of this trade with England is reflected in Christopher Bellew's business dealings. London was the English import center, taking over 60 per cent of provisions shipments; in 1795, Bellew, along with other Irish merchants, had £8,000 invested in 4,000 sides of bacon there and in 1797 was 'laying out money in bacon and hogs'. The ports of the south and northwest also carried on a significant amount of Irish business, and Bellew had correspondents in Liverpool as well, dealing in oats and beef. Butter, however, was the most important commodity; by the close of the century, the value of shipments to England was £700,000. Again, trade was centered on London; cheesemongers there distributed much of the quantities imported to inland country merchants. By 1795, the 1,000 casks of butter Bellew was purchasing were intended for this London market as well as Cadiz.

Generally, the business dealings of Irish merchants were on a modest scale, and those in the Anglo-Irish trade relied more on filling commissions for their English counterparts, who had more capital and better discounting facilities, than on shipping to England on their own accounts. For example, Christopher Bellew's butter shipments were on the commission of London cheesemongers whose trade, as he complained to Michael Bellew, 'I have to solicit yearly as others are applying to them.' Yet, he was also among those Irish merchants able to trade with their own resources; his dealings with his correspondents in Liverpool and London in oats, beef, and bacon appear to have been on his own account.

The general themes of Christopher Bellew's correspondence with his uncle and cousin in Galway are almost exclusively business-oriented; they include the prices of commodities, reports on business in general and that of Dublin in particular, and the difficulties involved in discounting bills and obtaining long-term credit. The latter topic provides a good illustration of the family resources available to a merchant with landed gentry connections.

The economic structure of eighteenth-century Ireland, especially with regard to banking, was relatively undeveloped, which often proved a disadvantage to the merchant community. Although the volume of business and trade in Ireland increased steadily from the 1720s through the 1790s, there was no accompanying increase in structured banking facilities, especially those providing for the discounting of bills of internal and external exchange.[104] From 1759 to 1793, there were only four or five private banks in Dublin; the Bank of Ireland was not established until 1783. Merchants eased the situation in part by selling bills, and this process continued into the 1790s, with much of the discounting done by private houses. Generally, bills of 31 days were the norm; those of more than 61 days were often extremely hard to negotiate. The difficulties often encountered by a merchant seeking to discount bills were recounted, with only slight exaggeration, by the anonymous author of *A View of the Present State of Ireland* in 1789:

The interests of the merchant and the community are sacrificed to the convenience and profit of a few individuals...The caprice of a partner, the pretended settlement of their accounts, the dread of an approaching linen market, the failure of some merchant, causes them without any notice to forbear discounting. The anxious merchant turns over his bills, places the best uppermost, and, like some unfortunate criminal dragged to execution approaches with a pallid cheek and trembling hand, the counter of the banker ...[105]

In periods of economic downturns, when the demand for conversion of paper into cash was high, the Dublin banks and private houses were reluctant – indeed, sometimes unable – to discount even short-term bills, and those merchants holding bills with more than two months to run found themselves in dire economic straits. Such a commercial crisis occurred in 1796–97, brought about by unstable political conditions and the threat of invasion from France, and Christopher Bellew was among the Dublin merchants who found themselves in the situation described by the anonymous pamphleteer.

As early as 1793, Bellew had reported to his Galway relatives that the banks had stopped discounting for a time. In 1795, he complained of the difficulty in passing bills on the change,[106] procuring money, and negotiating bills, adding that there was no profit in speculation (a reference to the practice of purchasing bills in areas with lower rates of interest and paying in bills bought in areas where the rates were higher). During the height of the crisis in late 1796 and early 1797, his difficulties became acute: the national bank ceased discounting and the private banks were unable to accomodate all the merchants. In September of 1796, Bellew wrote his uncle that 'the situation in Dublin is such that [a] person must not only be prepared for his own engagements but also for the bills he passes for few are now able to pay them punctually, not for want of means as they all have plenty of property but for want of discount'. As a temporary expedient, he requested Michael Bellew to draw bills in Galway for 50 days. In February of 1797, 'bills longer than 21 days will not be done at the banks' and it was 'impossible to raise money on the best paper'. Again the private banks were unable to discount; the national bank refused to. Bellew offered his bankers £17,000 in England and Irish bills, but they 'were not able to discount a shilling'. However, that same month, his gentry relatives were able to provide aid; Michael Bellew sent sundry notes amounting to £1070, much to his nephew's relief. Recovery came at last in June of 1797.

As this account of the activities of eighteenth-century Galway families has demonstrated, the involvement of members of the Irish Catholic gentry in trade and commerce was extensive and diverse. For those in the merchant communities abroad, it was also closely linked with the country they had left. On the continent, they served primarily as import-export agents in close business association with relatives, friends, and co-religionists in Ireland as well as England.

Links with Ireland of a non-commercial nature were also strong. Although members of the merchant communities abroad often established marital ties with families in their countries of residence, the number who chose to marry within their commercial colonies, like Patrick Bellew, or among families in Ireland is notable. Further, it is likely many considered their overseas residence only temporary: Henry Blake of Montserrat, Patrick Bellew of Cadiz, Luke Bellew of Bordeaux, and George Moore of Alicante, all from Connacht families, returned to their homeland, usually after having made sufficient profits abroad.

In Ireland, the younger sons of gentry families contributed to the rise of a Catholic middle-mercantile class, and some of the landed gentry themselves enthusiastically embarked upon business enterprises, if not always with the same degree of success illustrated in flour milling.[107] The reciprocal benefits of the relationship between those family members who maintained their lands and those who went into trade and commerce were important and varied. Merchants could provide their landed relatives with foreign commodities, aid in establishing credit and passing bills of exchange, serve as factors for country produce, and generally add to the family wealth in land – by not having to be provided for from it. The landed gentry in turn could supply the capital necessary to initiate a mercantile career, provide business contacts within their counties, and on occasion, as we have seen, offer financial aid in times of need.

This involvement of the Irish Catholic gentry in mercantile affairs is in interesting contrast to the relative lack of it among their English counterparts. While English Catholics were merchants, manufacturers, and bankers, gentry families do not appear to have contributed significantly to their numbers. There are of course examples of participation in industrial and mercantile affairs; some were successful in coal mining and the import of mahogany and timber, but the gentry were never particularly conspicuous in trade. Among many English gentry families, medicine and law were considered the only socially acceptable careers for younger sons, and those who chose neither must surely have placed a financial burden on the family.[108]

The attitude of the Irish Catholic gentry toward trade and commerce as acceptable careers was obviously quite different, although social distinctions were made between the activities of a merchant and those of a mere tradesman. While Sir Patrick Bellew of county Louth was eager to further the fortunes of a relative, Garret Bellew, by placing him 'in the mercantile way at Cadiz' through Patrick Bellew, he was not pleased when Garret's brother John married the daughter of 'some man who sold garden seeds in Christ Church Lane'. Despite the rumours of a favourable financial settlement, he told Michael Bellew that, 'I must own my pride suffers a little on account of the alliance'.[109] However, the gentry were certainly not disdainful of the type of commercial enterpise described in this chapter. They regarded it as an extremely useful outlet for the energies and industry of younger sons and relatives, one that could also contribute to the family fortune as a whole. Thus, mercantile involvement proved to be a significant factor in maintaining the financial resources, indeed the vitality, of the Catholic gentry in the eighteenth century.

'It Is Time for Us to Speak Out like Men': The Gentry and Catholic Relief

Throughout almost all of the eighteenth century, Catholics were effectively denied the constitutional means by which to alter penal leglislation, for those laws governing Catholic participation in civil life were all-encompassing and totally restrictive. They were designed to ensure that Catholics had no measure of political power, either as voters or as holders of office on a national or local level.

Catholics had been excluded from the Irish parliament by an English act of 1691, which required a member of parliament to make a declaration against transubstantiation and also to take an oath that the doctrine of the papal power of deposition was heretical. They were also barred from serving on grand or petty juries, or acting as magistrates, sheriffs, or constables. Catholics had nonetheless been permitted to vote in parliamentary elections from 1692 by taking an oath of allegiance and, from 1703, by taking an additional oath of abjuration, acknowledging Anne as rightful sovereign and denying James' right to the crown.[1] However, they were deprived of this right in 1728, when legislation prohibited their voting, regardless of any oaths they might take.

Catholics were also barred from the profession, that of the law, by which they might be assumed to acquire civil influence. Barristers were required to take the oath of 1691 by both English and Irish statute. Legislation also prohibited Catholics from becoming solicitors. These laws were less effective, however, than the ones which forbade Catholics to vote or hold office. Archbishop Hugh Boulter complained in 1728 that the legal profession was dominated by nominal converts said to have purchased certificates stating they had taken the sacraments in the Church of England or Ireland in order to be admitted to the bar.[2] Moreover, numbers of Catholics in the eighteenth century entered Inns of Court in Ireland and England and pursued legal studies to receive certification of competency as conveyancers.[3] Although they could not plead cases, they were qualified in the law and could provide legal advice to their fellow Catholics. Nonetheless, despite presumed Catholic sympathizers among 'convert' barristers (and even here, additional requirements beyond certificates were demanded)[4] and the opportunity for circumscribed participation in the legal profession, the law could not serve Catholics, as it could their Protestant counterparts, as a means of acquiring influence in civil or political life.

These penal laws were to remain in effect after others had been repealed or fallen into disuse. The Protestant government was, quite early in the eighteenth century, prepared to allow Catholics to practise their religion with little interference, and, as will be seen, by the late 1770s and early 80s, to allow them to participate fully in economic life. However, for many Protestants, in positions of power and out, this was the furthest they were prepared to go. They were adamantly opposed to measures of relief that would allow Catholics any political power, even within the eighteenth-century system of government that decidedly assured the majority would not rule.

However, it should not be assumed that landed Catholics were totally without means of exerting influence in a political system that barred them as voters or office holders. As substantial landholders in Louth and Galway, the Catholic Bellews could at least influence their freeholders in political matters in much the same way as Protestants. In March 1768, Sir Patrick Bellew, in a letter to Michael Bellew, discussed his and his relatives' electoral strategy in Galway for the upcoming elections:

> I hope Mr. Daly will carry his election. I was obliged to promise my neighbours here, the Fortescues, that I would do all I could for Billy Trench, so beg you'll speak to Grace if he means to pay me any compliment for his freehold, to vote for him and Denis Daly, and if you and Dominick Bellew can influence any ... I am determined to make a score of freeholders at Newtown Bellew, which I shall certainly give for the future to Daly and Robin French of Monivea who I think very deserving of his country's favour.[5]

The significance of this electoral activity lies not just in a Catholic landholder influencing the votes of his freeholders, but in the Bellews' choice of candidates to support. Sir Patrick's characterization of his support for Trench as an obligation as opposed to what appears to be more whole-hearted support for Denis Daly and Robert French might also reflect shrewd assessment of their respective support for Catholics. The Trench family was of Huguenot origin; Daly and French, however, were from families who had conformed only one or two generations earlier, and branches of their families remained in the Catholic faith. While French seems to have been a sincere supporter of the Protestant interest – and faith – he was also among those who viewed mitigation of the penal laws with favour;[6] Daly was also sympathetic toward relief, to the point of being included in what the earl of Charlemont termed a 'Popish party' in the Commons. However, exerting influence was still qualitatively different from participating in a political system. This final civil barrier would not be over-come until the very end of the century, and even then Catholic success was limited.

The granting of Catholic relief was a process both piecemeal, occurring in several stages, and complex. Its complete analysis requires discussion of a daunting number of topics: political machinations and manoeuvreing in both Ireland and Britain,[7] the mentalités of Catholic activism and Protestant ob-struction,[8] the Volunteers and the United Irishmen and the connections be-tween individual Catholics and both, and the role of organized bodies such as the Catholic Committee in pursuit of relief. Not least, such an analysis in-volves consideration of the impact of events external to Irish politics which brought about change. While some of these topics will be explored in order to provide an adequate historical context, the focus here will be on the place of the Catholic gentry in the movement to dismantle the structure penal legisla-tion had erected.

Many historians have justifiably observed that Catholic opinion, articulated of course by a relatively small segment of the Catholic population (and done so frequently in their own interests), was divided as to the best way to ap-proach amelioration of their condition. As in any reform movement, there were those eager to take advantage of every favourable opportunity to promote change and those reluctant to proceed too quickly. The more activist approach is usu-ally ascribed to middle-class merchants and professionals, the conservative outlook to the aristocracy and gentry. Although this division tends to overlook the gentry background of many Irish merchants, the characterization contains some validity. Catholics who had retained their lands might well have pre-ferred to place their hopes for relief on the good will of the Irish and British administrations, rather than through agitation that might prove alienating.

As with most simple dichotomies, however, this one is misleading, mask-ing the complexity of the attitudes of the gentry toward reform and the best ways to achieve it. It is based in part on their sometimes dismissive, sometimes stormy, relationship with the Catholic Committee, the first organized body to promote the Catholic cause. This exclusive focus on organized attempts to bring about change has often obscured other avenues used by the aristocracy and gentry, notably the social and political connections with which their status provided them. Indeed, it has been observed that the negotiations with the Irish government involving the first two substantial measures of Catholic relief, in 1778 and 1782, were conducted by the Catholic gentry and bishops, with the Committee playing a subordinate role.[9] Such a focus also overlooks the ability of some of the Catholic elite to employ both Committee membership and those other connections in an attempt to achieve their goals. Finally, such a dichotomy fails to reflect the changing nature of gentry participation in the reform movement from the relatively placid 1760s through the turbulent last quarter of the century.

An examination of the role of the Bellews in the movement to bring about Catholic relief illustrates well all of these aspects of gentry involvement. Sir Patrick Bellew of the Louth branch was a prominent member of the Catholic Committee from the 1770s, yet he also established connections with the Volunteer movement through his personal acquaintance with Frederick Hervey, the earl of Bristol and bishop of Derry. As a result of his activities, Bellew was considered a dangerous radical by Dublin Castle in the 1780s. However, a decade later, he was castigated as a conservative by some of his fellow Catholics and briefly seceded from the Committee in a split occasioned by disagreements over the proper pace and nature of reform. It was his younger Galway relative, Christopher Dillon Bellew, who played an activist role in agitation to bring about what would be the last eighteenth-century measure of Catholic relief.

The activities of the Bellews from the 1760s through the 1780s in support of reform can be traced in part through family letters, particularly those of Sir Patrick to Michael Bellew. Their correspondence, a part of which is preserved in the family papers,[10] begins in 1762 on a pessimistic note. Writing from his Louth seat of Barmeath, Sir Patrick responded to his kinsman's curiosity as to whether 'anything is in agitation for us in Parliament'. A bill to loosen restrictions on Catholics' holding judgments and investing in mortgages on land had been introduced in the previous parliamentary session. However, it was defeated, and Patrick Bellew, although hopeful for the granting of some indulgence, had learned from his informants that nothing would be done in the current session of parliament: the government and a majority of both houses were against 'talking any more of ourselves'. According to Sir Patrick, this 'inclines many of our persuasion to think of breaking ground in order to settle in other countries of liberty and equality'.

Despite this set-back, Sir Patrick engaged that same year in extra-parliamentary efforts to work for government favour – from a different source. He was among those Irish Catholic nobility and gentry who requested the British administration to permit Catholics to enroll in military service to the crown, a timely request in view of the manpower demands of the Seven Years War. The law excluding Catholics from the army was not changed, and the government was unwilling to take any measures to allow Catholics to serve as officers, but it did support the landed classes' proposal to enroll seven Irish Catholic regiments to serve the allied army of Catholic Portugal.[11] The proposal died, in the face of the Irish parliament's disapproval and the approaching end of war,[12] but is a reflection of the traditional approach of the gentry and aristocracy: attempts, through demonstrations of loyalty, to elicit favourable attention from the British government in the face of the Irish parliament's intransigence toward reform. In 1762, the approach was unsuccessful. However, in view of the fact that most significant relief would come during periods of war, in which the British administration felt it necessary to conciliate Catholics in Ireland for reasons of security, it was a tactic that should not be dismissed lightly.

There was, however, another avenue available after mid-century for gentry Catholics seeking reform and relief. A representative body to plan action on the Catholic behalf had been created as the result of efforts by three men: Charles O'Conor of Belanagare, a gentry scholar and antiquary from Connacht;[13] John Curry, a Dublin physician; and Thomas Wyse, a member of a Waterford mercantile-gentry family. In the late 1750s, they met with other like-minded Catholics in Dublin to discuss formation of an association to direct Catholic affairs, and in 1760, the General Committee of the Catholics of Ireland was selected and directed to promote the Catholic cause and seek mitigation of the penal laws. It was composed of representatives from Dublin parishes and some of the larger towns, with admission open to those country gentlemen and nobility who wished to attend.

Initially, however, many of the aristocracy and gentry tended to distance themselves from the Catholic Committee (as it would come to be known). Shortly after its inception, the few who had established connections briefly severed them over the proper wording of an address of loyalty to George III; Lord Trimleston led a group of Meath and Westmeath gentry who submitted their own separate address.[14] After this contretemps, the Committee ceased regular meetings until 1767; even after their resumption, the gentry remained relatively uninvolved. Perceptions of the Committee as unimportant, or conversely, a lower-class threat to their traditional direction of Catholic affairs were undoubtedly factors. Provincial resentment of Dublin also played a part, illustrated well by a letter from the Catholic archbishop of Tuam to Charles O'Conor. The 'gentlemen of Dublin', he wrote testily, 'assume an authority which I think they have no right to do: that is to put everything their wise heads suggest in the name of the kingdom.'[15] Whatever the reasons, both the composition of the Committee and its programs reflect the absence of the landed classes from the late 1760s into the 1770s.[16] With only a few exceptions, merchants, drapers, and others of the commercial class predominated at the Committee's irregular meetings held in Dublin coffee houses. They concerned themselves with relief for beggars and, from 1766, the issue of quarterage, the tax imposed on quarter-brothers of guilds, the majority of whom were Catholic. The Committee coordinated opposition to its collection and raised money for legal expenses.[17]

Sir Patrick Bellew's initial involvement with the Committee was less than auspicious and reflects its internal divisions. Charles O'Conor referred to Bellew as 'your chairman' in a letter to Dr Curry in January of 1763. At the time, Sir Patrick was engaged in the delicate task of mediating between Lord Trimleston and the Committee: Trimleston had expended £300 of collections without adequate consultation with its members and was reluctant to return it after the breach in relations.[18]

Bellew would, however, assume an active role in the Catholic Committee as its composition began to change. Perhaps in response to the first partial relief from the provisions of the penal laws affecting land, the so-called 'Bog Act' of 1771,[19] or from a perceived need to reassert their authority in the direction of Catholic affairs after the success of the Committee in the quarterage campaign, the aristocracy and gentry took an increasing interest in the Committee and its activities. In 1773, the Committee was reorganized under the guidance of Lord Kenmare and the direction of business was delegated to a select committee; this was to be the vehicle for the landed classes' reassertion of influence. The select committee, deliberating in private from June 1775 to June 1778, appears to have been controlled by the landed gentlemen, although several middle-class members worked with them.[20] By 1778, assimiliation of the nobility and gentry into the Catholic Committee was marked. The new select committee of that year, appointed to a two-year term, had 25 members. Of this number, three were peers, one a baronet, and ten were country gentlemen; among the latter was Sir Patrick Bellew.[21] Its meetings were chaired by such members of the Catholic aristocracy as the earl of Fingall, Viscount Gormanston, and Lord Kenmare, and many landed gentry not appointed to the select committee itself attended its meetings. Although, with the expiration of the two-year term, formal control of affairs returned to the General Committee, the voice of the landed classes remained a strong one.

In 1777, returning to traditional forms of gentle agitation, the Catholic peers and over three hundred landed gentry presented a petition to George III. In it, they proclaimed their steadfast loyalty, but enumerated the disabilities under which they continued to labour: the restrictions on land purchases and rentals, the threat of the discoverer, and above all, the 'pernicious privilege' offered the eldest son on his conformity of forcing an estate's entail against the wishes of his father.[22]

The British government in the late 1770s would prove to be receptive to Catholic requests for relief. With fears of Jacobitism long receded, its concerns about Irish Catholics were far different from those of the Irish parliament. The position – and protection – of Ireland in the empire was the paramount issue, particularly as relations with the American colonies worsened and fears of French involvement increased. When those relations ruptured, the loyalty of at least the Catholic elite during the American War for Independence did not go unnoticed.

Sir Patrick Bellew and Michael Bellew took part in the agitation for repeal of the penal laws in 1777–78; both signed the petition to the king in 1777.[23] Sir Patrick contributed funds and worked in both Ireland and England for relief. In two letters from London in 1788, he kept Michael Bellew informed about progress, or its lack, on the political front. In February of 1778, his reaction to Lord North's conciliatory motion in the Commons reflected the general lack of sympathy among the Catholic elite for the American cause: 'tho mortifying it is to give up so much to the Americans, yet it is universally believed they will reject it', refusing all terms short of independence. After brief mention of the popular opinion that a French war was inevitable and the resultant fall of stocks, his next comment revealed a perhaps unconscious linkage between concilation of Americans and a refusal to do the same for Irish Catholics: 'Nothing will be done for the Roman Catholics after all their hopes, the Ministry are afraid to meddle in their affairs'.

Bellew's pessimism, however, was unfounded. The British government, to secure Catholic loyalty and ensure support for recruitment of Catholics, was prepared to move. In May of 1778, the Commons assented to Saville's relief bill for English Catholics; it would become law in June. As one recent account of Catholic relief in 1778 has asserted, 'the English Catholic Relief Act of 1778 was passed with Irish Catholics in mind'; in the debate over the bill, Lord Beauchamp, a former Chief Secretary for Ireland, expressed the hope that it would be 'an example to the Irish parliament'.[24] In a letter to Michael Bellew in April of 1778, Sir Patrick would virtually echo Beauchamp's words, hoping English Catholic relief would serve 'by way of example to your Irish Parliament', adding that a relief bill would shortly be introduced. After spending nine months 'at a very heavy expense to this affair', passage, he stated, 'will make us a happy people', with liberty to purchase, take leases of any time, and 'abolish the gavel, that infernal act'. The date of Bellew's letter, 23 April, almost a month before the introduction of Saville's bill, would appear to indicate that he was extremely well-informed as to government planning on both sides of the Irish Channel, perhaps through the London agent of the Catholic Committee, Daniel MacNamara. Indeed, shortly after, on 5 June, Luke Gardiner introduced a measure for Catholic relief into the Irish Commons. The Catholic Committee organized the collection of £2,000 to aid in its passage,[25] and with government support and the efforts of Irish MPs Henry Grattan, Barry Yelverton, and Sir Hercules Langrishe, the first major Irish Catholic relief measure became law. On taking an oath of allegiance to the Crown and making a prescribed declaration against papal temporal or civil powers, Catholics could take leases on land up to 999 years and inherit and sell lands on the same footing as Protestants. Although the freedom to purchase fee-simple lands (and with it, political rights) still remained to be won and other penal laws remained, expectations for further concessions had now been raised and the Catholic Committee began to raise more money to fund further reform efforts.

Both Sir Patrick and Michael Bellew took the oath of allegiance to qualify for the provisions of the relief act[26] and were involved in the Committee's planning for future relief. By this time, the Galway branch of the family may have begun to participate in the Committee's affairs. A Michael Bellew attended a meeting of the select committee on 7 December 1779 and was among the signatories to a resolution for employing lawyers to prepare plans for further relief. In the select committee's next meeting on 21 December, Sir Patrick Bellew was appointed to oversee collection of funds in Drogheda for legal expenses.[27]

By the third quarter of the eighteenth century, a distinct Catholic interest group had emerged, its concerns articulated by both the landed and mercantile classes, working both within and outside the Catholic Committee. At the same time, a new group of Protestant leaders had emerged who were more sympathetic to at least some of its goals. While Henry Flood and the earl of Charlemont were disposed to accept and further plans for complete religious toleration and loosen restrictions on Catholic landholding, this was the highwater mark of their liberalism. Now, a group of Protestants more favourable to Catholic expectations of further relief was gaining in prominence. In the Irish parliament, such men as Henry Grattan, Luke Gardiner, Sir Hercules Langrishe, and John Hely-Hutchinson formed, in Charlemont's phrase, a 'Popish party'; outside of the Commons, the eccentric but influential Frederick Hervey, earl of Bristol and bishop of Derry, urged accommodation with Catholics. Moreover, a movement seeking greater autonomy for Ireland within the British empire would soon develop, led by many of these men. A related concern of these 'patriots' was reform of the Irish government and franchise, which would ultimately lead them to the most crucial issue of all – the place, if any, of the majority Catholics in either a reform movement or a reformed political system.

From the inception of the Catholic Committee in the 1760s, its members, despite their occasional divisions, had worked for relief by themselves, pursuing their own aims. Beginning in the early 1780s, however, certain of the Committee's members were to become directly involved with these Protestant movements for reform – with the attendant problem of ensuring that Catholic aims might be accommodated within them. The first of these rapprochements was made with the Irish Volunteers, and a decade later, with a more radical group, the United Irishmen. Both of these involvements would bring about division between forward and conservative Catholics on the Committee; the last would bring about an open breach.

In the 1780s, Sir Patrick Bellew would be in the forefront as part of an activist group on the Catholic Committee who saw the hopes of the Catholics tied to those of the Volunteers. His personal acquaintance with one of the Volunteer leaders, the Earl-Bishop of Derry, would be the link between Catholic and Protestant reformers. The Volunteers were a citizen army raised for the defense of Ireland in 1779. Their military prowess would be untested, as foreign invasion threats never materialized. However, the influence of their numbers – perhaps some 50,000 - was great, and the Volunteers soon made their presence felt in Irish politics. They lent their support to the 'patriots' in the Irish parliament in their proposals for free trade and a more independent parliament and judiciary. Leading 'patriot' Parliamentarians such as Charlemont, Grattan, and Flood were also members of Volunteer corps. Aided by a change of government in Britain, with a Whig ministry under Rockingham replacing Lord North's, these leaders succeeded in obtaining their goals, embodied in the so-called 'Constitution of 1782'.

Further measures for Catholic relief also accompanied the campaign for political concessions from Britain. They have also been seen as intertwined: as part of a calculated plan to show the unity of all Irishmen behind the demand for legislative independence.[28] In February 1782, Luke Gardiner introduced a second bill to repeal or modify the penal laws, and Sir Patrick Bellew was again active in its support. After the bill's passage through the Commons, he wrote to Michael Bellew in April as it came before the Lords, complaining that 'friends in town' had not been as active as they could have been. According to Bellew, they should have had a list of peers and 'sounded every one of them' as well as inquired about proxies. One lord in particular, Strangford, could be 'had for money, which if wanting ought not to be neglected.[29]

Despite Bellew's concerns, Gardiner's proposals became law. In their final form as the Catholic Relief Acts of 1782, they granted Catholics the right to purchase lands freehold, formally repealed many measures (long since obsolete) restricting the activities of the Catholic clergy, permitted Catholics on taking an oath of allegiance to become schoolmasters and private tutors, and restored the right of Catholic laymen to be guardians to Catholic children. If Sir Patrick Bellew was at similar 'great expense' in his support of relief in 1782 as he had been in 1778, he did not mention it to Michael Bellew. However, the possibility of his being either recompensed by the Catholic Committee or funded by them for his efforts is suggested by an entry in the Committee's minutes, directing the treasurer to 'hold the sum of £50 str. at the disposal of Sir Patrick Bellew'.[30]

In his letter of April to Michael Bellew, Sir Patrick also regretted not sending 'an express to Lord Bristol' for closer coordination of the relief bills' support. This is the first mention in the family papers of his association with Frederick Hervey, which dated from 1780 or perhaps even earlier. Lord Sydney, writing to the duke of Rutland in 1784, remarked that he knew Bellew 'long ago' and used to see him in Suffolk, 'at that time a good deal with the Bishop of Derry'.[31] Hervey was among the most tolerant of the church of Ireland clergy; on his translation to the see of Derry in 1768, he cultivated friendships with Dissenters and Catholics alike. He considered favourable relations with the Irish Catholics in particular of vital interest to both Ireland and England and lent his support to the measures for Catholic relief in both 1778 and 1782. The earl-bishop would also come to envision a union of Catholics and Dissenters to achieve Irish goals of reform, even including Catholic political emancipation, points of view the Irish and British governments viewed with alarm. By 1782, he was also involved in the Volunteer movement, especially strong in the North.[32]

Although, as will be seen, the Catholic Committee itself would maintain a studious official neutrality in the contest between reformers and government, individual Catholics would feel no such constraints. Members of both the Volunteers and the Committee, including Bellew and Hervey, would briefly unite in their goals – reform and emancipation. Although their efforts would be defeated, their co-operation provided a model for a latter rapproachment of Protestant and Catholic which would result in further Catholic gains. However, in order to understand the nature of this first alliance, and its ultimate frustration, it is necessary to discuss briefly the relationship between the Irish Volunteers and the Irish Catholics.

Although the law forbade Catholics to bear arms and thus formally excluded them from any citizen militia, they were generally supportive of the Volunteer movement, providing funds for arms and equipment. However, from 1781, Catholics, despite the law, were permitted to enlist in several Volunteer corps. In turn, there was support from some Northern elements of the Volunteers for Catholic relief. The Volunteers of Ulster had called a convention at Dungannon in February of 1782; at a prior meeting at the earl of Charlemont's Dublin house, he, Flood, and Grattan, all leaders of Ulster corps, met to draw up resolutions in support of 'patriot' proposals in the Irish pariament. Included among them was one conciliatory to Catholics, proposed and drafted by Grattan over the opposition of Flood and Charlemont. As approved by the Dungannon Convention, it stated that

> as men and as Irishmen, as Christians and as Protestants, we rejoice in the relaxation of the Penal Laws against our Roman Catholic fellow-subjects, and that we conceive the measure to be fraught with the happi-est consequences to the union and prosperity of the inhabitants of Ire-land.[33]

By the end of 1782 and the beginning of 1783, their 'patriot' goals achieved, the Volunteers were to undergo significant changes – in the composition of their ranks and in the thrust of their political activities. Although the Volun-teers were to remain overwhelmingly Protestant, the number of Catholic mem-bers continued to increase. Corps in Limerick and Cork invited Catholics to enroll, and in the west, the Raford Brigade of Colonel Denis Daly MP and the Clanricarde Cavalry, led by his relative Peter Daly, opened their ranks to Catho-lics.[34] Of even greater significance in the events of 1783–84, John Keogh and Thomas Broughall, both merchant members of the Catholic Committee, joined Volunteer corps in Dublin.[35] At the same time, greater independence of the Irish parliament having been won, the Volunteers became active in plans for its reform; enlargement of the franchise was considered of particular importance.

However, proposals for reform of the political system brought with them the fateful question of Catholic participation. For some, notably the earl-bishop and certain of the Northern Volunteers, parliamentary reform and Catholic emancipation were inseparable, for the only way to achieve the former was to concede the latter. Even among this group, support was qualified: only Catho-lic property-holders worth £50 per year were to be enfranchised, ensuring that the Protestant establishment would not be seriously challenged. Their views were, however, as future events would show, by no means those of the major-ity of the Volunteers, who regarded Catholic suffrage as the deathknell of Prot-estant domination, regardless of the necessity of Catholic support in achieving reform.[36] This thorny issue would not only cause problems for the Volunteers but also create division within the Catholic Committee, which had not openly declared its views on Volunteer proposals.

A Grand National Convention of the Irish Volunteers planned to meet in Dublin in November of 1783 to prepare resolutions for parliamentary reform, and a split in leadership was soon evident.[37] Grattan refused to participate; Charlemont also disapproved of such a meeting, but considered his position as head of the Ulster Volunteers necessitated his presence. He also feared a radi-cal element might otherwise make its presence felt, for the earl-bishop, whom

Charlemont strongly disliked and distrusted, was a delegate from the London-derry Corps and the town of Belfast. Charlemont knew that Hervey was likely to introduce the question of the Catholic franchise, and, hoping to keep the Convention in the hands of the moderates, had himself elected president. On the second day of the Convention's sitting, the issue of the Catholic vote was indeed introduced, but in a totally unexpected way, and one that ended any chance of serious discussion. George Ogle, an MP and Volunteer delegate from Wexford, informed the delegates that he had received a communication from a Catholic peer disclaiming on the part of Catholics any further concessions beyond those they had previously gained. With the Catholic supporters in the Convention in disarray, the session was adjourned.

Rather remarkably, despite the fact that the Catholic Committee was in session at the same time as the Convention, no meeting had been called previ-ously to plan any kind of strategy or make clear their attitude toward any relief proposals that might have been brought forward.[38] Nonetheless, interest was obviously keen; 46 members, many of whom were country gentlemen not nor-mally in Dublin, were in attendance, and Volunteer allies were prominent – John Keogh; Richard McCormick; and the Bellews, Sir Patrick and his two sons Edward and William. Sir Patrick was in the chair, and the response to the day's events in the Convention was quick. It was unanimously resolved

> [That] the message relating to us, delivered this morning to the national convention, was totally unknown to us, and unauthorized by us.
>
> That we do not so widely differ from the rest of mankind, as, by our own act to prevent the removal of our shackles.
>
> That we shall receive with gratitude every indulgence that may be extended to us by the legislature, and are thankful to our benevolent coun-trymen for their generous efforts in our behalf.

Bellew was requested to present the resolutions to Hervey to be communicated to the Convention.[39]

At the next session of the Convention, Ogle, a strong opponent of Catholic relief, revealed that his statement was based on information received from Lord Kenmare's cousin, Sir Boyle Roche. Roche then told the delegates that Kenmare had sent him the message disclaiming any Catholic wish for the franchise. The earl-bishop immediately produced the resolutions of the Catholic Committee, and a few days later, Kenmare himself sent a letter stating he had made no such communication. (Roche would later explain that he considered the crisis so great that Kenmare and other Catholic leaders should have stepped forward to make such a statement and that since he, Roche, knew the 'sentiments of the persons in question', considered this sufficient justification for inventing the message.)[40]

Attempts were made to bring up the issue again. According to Charlemont:

> The Bishop again renewed the Catholic question, in which he was warmly supported by many of the Connaught and by some of the Munster delegates, while even a few of the Northern Dissenters, by their speeches and acquiesence, appeared already to indicate the approach of that strange madness by which they were, not long after, actuated.[41]

At the Catholic Committee's meeting on November 15, with 50 members present and Sir Patrick Bellew again in the chair, the resolutions given the earl-bishop were confirmed and a strong statement that the Committee represented the voices of all Irish Catholics was made.[42] Nonetheless, Catholic protestations and the efforts of their supporters were in vain. Roche's 'communication' made it possible for the Convention to regard Catholic opinion as divided (which, as will be seen, it indeed was) and sidestep further discussion of Catholic political rights, an issue which threatened to split the Volunteers. The *Dublin Evening Post* summed up the affair: 'there scarcely seems a doubt that the Convention have got rid of a matter which was likely to harass them exceedingly.'[43]

The Volunteer Convention adjourned on 2 December, but with its goal of reform dashed. The Irish parliament rejected its proposed bill, which made no reference to Catholic suffrage, and later attempts by Flood to reintroduce it also failed. However, the spirit of reform continued unabated, particularly in the north, where Belfast corps openly enlisted Catholics, and in Dublin, where more radical Volunteers in the 'Liberty Corps' led by Napper Tandy did the same. In the Catholic Committee, a division between conservatives content with the concessions already gained and those eager to continue the rapproachment with the northern Volunteers surfaced. One of the more conservative Catholic leaders alarmed at the effect of such a Catholic-Dissenter alliance was Lord Kenmare. Although he had disclaimed any involvement in Roche's concocted communication, his sentiments were nonetheless those Roche had imputed to him. Indeed, in a letter published in the *Freeman's Journal*, he declared himself content with the relief measures passed in 1778 and 1782.[44] After a conversation with Thomas Orde, the Irish Chief Secretary, Kenmare requested a select committee meeting for May 6. There, he warned of the consequences of continuing ties with the more radical Volunteers, presumably reflecting government opinion. However, his suggestion of a formal declaration of loyalty to the government was rejected.[45]

Kenmare's concern with adhering to constitutional process rather than flirting with extra-parliamentary pressure-group politics was shared by a number of Catholics, including Michael Bellew's cousin Christopher Kelly Bellew. In a letter of May, 1784, Bellew regarded it as 'more constitutional *and* prudent to negotiate with Parliament, not the Convention', warning that patriotism and passions were short-lived and selfishness and self-interest would inevitably set in. The need was for more expeditious behaviour and better timing, which offered the only chance of further concessions in the 'present struggle between constitutional and republican principles'. In a very prescient conclusion, he observed:

> the great power of government in Ireland, consists in the remaining Penal Laws, which by relaxing at pleasure, and throwing into the scale may preserve the balance of the Constitution. This is a power of too valuable a nature to be sported with, or squandered away. Government know it, and if ministers are wise, every future relaxation must be the work of inevitable necessity ...

Christopher Kelly Bellew's sentiments were not shared by his kinsman Sir Patrick Bellew, who continued, with John Keogh, to attend the Catholic Committee meetings held during the spring and summer of 1784 while Volunteers in Dublin led by Napper Tandy continued to push for reform. Significantly, Kenmare and most of the gentry who had attended the meetings in 1783 were absent. Lord Kenmare continued to work for a declaration of loyalty to the Irish administration, but was again frustrated. In letters to Sir Boyle Roche, he complained that 'our people are still frightened of shadows and when pressed ... to disavow this claim of election franchise the answer we get is "shall we reject the offers of our most ancient enemies?"'[46]

The Irish government was disturbed as well over the persistence of the relationship between individuals in the Volunteers and on the Committee. The intemperance of the earl-bishop in particular caused him to come under suspicion, as did his Catholic ally Sir Patrick Bellew. The British Southern Secretary Lord Sydney wrote to the Irish Lord Lieutenant Rutland in September of 1784 concerning Hervey's activities and 'a popish committee with Sir Patrick Bellew at their head'. Sydney sought further information about those who 'disavowed the declaration of Lord Kenmare and asserted that they were the real heads of the Roman Catholics and declared that nothing less than a general participation in the rights of citizens would satisfy them'. Rutland replied in October that Hervey's 'conduct has indisputably rendered him a fit object to be dealt with by law ...' As for Bellew, Rutland believed he carries his ideas of mischief as far as any Catholic in Ireland. I have not as yet had occasion to name him to your Lordship, because as yet nothing specific or direct against him has come to my knowledge. But you may be assured I have not been inattentive to his motions. Should the Catholics persevere in carrying their ideas to an improper extent, it might not be impolitic to suggest to them the possibility of repealing those Acts which were made in their favour.[47]

Rutland's concerns should be placed in the context of failed administration attempts to persuade members of the Catholic elite to issue an address of loyalty distancing themselves from the Volunteers. The Catholic Committee as a body had committed itself to a policy of non-intervention in the struggle between government and reformers, and the aristocracy and gentry followed suit. This strategy was developed at meetings in the summer and fall at which Bellew, along with Gormanston and Fingall, were in attendance; one in September was even held at Barmeath. By November, there were even rumours being reported in government circles that Bellew was at the head of a Catholic association he was supplying with arms.[48]

Although Sir Patrick Bellew was certainly in favour of Catholic relief, and willing to use his friendship with the Earl-Bishop to get it, the government's assessment of him as a dangerous radical, or at least the sort they feared in November, was incorrect and manifestly exaggerated. Bellew appears not to have been in total agreement with the Earl-Bishop as to the degree of Catholic activism in pursuing the franchise,[49] placing his hopes in the Catholics being the object of pursuit by both reformers and the Irish government. Writing to Michael Bellew in November of 1783, while the Convention was still sitting, he analyzed the situation in these terms:

Convention will do nothing or next to nothing. Government has a majority among them it is believed. The Roman Catholics are objects of the wishes of both parties and if they go on in the decent and manly manner they have done of late, my opinion is that they may make their terms.

By March of 1784, while hopeful of Irish Catholic admission to the bar and army, he advised his kinsman that Catholics 'must not think of having a right to vote'. It is difficult to see Bellew's views in 1783–84 as radical. Despite the flaws in his assumptions, they simply reflect an assessment of circumstances that had led to Catholic relief in the past and promised to do so in the future.

In any event, the fears of Kenmare and the Irish government over an alliance of radical Volunteers and Catholics were soon to be calmed. With proposals for reform repeatedly rejected, the fervour of the movement abated, and traditional Protestant fears of Catholic political power reasserted themselves. For example, the Dublin Volunteers in June of 1784 had resolved to extend the right of suffrage to the Catholics and made plans for a National Congress of Reformers in October to urge such a policy. The established and respectable Volunteer leaders, disturbed at the radicalism of some of the corps and determined to put an end to extra-parliamentary influence, disassociated themselves from the October meeting. It broke up, inevitably, over the Catholic question.

After the failure of the Reform Congress, Sir Patrick Bellew apparently gave up his hopes for any benefits to be derived from association with the Protestant reformers. In a Catholic Committee meeting on 25 March 1785, with Bellew in the chair, a motion was made that Catholics should withdraw from the Volunteers, but that further relief should be pursued through, pointedly, constitutional means. With approval likely, the activist John Keogh moved for an adjournment, rallied support, and defeated the motion in a second meeting. Significantly, Sir Patrick Bellew and the gentry had supported it.[50]

After 1785, the heated issues of reform and Catholic relief would be shelved for a time. However, the entire affair had changed relations among the Catholic Committee, the Catholic elite, and the Irish government. When the Committee and the aristocracy and gentry had been content to present addresses of loyalty, they had been viewed as useful means of dealing with Catholics in general. The rapprochement with Protestant reformers and Catholic refusal to totally dissociate themselves from reform had changed things. On the one hand, with the failure of the reform movement, the government could for the time being safely ignore the Commitee; on the other, the involvement with the Dissenters and the flirtation of some of the Committee members with reformers of the ilk of the earl-bishop and Napper Tandy had been alarming. For the immediate future, proposals and resolutions emanating from the Catholic Committee would be viewed with suspicion.

On the Committee's part, members like Bellew, Keogh, and McCormick had been politically naive, mistaking the views of a radical segment of the Volunteers for those of the majority.[51] Nonetheless, their involvement with those Northern Dissenters in Belfast most favourable to their cause would become the basis for another temporary alliance a decade later with a much more radical opposition group: the United Irishmen.

After the failed connection with the Volunteers in the mid-1780s, the Catholic Committee took little part in political activism, meeting only eight times in the five years after 1785. Sir Patrick Bellew continued to attend its infrequent sessions; in September 1788, he and two of his sons, Edward and William, were appointed to a subcommittee of 25, 13 of whom were nobility or country gentlemen, charged with overseeing the Committee's immediate business, such as it was.[52] By 1790, however, several factors – both domestic and foreign – had combined to make Catholics hopeful of further relief. Radical agitation for parliamentary reform including expansion of the franchise had started anew. Moreover, the reform fervour generated by the French Revolution prompted the British government to consider conciliation of the Catholic majority of Irishmen, both by way of example and as a deterrent to the spread of republican priñciples.

In consequence, Irish Catholics began efforts to seize their opportunity, efforts that would continue from 1790 to 1793 and result in two Catholic relief acts. Sir Patrick Bellew and his sons William and Edward; Christopher Kelly Bellew; and Christopher Dillon Bellew, Michael Bellew's eldest son and heir, would all participate, both through the Catholic Committee and their personal capacities as members of the Catholic gentry. Their activities and sentiments as recorded in family correspondence, minutes of the Catholic Committee, and contemporary accounts are a reflection of the outlook of their class: an obvious desire for reform and political emancipation that would almost certainly benefit themselves, but also a degree of hesitancy about the best way to proceed. Their attitude toward the latter often oscillated from an innate conservatism to a desire for a more activist approach, and the Galway and Louth branches of the family would briefly part philosophical ways over the direction of the Catholic Committee in obtaining political emancipation.

The participation of Christopher Kelly Bellew in the Catholic Committee in 1790 and 1791 is a good example of the mixed attitudes and emotions with which some of the gentry regarded agitation. From 1790 to 1792, Bellew appears to have divided his residence between Ireland and England, and his correspondence provides an interesting view of Catholic affairs from both countries.

Christopher Kelly Bellew of Mount Kelly in Galway was a country gentleman and a lawyer as well, having studied at Inner Temple at the English Inns of Court.[53] Because of his religion, he was, however, unable to become a barrister or a solicitor. In 1784, he had despaired of the bar ever being opened to Catholics, remarking to his cousin Michael Bellew that two-thirds of the Commons were lawyers and 'they are not so encumbered with business as to make them think a division of it necessary'.[54] By 1790, he seemed to share in hopes of further relief, although he agreed with Michael on the dangers of a divided approach: 'divisions among our sectaries turns them into a complete butt of ridicule for the rest to laugh at'.[55]

At a meeting of the Catholic Committee on 20 January 1790, 'Counsellor Bellew' was appointed to a subcommittee to draw up a congratulatory address to the new Lord Lieutenant, the earl of Westmorland.[56] He also proposed a resolution 'to take into consideration the best and most proper means to apply for further advantages for the catholics of this kingdom', and was thanked by the Committee for his attention to Irish Catholic interests. At the next meeting of the Committee on 26 January, which Bellew also attended, it was resolved that 'the present is a proper time for exertion on behalf of the Roman Catholics of Ireland towards the attainment of a repeal of the Penal Laws now in force against them.'

Bellew's activism would, however, soon be tempered. In the spring of 1790, new elections to the Catholic Committee were held, which brought a strong representation of those, mostly from the merchant-professional class, favouring a more forceful approach to relief. Joining such long-time forward Committee members as John Keogh, Richard McCormick, and Edward Byrne were Theobald McKenna, James McNevin, Edward Sweetman, and others who would later become prominent in radical movements, including the United Irishmen. They brought with them resolutions and instructions from their districts pressing for a petition to parliament for 'a redress of their grievances'. On 18 February 1791, a committee of twelve was appointed to consider measures to carry out the demands expressed in the resolutions. Bellew was appointed, as was the session's chairman, the earl of Fingall, and a county gentleman, Richard Strange; however, so too were Keogh, McKenna, Byrne, McCormick, and Charles Ryan, all activists. Within weeks, there was disagreement over 'the best and proper means to apply for further advantages'. At the next meeting of the Catholic Committee on 1 March, the sub-committee announced that two of its members 'had refused to cooperate in carrying into effect the measures committed to their care'. The two dissenting members were the country gentlemen, Richard Strange and Christopher Kelly Bellew.

The strain between conservative and popular elements was manifested in an even more obvious way two weeks later, when a deputation from the Committee met with Chief Secretary Hobart to discuss relief.[57] After considerable effort, they had persuaded Lords Kenmare and Fingall to accompany them. Kenmare was no more an activist in 1791 than he had been earlier; besides, as Westmorland reported to the British government, 'Lord Kenmare and the superior Catholics expect to obtain further privileges, which they understand the Catholics are to be given in England by the agitation of that question ... and by his Majesty's kindness'.[58] To the deputation's chagrin, Kenmare declared, according to their subsequent report of the meeting, 'in the name of the Catholics, intentions different from what they had resolved upon'. (Kenmare probably stated his own view: that the Catholics were satisfied with relying on the good will and initiative of the government for further relief.) However, the other deputation members produced the specific proposals for relief derived from the new Committee members' instructions from their districts. They included admission to the bar, the capacity to serve as justices of the peace and on grand and petty juries, and the enfranchisement of those in the counties who were £20 freeholders or 40-shilling freeholders who either rented or cultivated a farm of £20 per year.[59] Kenmare would write to Hobart a day later that he and Fingall had not seen the resolutions and asked that 'we may not be considered *by our presence* there as parties or approvers of such proceedings; had we foreseen them, we should not have been there'.[60] The obvious difference of opinion did the Catholic cause little good.

With the reluctance of the aristocratic and conservative element to push actively for relief evident, the activists on the Catholic Committee began contacts with the Dissenters of the north, particularly those in Belfast who had been favourable to their cause in the 1780s. By the 1790s, elements of the Volunteers had turned from liberalism to radicalism. Influenced by the ideals of the French Revolution, such men as Dr William Drennan and Theobald Wolfe Tone had begun to formulate a democratic program for a reformed Irish government, one in which no religious distinctions were to exist. In order to carry out such reform, Dissenters were urged, in Tone's influential pamplet *An Argument on Behalf of the Catholics of Ireland*, to unite with the Catholics and support their claim for the franchise. By the summer of 1791, northern radicals had begun making overtures to John Keogh and other members of the popular element of the Catholic Committee.

This did not pass unnoticed by the Irish government. Westmorland warned the British administration that 'the language and bent of these Dissenters is to unite with the Catholics, and their union would be formidable'.[61] Such a union also alarmed the more conservative members of the Catholic Committee. It also disturbed Sir Patrick Bellew and his sons. Although, in the mid-1780s, Sir Patrick had been in the forefront of the activist attempts to use connections with the Irish Volunteers to obtain relief, he now joined the group led by Kenmare in opposition to entanglements with radicals of the 1790s. As early as April 1791, the Louth Bellews' dissatisfaction was noted by Christopher Kelly Bellew; in a letter to Michael Bellew from England, he remarked he was sorry to hear in a letter from William Bellew that 'there are differences ... subsisting [on] your side'.

However, encouraged by the passage of Catholic relief in England in the spring of 1791 which repealed restrictions on Catholic worship and education and granted Catholics admission to the bar, the activists on the Catholic Committee continued to press for petitions to parliament and the enlistment of public support for Irish Catholic relief. They appointed Richard Burke, son of

Edmund Burke, to act as their agent in England; at the same time, their relations with Northern radicals became closer.

In October 1791, Wolfe Tone founded the Society of United Irishmen in Belfast to work for the new Ireland he envisioned, and in November a branch of the society was established in Dublin under the secretaryship of Napper Tandy. The same month, a new, more democratic Catholic club, the Catholic Society of Dublin, was founded. Some of their members, notably Theobald McKenna and James McNevin, were in regular contact with the Dublin United Irishmen,[62] and William Drennan asserted that the new society 'will form a balance against the aristocratic influence in their regular committee, and as many of them are members of both, they will be enabled to direct the committee as they choose'.[63] The new Catholic Society's declaration of principles, written by McKenna, called for the abolition of the entire penal structure. The influence of the activists on the Catholic Committee grew steadily stronger, and a concerned member favourable to the conservative Kenmare approach informed Dublin Castle that the Committee was in the hands of the 'factious and popular party' and 'gentlemen of production and property have no weight'.[64]

In December 1791, events came to a head. From late November, Richard Burke and John Keogh, the latter now emerged as the leader in the Catholic Committee, had been participating in discussions with the British government with the help of Thomas Hussey, a Catholic ecclesiastic in favour with the administration. On 22 November, Christopher Kelly Bellew, in London, reported to Michael Bellew that he was to dine with Dominic Rice, a newly arrived emissary from the Committe, and Keogh at Hussey's. With the granting of English Catholic relief, Bellew had been called to the English bar,[65] and was now, in contrast to his conservative attitudes toward the Catholic Committee in the beginning of the year, in an activist mood. Referring to Rice's mission, he commented that 'this is the situation which William Bellew (if he had common judgment) ought to fill'. Hussey had introduced Keogh to Edmund Burke and an undersecretary in the government; 'he was well received, but nothing done in the way of business.'

However, the British government, having just granted relief to English Catholics, and conscious of the need for Irish loyalty in the face of an unsettled Europe, was disposed to support conciliation. On 15 December, Bellew excitedly informed his cousin of

> an event that has just this moment been communicated to me, 'tis nothing less than that the Cabinet of this country have agreed to give the Irish Catholics the bar ... the Army and Navy, a right of sitting on grand juries ... on the right of franchise, they have been divided. Mr Pitt, Lord Grenville,

and Mr Dundas in favour of it under certain restrictions, the rest of the Cabinet being the majority against it. My authority is *Mr Hussey*, who comes from young Edmund Burke [Richard Burke] the agent employed in this business, to borrow Mr Tone's pamphlet which had been sent me from Ireland. How far this is an absolute fact I can't say, but certainly through a more authentic channel it could scarcely come. I hope to hear that Kitt [Christopher Dillon Bellew] and you will be on the next grand jury ...

He remarked that his sister Julia had just had a visit from Mrs. Keogh, 'nothing less than laced liveries', and, conveniently forgetting his earlier alliance with the conservatives, asked 'Where are the great Kenmares and Fingalls now?'

Ironically, two days after Christopher Kelly Bellew's jubilant letter was written, the Kenmares and Fingalls – and the Louth Bellews – would try one last time to brake the activists on the Catholic Committee. On 17 December, William Drennan informed his brother-in-law in Belfast that 'a Kenmarish, or, as the wits say, a Banshee resolution is to be brought into the Catholic Committee this night by one of the Bellews, but there is little fear of defeating it ...'[66] At the night's meeting, chaired by Edward Bellew (his father Sir Patrick was in ill health), his younger brother William introduced a resolution openly disavowing the declaration of the Catholic Society which had alarmed the government.[67] In the debate that followed, Bellew and his supporters urged official disassociation from the 'turbulent principles' of the Catholic Society. His opponents argued that they had already disavowed connection with McKenna's publication; they would make no new statement which 'might seem to imply a doubt rather than serve their cause'. On a resolution simply stating that a petition to parliament drawn up earlier was reflective of Catholic sentiments and which assured their loyalty and attachment to the constitution, Bellew and his supporters, unable to get their own resolution through, called for a division. As Drennan predicted, they were defeated soundly, 90–17. The 17 in the minority, including William and Edward Bellew, walked out of the meeting. The irony of one of the Committee's final resolutions of the evening was presumably not lost on the Bellews. It was decided that the Committee resolution of 15 November 1783 be confirmed, which stated that the Committee was the 'medium through which the voice of the Roman Catholics of Ireland has been conveyed and the only one competent thereto'. This 1783 resolution had been passed in the midst of the Volunteer Convention at a meeting chaired by Sir Patrick Bellew.

That night the 'seceders' met with Sir Hercules Langrishe, a long-time moderate advocate of Catholic relief and a government supporter, and began preparation of a loyal address. As presented to the Lord Lieutenant on 27 December, it stated that the undersigned would 'rely with confidence on our past as a pledge for future conduct'. While it was made clear that some form of relief was expected in the next parliamentary session, it was resolved that 'grateful for former concessions, we do not presume to point out the measure or extent to which such repeal should be carried, but leave the same to the wisdom and discretion of the legislature ...' Disclaiming 'every word or act which can directly or indirectly tend to alarm the minds of our brethren, or disturb the tranquillity of the country', the address listed 68 signatories, mostly landed aristocracy and gentry, but several Dublin merchants as well. Among the 68 were Lords Fingall, Kenmare, and Gormanston, and Sir Patrick Bellew with his two sons Edward and William.[68]

Reaction was swift and showed that the seceders had misjudged general Catholic opinion. The address was condemned by meetings in the Dublin parishes and in addresses from both counties and towns. The Catholic Committee responded by resolving unanimously that 'Lord Kenmare has entirely forfeited our confidence by his late conduct, in procuring by his own exertions and those of his emissaries certain insidious and servile addresses, calculated to divide the Catholics of Ireland', and took Kenmare off the Committee.[69]

The seceders were ultimately rewarded, but not in the way, and to the extent, they had hoped. The British government was willing, as Christopher Kelly Bellew's letter had accurately reported, to grant Irish Catholics the right to serve on grand and petty juries and carry arms, to lift restrictions on Catholic education, to allow free exercise of the professions and trade, and to permit a limited suffrage. However, the Irish Cabinet, particularly Westmorland, alarmed at the likely reaction of Protestants to sweeping relief, modified this program considerably.[70] The Irish Relief Act of 1792 permitted Catholics to become solicitors and barristers, lifted restrictions on education, and repealed the statute placing a limit on the number of apprentices a Catholic could have. Provisions for sitting on grand juries, carrying arms, and, most important, sharing in the franchise were excluded.

Some Catholics were content with the limited relief; Christopher Kelly Bellew was now carrying out legal business for Lord Petre, a prominent English Catholic, and hoped that it would '[introduce] me to the first Catholic connection in England'. Planning at long last to enter the Irish bar,[71] he observed to Michael Bellew that Catholics should have been satisfied with what they had gained. This was an attitude shared by Westmorland, who complained in a letter to Lord Melville that the activists on the Catholic Committee 'endeavour as much as possible to represent that the English government wish to give them everything and that they were only stopped by my representations, the principal people are sensible that to Government only are they endebted for what has passed'.[72] The reaction of the majority of Catholics, however, was not the one of satisfaction Christopher Kelly Bellew urged or the one of gratitude Westmorland expected. Moreover, many of those who had signed the address to the Lord Lieutenant and expected greater concessions felt betrayed by the government.

The Catholic Committee had petitioned parliament, while the relief bill was being debated, to include Catholic suffrage; their petition was overwhelmingly rejected, and a petition from the Belfast United Irishmen calling for the repeal of all the penal laws met a similar fate. Moreover, Committee members were angered by implications made during the parliamentary debates that they were not the true representatives of the Irish Catholics. In response, the Commitee embarked on an ambitious plan for new elections. Under the new system, country gentlemen were no longer to sit at large and at their pleasure; county delegates as well as those from the towns were now to be elected. They would be chosen by electors, themselves chosen by the voters of each parish. A convention of delegates who reflected Irish Catholic opinion country-wide would then assemble in Dublin to consider means for further relief.

The split in the Catholic Committee had left the activist elements in control, with freedom to pursue this program. Moreover, their control and direction was a reflection of the new political importance of the merchant-professional class. Edmund Burke, a warm advocate of Catholic claims, marked their emergence. In a letter to his son Richard, himself in the midst of the turmoil as the agent for the Committee, Burke observed that 'a new race of Catholics have risen by their industry, their abilities, and their good fortune to considerable opulence, and of course to an independent spirit'. He warned that the 'old Standard Gentlemen' would be wise to cooperate with them 'in everything rationally proposed for their common benefit'. He urged Richard to make them aware that remaining aloof would be 'so perfectly contrary to their dignity and their interests'.[73]

Some of the seceders were having similar thoughts; in June of 1792, Lords Kenmare and Fingall assured the Catholic Committee that they 'should receive no further opposition from them in their laudable efforts for Catholic emancipation and that they now saw the strong propriety of your measures and sincerely wished your proceeding successful'.[74] Many of the gentry returned to the Committee, but the leadership would remain in Keogh and Byrne's and other activist hands. Moreover, although some of those who had signed Kenmare's address to the Lord Lieutenant in December 1791 would sit in the convention called by the Committee in December 1792, it would be as elected representatives of their counties. As a further indication of a change in direction, Richard Burke was eased out of his position; the new assistant to the Committee would be Theobald Wolfe Tone.[75]

In order to assure full representation for the upcoming Catholic Convention, both Tone and Keogh canvassed potential trouble areas. Tone was sent to secure Galway and Mayo, counties which had supplied eleven signatories to the address of December 1791. With Thomas Broughall, he travelled to Ballinasloe in October 1792 to meet with Catholic gentry of the two counties. Sir Thomas French, a neighbour of the Bellews and one of the country gentlemen who had sided with the Catholic Committee in the schism of 1791,[76] chaired the meeting. According to Tone, French questioned the approval of Lord Fingall to the new method of election, 'inasmuch as he has been well assured, on good authority, (the Bellows [*sic*] (*Rascals*) and Donellan of Bally Donellan, as we suppose), that such assertion arises from misconception'. Tone, however, won over the gentry to the Committee, and plans were made for county elections. Tone's notes of the meeting concluded optimistically:

> Galway is now finally settled, and Mayo in a fair way. They are the two great Catholic counties in Ireland, and the cream and flower of the Catholic gentry. They have been, hitherto, rather adverse to the General Committee, from the bad spirit of aristocracy, which has done the cause so much mischief by producing disunion; but we trust we have now fairly beat the Castle out of Galway ...[77]

The Bellews who, according to Tone, were spreading dissension were most likely the Louth branch: Sir Patrick and his sons (and perhaps Bishop Dominick Bellew, who shared the concern of the western bishops over what they perceived as the Committee's drift toward radicalism).[78] Neither Michael nor Christopher Dillon Bellew had signed the address to the Lord Lieutenant, and if Christopher Dillon's sentiments were with the seceders, he was reconciled to the Catholic Committee much earlier than most of the gentry. His name appears in the minutes of the Committee for 31 March 1792 as one of the gentlemen to be contacted to request collection of funds in their counties.[79] Moreover, he, Christopher Kelly Bellew, and Sir Thomas French were elected as delegates to the Convention from county Galway, and Michael Bellew's eldest son would play a prominent role there.[80]

Preparations for the Catholic Convention had alarmed Westmorland as had open support for the Catholics from Belfast and the United Irishmen. Protestant reaction was also strong: freeholders from six counties and grand juries from seventeen issued resolutions condemning it. The manifesto of the Corporation of Dublin was especially vehement. In response, Keogh, McNevin, and

Charles Ryan addressed a mass meeting of Catholics in Dublin to shore up support for the Convention. In attendance was Dublin merchant Christopher Bellew, who reported to his cousin Christopher Dillon Bellew on November 6 that 'we had a great meeting last Wednesday which was attended by all the respectable Catholics of Dublin ... Dr. Ryan's speech is much talked of'.[81]

With over 200 representatives in attendance, the Catholic Convention met on 3 December at Tailors' Hall in Back Lane. Edward Byrne was in the chair, and Christopher Dillon Bellew and Sir Thomas French were appointed to be among the six succeeding chairmen.[82] It was immediately decided to petition the king for the relief denied by the Irish parliament. As an indication of the delegates' enthusiasm, the original petition for participation in the franchise and on grand juries was amended to ask for full relief. A debate then followed over the method of presenting it. Petitions and addresses were normally given to the Lord Lieutenant who transmitted them to the king. This, however, no longer satisfied some of the delegates, including Christopher Dillon Bellew. According to Wolfe Tone's account of the proceedings, Bellew, 'a spirited young member, whose property gave him much, and his talents and virtues still more, influence in the assembly, and who represented a county, perhaps the first in Ireland for Catholic property and independence', moved that the petition should be presented directly to the king by a deputation from the Convention.

Some delegates urged caution, counseling that the traditional channels should be used. However, negotiations with Dublin Castle broke down, as Westmoreland intimated his reluctance to transmit a petition he had not seen or studied. As a consequence, Bellew claimed he had lost confidence in 'men who kept no faith with Catholics', a statement that might also have been a reference to the manner in which his seceder relatives had been disappointed by the Irish government. In strong language, he argued his case:

> It has been said my plan is disrespectful to administration. I answer, *it is intended to be so*. It is time for us to speak out like men. We will not, like African slaves, *petition* our taskmasters. Our Sovereign will never consider it disrespectful, that we lay before his throne the dutiful and humble petition of 3,000,000 of loyal and suffering subjects. For my part, I know I speak the sentiments of my county. I wish my constituents may know my conduct; and the measure which I have now proposed, I am ready to justify in any way.

Bellew's motion was carried, and on 7 December, a deputation of five was elected to present the petition to George III. It consisted of John Keogh, Edward Byrne, Christopher Dillon Bellew, Sir Thomas French, and another country gentleman, James Devereaux of Waterford. They set out by way of Belfast, where they were greeted enthusiastically, and through Scotland, arriving in London on 24 December.

On 15 December, Bellew's merchant cousin Christopher wrote him a letter that he hoped would meet his arrival in London. In it he expressed the hope that 'we shall soon hear the success of your embassy' and reported the general opinion that the deputation would be met graciously, 'tho' some great men here have indirectly indicated that the petition will not be received'. His letter also indicates the Irish administration's precautions in Dublin: 'from every appearance Government seem much alarmed. The Castle Guard's now relieved with two pieces of cannon, in the Barracks nobody but a soldier is allowed to walk. There are 24 pieces of cannon in one of the squares'. Employing rhetoric similar to that used by his cousin in the Convention, Christopher Bellew asserted that 'every citizen at this side will be anxious to know our fate, whether we are to be free citizens or slaves'.

On 2 January 1793, the Catholic delegation was presented to the king at a levee where he received their petition, and they had two interviews with the Home Secretary Henry Dundas. Dundas was non-committal, implying that the extent of a relief measure would be up to the Irish parliament, but gracious, assuring the delegation that their requests would be heard. Nonetheless, the assurances came at a price: the understanding that Catholics would dissociate themselves from 'dangerous associations', a clear reference to the United Irishmen.[83] The delegation returned to Ireland in mid-January and Catholic hopes were high for relief. A Dublin friend wrote to Michael Bellew on 20 January that he was happy to hear of 'the safe arrival of Mr Christopher from his embassy, and to congratulate you that I believe every part of it will be granted. Our country, though the last expected, has come forth in a most spirited manner in spite of Aristocracy'.

Indeed, the popular element of the Catholic Committee had shown political acumen in 1791–93. John Keogh, their leader, had no doubt learned a lesson from the failed alliance of some Committee members with the Volunteers in 1783–84. He had followed the same counsel Edmund Burke had given his son Richard in 1792 regarding Catholic dealings with the more radical Protestants: 'Let them be united in *themselves* – and thankful to, without being in a confederacy with, the dissenters'.[84] Keogh attended United Irish meetings and in July 1792 joined the Belfast anniversary celebrations of the fall of the Bastille with Richard McCormick and Theobald McKenna. He and the other activists on the Committee accepted United Irish and radical support and welcomed their petitions for repeal of the penal laws. However, Keogh never officially joined the United Irishmen, and, while the Convention was in session, a delegation from the Society with a resolution of support was not permitted to address it, but received politely in an antechamber.[85]

The nature of Catholic-Dissenter and Catholic-United Irish relations in this period were viewed quite differently by two United Irish leaders. Wolfe Tone was willing to modulate more radical views in order to effectively serve Catholic relief. During the Convention, he ignored requests from Belfast for information about its proceedings.[86] Yet, his commitment to the Catholic cause often led him to overlook the tenuous nature of the association. In contrast to Tone, who counselled patience with Catholic reluctance to openly join the United Irishmen, William Drennan mistrusted Catholic motives. As early as December 1791, he commented that:

> the Catholics wish to have two strings to their bow – a *part* to treat with Government, a *part* to ally with us – and if one string cracks, why, try the other. This is good, and *perhaps* fair archery. None pledge, but those who come among us, and it is easy for the body at any time to disclaim them, if Government is gained, and to back them if Government holds out; but, at any rate, to use them as a bugbear to the minister who is alarmed, not surely at what *is* , but what *may be* the consequence of this new style of speaking.[87]

Drennan's assessment was probably the more realistic one. The Catholic Committee could use the threat of an open union as leverage with the Irish government, but by keeping the Committee at a discreet distance from the United Irishmen and welcoming moderate country gentlemen back into their ranks, appear in England as the reasonable, moderate voice of a united Catholic body.

Christopher Dillon Bellew, on his return to Dublin, appeared to have been confident of success. In mid-January, he requested an interview with Chief Secretary Hobart where he delivered a paper which, according to Hobart, 'he conceived to be the substance of what had passed between Mr Dundas and those gentlemen [the Catholic Convention delegates]'. Bellew asserted that

> the delegates had received the most unequivocal assurances of the sense entertained by His Majesty of the justice of the Catholic claims as set forth in their petition, and of the wishes of government in England to give them every support, so far as those wishes could be expressed consistently with the independence of the legislature of both countries.

He offered his opinion to Hobart that 'nothing short of being on a footing with other Dissenters would satisfy the Roman Catholics'.[88]

The attitude of the British government and its Prime Minister Pitt toward relief was indeed favourable. England was on the brink of war with France, and Irish loyalty of all denominations was required. The government was also not particularly pleased with the Irish administration's handling of Catholic matters: Dundas in a dispatch to Westmorland pointed out that the concessions urged in 1792 which might have quieted the question were now not likely to work. He strongly urged that the Lord Lieutenant and his cabinet 'give a candid and liberal consideration to the whole of this subject and to weigh well the consequences of leaving behind any sore part of this question'.[89] The concessions he suggested were enfranchisement, jury service, and admission to specified civil offices.

On 4 February 1793, Chief Secretary Hobart brought in the long-awaited Catholic relief bill. As enacted in April after considerable debate (some 72 MPs spoke), it enabled Catholics to participate in the franchise on the same terms as Protestants, to keep arms subject to specified conditions, and enroll for degrees at Dublin University. It opened certain civil and military offices to Catholics and repealed the laws excluding them from the magistracy. Wolfe Tone regarded it as an important relief measure for the Catholics, but a 'mutilated one', for it still withheld almost all the high government and judicial positions – privy councillor, King's Counsel, high sheriff, Lord Lieutenant of the county, and general of the staff. Most important, no Catholic could take a seat in the Irish parliament. The new Catholic voters were to elect the old Protestant candidates.

The contradiction in allowing 40-shilling freeholders to vote, while barring the Catholic gentry and nobility from the Commons and Lords had been discussed during debate over the bill. One MP asked

> Will the Catholic gentleman – a man of education, of ambition, perhaps of distinguished ability – acquiesce in a decision which admits the most ignorant and turbulent of his co-religionists to an equality with Protestants in respect to the suffrage to which alone in political life they could assume, while he is himself marked out as inferior to the Protestant gentry by his exclusion from Parliament?

Another put it more succinctly, claiming the bill 'courts the Catholic rabble and insults the Catholic gentry'.[90] Nonetheless, a proposal to admit Catholics to parliament was defeated, 163–69.

The limited civil and political emancipation also occasioned stormy debate in the Catholic Committee when it reconvened after the bill's passage.[91] Questions were raised over the conduct of Keogh and the delegation and subcommittee entrusted with discussions with Irish government officials. Edward Sweetman, an activist Committee member and a former United Irishman, asked, 'The demand of Catholics was total, why was the relief partial?' John Keogh, supported by Thomas Braughall, defended the Catholic deputation's conduct during their meetings with Dundas (one of its members, James Devereaux, interrupted to add plaintively, 'We could not drive him to an answer') and subsequent meetings with Chief Secretary Hobart. Keogh argued, probably correctly, that a bill for total emancipation would have failed. Reminding the Committee that they had much to rejoice in, he asserted that what had been lost could be obtained by what they had won – the elective franchise. Keogh's willingness to accept the relief act was shared by not only Edward Bryne, but the country gentlemen who had worked with him, including Christopher Dillon Bellew and Sir Thomas French. Although those discontent with the limited relief managed to pass a resolution to cooperate in loyal and constitutional means to obtain parliamentary reform, the Catholic Committee as a whole was also content. They voted £1500 and a gold medal to Wolfe Tone, a plate to the value of 500 guineas to each of the five delegates who had carried their petition to England, and an address to the king thanking him for relief. They then dissolved the Committee as a mark of respect on 25 April 1793.

The divisions over the question of further reform of the parliament and complete relief were not completely forgotten, however. At a Dublin dinner in 1794 to commemorate the late Catholic Committee, the conservative and activist differences again reappeared, this time dividing landed and mercantile Bellews. As Christopher Kelly Bellew indignantly wrote to Michael Bellew, he had been 'called an *aristocrat*', having opposed the suggested toast of parliamentary reform as the last wish of the Catholic Committee. 'We had great debating, and it ended as usual in splitting into two parties, and having two separate dinners; however, we had the majority and most decidedly in point of respectability, though we had Doctor McNevin, Henry Taaffe, and Christopher Bellew against us'.

For the Irish Catholic gentry, the results of the political agitation of the last quarter of the eighteenth century were bittersweet. Complete freedom in landownership had been gained, the professions had been opened, and suffrage had been won; nonetheless, the gentry were still denied the full degree of political participation their Protestant counterparts possessed. They could not enjoy the status and leadership offered by a political career – they could not sit in the Irish Commons or hold the highest offices. Moreover, although a number of their class, including Christopher Dillon Bellew, had been active in the Catholic Convention of December 1792, the secession of some from the Catholic Committee a year earlier had been damaging to their influence. While their return and support of relief proposals had been welcomed and the gentry would continue to be active and influential in Catholic affairs, their leadership role in the Catholic political body had been briefly co-opted by a 'new race of Catholics', a harbinger of things to come.

In the closing years of the eighteenth century, attempts to win what had been denied in 1793 would fail, as events rapidly overtook the social and political framework within which Catholic agitation had operated. On-going war with France, the Irish Rebellion of 1798, and resultant concern with the security, as well as the constitutional and economic position, of Ireland within the British empire brought about union with Great Britain in 1800 and the end of the Irish parliament. Pitt's plan to admit Catholics to parliament as a provision of union attracted the support of many of the Catholic gentry, including the Louth Bellews. However, such hopes were dashed by George III's intransigence and deeprooted conceptions of the unity of British church and state.

Catholic agitation would not bring about final emancipation until 1839.[92] In Ireland, that emancipation was not the result of pressures on an Irish parliament – the expectation of the Catholic gentry in 1793 – but from a calculated election campaign for a seat in Westminster. Moreover, that campaign would not be led by a representative of the old aristocratic and gentry families who had influenced Catholic affairs throughout much of the eighteenth century. It would be led instead by an O'Connell, aided by new forces which would shape much of nineteenth-century Irish political life – the Catholic clergy and the Irish peasantry.

'To Preserve the Religion of Our Posterity'

The Bellews of Mount Bellew were, despite the penal laws, among the more successful Catholic gentry families of eighteenth-century Ireland, if success is measured in terms of the aspirations of a landed class. They maintained their estates and, as progressive landlords, improved their lands. Their holdings provided them with a good living, from which Michael Bellew was able to build a substantial country house and purchase additional lands with the repeal of the penal laws restricting Catholic landownership. Younger sons did not challenge the transfer of the estate – as was their right under the law – but entered trade and commerce. In all these circumstances, the penal laws did not directly affect the Bellews' status as gentry.

The family, however, did not remain untouched. Accommodation to the penal structure was necessary and can be identified in almost every area of the Bellews' life. Land could be rented only on limited terms, unless subterfuge was used. The transfer of lands from one generation to another required at least a minimum of circumspection and care. A career in the military meant service abroad, in the armies of France or Austria. A higher education, either clerical or lay, also required residence on the continent: Christopher Dillon Bellew and three of his four younger brothers were educated in France.

The existence of the penal laws, then, resulted in a life which was rarely, if ever, uncomfortable, but it was one which could never be completely secure. Even if there was a conscious intent, as there was on the Bellews' part, to ignore or circumvent the laws governing landholding, they had to be taken into consideration – often involving legal expense – in each and every transaction involving the land – the constant basis of their economic and social status. Moreover, those provisions offering favourable terms of inheritance and land disposition to family members who conformed could also threaten the religious solidarity of the family. Andrew French's concern that the terms of his father-in-law's will would offer a temptation to his daughters to abandon their faith, was, based on the experience of other Catholic landed families, valid.

Other effects of the law are more difficult to illustrate or quantify, but are

175

nonetheless important. The Bellews' life was most certainly not one of oppression, but it was one of accommodation and frustration. The references in the family correspondence to the penal structure, before the movement for reform had brought at least partial success, are striking. Michael Bellew, head of a Catholic family remarkably successful in this period, could, in 1767, consider leaving for France to, in the words of his brother-in-law Andrew French, 'preserve the religion of our posterity'. Sir Patrick Bellew, disappointed at the defeat in 1762 of a slight measure of Catholic relief, could complain that it 'inclines many of our persuasion to think of breaking ground to settle in other countries of liberty and equality'.[1] Here the psychological impact of the penal laws stands out in sharp relief. The wish of Andrew French that 'God will incline the hearts of our rulers to mitigate the penal laws; and thereby make us useful subjects',[2] underscores the importance of the legal structure as not just an economic, but a psychological, force in the life of the Irish Catholic gentry.

Did such frustration manifest itself ultimately in an increased political activism or radicalization? Certainly a lingering sense of resentment over events of more than one hundred years in the past is evident in the wording of the plaque placed on one of the Bellew flour mills erected in 1776: giving a brief history of the family, it states that John Bellew of Willistown 'was exempted from pardon for life and estate by Cromwell's Act of Parliament in 1652 for his inflexible constancy & zeal in the cause of his royal master against that bloody parricide & usurper ...' Yet, this is an echo of 'the old cause', rather than a radical new one. Moreover, while Sir Patrick Bellew of the Louth branch of the family took a leading role in attempts to bring about relief in the 1770s and 80s, it is difficult to see, as I have previously discussed, his activities as a major break with previous gentry strategies to promote change.

However, it is possible to see such a development in the Mount Bellew family. While Michael Bellew's generation relied on loyal addresses and oaths of loyalty, his eldest son, Christopher Dillon Bellew, and his brother Patrick's son, Christopher, had obviously different views about the best ways to bring about relief. The greater degree of activism illustrated by Christopher Dillon's participation in the Catholic Convention and Christopher's attendance at mass meetings of Catholics in Dublin is marked. Both employed rhetoric in their correspondence and public statements of a type very different from that of their older relatives. Certainly one contributing factor was the general trend of increased awareness of and interest in political structures and their reform in the last quarter of the eighteenth century, an awareness heightened by two revolutions – the American and the French. There may have been another factor: despite the oft-remarked caution and conservatism of the Galway gentry, younger family members, through participation in trade and the necessity of obtaining a higher education outside Ireland, were exposed to a much wider world and, perhaps, a much wider range of views and experiences. It is worth noting that Christopher Dillon Bellew had been provided with a first-class education abroad, and Christopher Bellew was a merchant, with international connections, carrying on business in the most politically-active city in Ireland. Of course, none of the activities of the younger generation of Bellews are manifestations of the type of radicalism associated with, for example, the United Irishmen. They do, however, point to a growing impatience and the willingness to engage in pressure-politics of a type unthought of just a decade earlier.

Most of this work has been devoted to an analysis of the Bellews as Catholic *gentry*, with an emphasis on their lands, their living from them, and related aspects of landownership. The former part of the equation deserves comment as well: that is, the Bellews as members of the Catholic faith. Family correspondence does not usually contain detailed discussions of religion or theology, and that of the Bellews is no exception. However, estate papers and family circumstances permit some conclusions. As in most aspects of eighteenth-century gentry life, tradition and continuity were prominent, and the Bellews' Catholicism exhibits both. Following the practice of many landed Catholic families, the Louth and Galway branches each provided a Catholic clergyman. With the advantage of gentry and familial connections, both pursued successful careers: Dominick Bellew became bishop of Killala, and Luke Bellew played an important role in the administration of the Irish College at Douai. In east Galway, Michael Bellew and his eldest son Christopher Dillon continued another kind of tradition. The presence of a large number of Catholic landholders in various places in Ireland assisted in parish organization and chapel maintenance; following medieval precedent, leading families in these areas were also patrons of the church and chapels were closely connected with Catholic estates.[3] Galway and the Bellews were no exceptions. Both Mount Bellew and Newtown Bellew had chapels, and in a cash and wages book covering expenditures in 1769–75, Michael Bellew noted payments in 1769 of 13*s.* for the thatching of the chapel and 3*s.*3*d.* for its upkeep. Regular payments were also made to the priest: for example, £1.2*s.*9*d.* and 11*s.*4*d.* were paid to Father Burke in 1770 and 1771. A generation later, Christopher Dillon Bellew had a new chapel constructed in the early 1820s and in 1825 brought in a community of Franciscans for 'the care and preservation of the newly-finished chapel'.[4] In its present form, St Mary's parish church in Mount Bellew village sits on the edge of what had been the Bellew desmesne.

The Bellews' religion set them apart from the majority of the Irish gentry. However, the sense of tradition that sustained them as a gentry family (as evidenced in the plaque tracing the family history – and the recurrence of the same christian names from generation to generation) also sustained them as Catholics. Christopher Dillon Bellew in mourning the death of a friend commented that he 'lived a Protestant, but I believe with some inclination to us'.[5] A Catholic who conformed in order to marry well was regarded by Christopher Kelly Bellew with scorn: 'young Browne of Castlebrowne has read his recantation, and by so doing has bartered his religion for a wife'.[6] The Bellews' continuance in the Catholic faith, notwithstanding the enticements of conformity offered by the penal laws, may well have been an enduring source of pride, one inextricably linked to their pride in family tradition.

However, the Bellews' Catholicism came at a cost. Despite their survival, success, and prosperity, there was one area in which accommodation or adaptation were of no avail: the penal laws excluded them from civil life. In this respect, the Bellews were ultimately frustrated. Vigorous, able Catholic country gentlemen were unable to exercise, particularly at the national level, the leadership to which their status would normally have entitled them. The activities of some of their Galway neighbours who had conformed provide a striking contrast: the great-grandson of Bryan Mahon of Castlegar, who converted before his death in 1719, was a justice of the peace and an MP. Patrick French of Monivea served as an MP from 1713–15; his son Robert was MP from county Galway from 1753–61 and for the town of Galway from 1768–76. John Daly of Carownekelly conformed in 1729; his son Denis of Dunsandle was mayor of Galway and enjoyed a distinguished parliamentary career as MP for the county. The Bellews, their equal as gentry, were not their equal as citizens.

By the time political and civil restrictions were lifted completely, the gentry's role in Catholic national leadership, while still important, was waning. Although Christopher Dillon Bellew's son Michael would be created a baronet in 1838 and his nephew T.A. Grattan-Bellew would be a Member of Parliament for county Galway (1852–57), the political – and social – system that had given the Irish gentry their influence was changing. In the late nineteenth and early twentieth centuries, the Bellews were no longer just Catholic landlords. Irrespective of their religion, they were Irish landlords, whose economic and social position, under assault by the peasantry and nationalistic political leaders, was becoming tenuous. With successive purchases by Land Commissioners and the Congested Districts Board, in programmes designed to ensure peasant tenure and rights, their Galway acres dwindled.[7]

The Mount Bellew estate was sold in the late 1930s; the house was demolished shortly after. The flour mill erected in 1776 has recently been torn down; its plaque has been preserved, embedded in a small monument in Bellew Park in the modern-day village. The only recognizable structures of the eighteenth-century estate remaining today are several stone walls and arches.

List of Abbreviations

The following abbreviations are used in endnotes; full citations are given in the bibliography:

Arch. Hib.	*Archivium Hibernicum*
CRSP	*Catholic Record Society Publications*
CSPI	*Calendar of State Papers Relating to Ireland*
HMC	Historical Manuscripts Commission
HO	Home Office Records (Ireland), Public Record Office, London
IHS	*Irish Historical Studies*
IMC	Irish Manuscripts Commission
Nat. Arch.	National Archives of Ireland, Dublin
NLI	National Library of Ireland, Dublin
NHI	*A New History of Ireland*, ed. T.W. Moody *et al.* (Oxford 1976–)

Spelling and punctuation in quotations have, in general, been modernized, although exceptions have been made to preserve the flavour of contemporary style. I have chosen the more generally accepted versions for the spelling of proper names, and, for the most part, the versions found in contemporary documents for local place names. 'Protestant' is used to refer to both members of the Church of Ireland and Dissenters, unless 'Dissenters' is used specifically.

The Bellew of Mount Bellew papers, the major primary sources used in this study, have recently undergone preliminary cataloguing and assigning of MS numbers. The bulk of research for this work was conducted when the papers, contained in some 20-odd boxes, were uncatalogued and largely unsorted. Wherever possible, new MS numbers have been cited; otherwise, dates of correspondence, etc. have been provided to facilitate location, as the material has been sorted in rough chronological order. All MS numbers in endnotes, unless otherwise specified, are to the Bellew of Mount Bellew papers.

Notes

INTRODUCTION

1 MS. 27,106.

2 See, for example, Robert E. Burns, 'The Irish Penal Code and Some of its Historians', *Review of Politics* 21 (1959), 276–99.

3 T.P. Power and Kevin Whelan, ed., *Endurance and Emergence: Catholics in Ireland in the Eighteenth Century* (Dublin, 1990), v.

4 S.J. Connolly, *Religion, Law, and Power: The Making of Protestant Ireland 1660–1760* (Oxford, 1992), 263; 312–13.

5 John Brady, 'Some Aspects of the Irish Church in the Eighteenth Century', *Irish Ecclesiastical Review* 70 (1948), and with P.J. Corish, *The Church under the Penal Code* iv in P.J. Corish, *A History of Irish Catholicism* (Dublin, 1971); Maureen Wall, *The Penal Laws 1691–1760* (Dundalk, 1961) rpt. in *Catholic Ireland in the Eighteenth Century: Collected Essays of Maureen Wall*, ed. G. O'Brien (Dublin, 1989). Most of Wall's research on the eighteenth century, published (particularly in *IHS*) and unpublished, has been collected in the above work. Future citations of Wall are to the latter edition unless otherwise specified. Nonetheless, it should be noted that exceptions were made for suspected sedition; the case of Nicholas Sheehy, a priest executed for alleged involvement in the Whiteboy movement of the 1760s in Tipperary, is a notorious example.

6 Wall, *Catholic Ireland in the Eighteenth Century*, 73–84. For a recent re-assessment, see David J. Dickson, 'Catholics and Trade in Eighteenth-Century Ireland: An Old Debate Revisited', in *Endurance and Emergency*, 85–100.

7 R.E. Burns, 'The Irish Popery Laws: A Study of Eighteenth-Century Legislation and Behavior', *Review of Politics*, 24 (1962) and S.J. Connolly, 'Religion and History', *Irish Economic and Social History*, 10 (1983), have warned of the dangers of viewing the penal laws as an attack on property exclusively. Conversion was an important goal as well. However, while religious zeal should certainly not be disregarded, the period in which the bulk of the laws was passed should be considered. It was in the aftermath of two rebellions within a fifty-year period led by the Catholic aristocracy and gentry, a period in which, I would argue, security was perhaps a more important concern than conversion. One could certainly argue that the latter could lead to the former, but the penal laws regarding property remained long after it became apparent they would not serve to convert the whole of the gentry.

8 The statistic for 1703 originated in J.G. Simms' study, *The Williamite Confiscation in Ireland, 1690–1703* (London, 1956), 195. As S.J. Connolly points out (*Religion, Land, and Power*, 147, n.10), the estimate of 5 per cent of lands remaining in Catholic hands by 1776 is Arthur Young's in *A Tour in Ireland* (Dublin, 1789 ed.), ii., pt.2, 44. It has been followed by most accounts – perhaps too faithfully, since it is based on a very general, unsupported comment ('nineteen twentieths of the kingdom changed hands').

9 Maureen Wall, *Catholic Ireland in the Eighteenth Century*, 27.
10 L.M. Cullen, 'Catholics under the Penal Laws', *Eighteenth-Century Ireland* 1 (1986), 27.
11 This is an approach exhibited in, for example, the county histories of Geography Publications and several of the essays in *Endurance and Emergence*.
12 See, for a recent reassessment of the relevant statutes and a valuable bibliography, W.N. Osborough, 'Catholics, Land, and the Popery Acts of Anne', *Endurance and Emergence*, 21–56.
13 Nancy J. Curtin, '"Varieties of Irishness": Historical Revisionism, Irish Style', *Journal of British Studies* 35 (April, 1996), 214.
14 Connolly, *Religion, Law, and Power*, 312.

CHAPTER 1: 'IN OPEN REBELLION'

1 Aidan Clarke, *The Old English in Ireland, 1625–1642* (Ithaca, New York, 1966), 15–16; Appendix I, 235–7. The accuracy of the term 'Old English' can, of course, be debated: not all were of strictly English or Anglo-Norman descent, nor were all Catholic. Generally, however, T.W. Moody's definition is a useful one: 'not exclusively composed of people of English descent but as constituting a political interest or party, Catholic in its religious identity but distinct in its political outlook from the Gaelic Irish or "old Irish"' (*NHI* iii, xlii).
2 *Burke's Peerage and Baronetage*, 105th ed. (1970), s.v. Bellew, 236–7; Edward MacLysaght, *More Irish Families* (Dublin, 1960), 33.
3 The Hon. Mrs Gerald Bellew, 'John Bellew of Willistown, County Louth and Clonoran, County Galway, 1606–1679. With some account of his troubles in Cromwell's wars', *County Louth Archaeological Society Journal* 6, no. 4 (1928), 230. A more recent account, drawing on both the private collection of Bellew family papers at Barmeath and the seventeenth-century Bellew of Mount Bellew papers in the *NLI* is that of Harold O'Sullivan, 'Land Ownership Changes in the County of Louth in the 17th Century' (unpublished dissertation, Trinity College Dublin, 1992), in which John Bellew figures prominently.
4 Clarke, *The Old English*, 31.
5 Margaret MacCurtain, *Tudor and Stuart Ireland* (Dublin, 1972), 128; Nicholas Canny, *The Formation of the Old English Elite in Ireland* (Dublin, 1975), 32–3.
6 Unless otherwise, or specifically, noted, the discussion of events to 1642 is based on Clarke, *The Old English in Ireland* and *NHI* iii, chapters VII-IX.
7 They frequently protested in terms indicative of their divided position. Following a proclamation by James in July of 1605 that commanded attendance at services of the established church and ordered the removal of all Catholic priests from Ireland by the following December (actions, it should be noted, which the government had no means to carry out), the nobility and gentry of the Pale petitioned the Lord Deputy asking for its suspension. They professed their loyalty and worried about the severities likely to follow in a 'mere [pure] matter of religion and conscience'. Among the signatories were three Bellews, including, from Louth, Patrick Bellew of Lisrenny. *CSPI 1603–06*, 362–5.
8 A succinct history of early plantation policy in Ireland can be found in Karl S. Bottigheimer, *English Money and Irish Land: The 'Adventurers' in the Cromwellian Settlement of Ireland* (Oxford, 1971), 1–29.
9 J.C. Beckett, *A Short History of Ireland*, 5th ed. (London, 1973), 69.
10 For a complete text of the Graces, see Clarke, Appendix II, 238–54.
11 For Wentworth's Irish career, see H. Kearney, *Strafford in Ireland 1633–41: A Study in Absolutism* (Manchester, 1961). Cf. T.O. Ranger, 'Strafford in Ireland: a Revaluation', in T. Aston, ed., *Crisis in Europe 1560–1660* (London, 1965).
12 Clarke, 110.

13 Clarke, 135–6; Wallace Notestein, ed., *Journal of Sir Simons D'Ewes* (New Haven, Conn. 1923), 84n.
14 M. Perceval-Maxwell, *The Outbreak of the Irish Rebelion of 1641* (Montreal & Kingston, 1994), 136–7; Clarke, 142.
15 Aidan Clarke, 'The Breakdown of Authority, 1640–41', in *NHI* iii, 288.
16 M. Perceval-Maxwell, *The Outbreak of the Irish Rebellion of 1641* is the latest full-length analysis of the rebellion and its origins. See 28–48 for the economic background.
17 HMC. *Ormond MSS*, n.s., ii, 4.
18 Sir John Temple, *The Irish Rebellion or An History of the Beginnings and First Progress of the General Rebellion Raised Within the Kingdom of Ireland* ... (London, 1646), 55–6. Temple was Master of the Rolls in Ireland. His account should, of course, be used with care; its inflammatory account of the massacres of 1641 is notorious. However, his observations of the role of the Old English in the initial stages of the rebellion (from a New English point of view) are valuable, as is the chronology he provides
19 MS. 31,883.
20 Perceval-Maxwell, 199–212.
21 HMC. *Ormond MSS*, n.s., ii, 4–5; Clarke, 163.
22 The depositions concerning the Bellews are in *Dowdall Deeds*, C. McNeill and A.J. Otway-Ruthven, eds. (Dublin, 1960), 329–30.
23 Temple, *The Irish Rebellion*, 60; HMC. *Ormond MSS*, n.s., ii, 36. Cf. Perceval-Maxwell, 242, who argues sufficient arms in the control of the gentry at the time of MacMahon's arrival in Louth, arms which were not used against him.
24 Clarke, 173; *Ormond MSS*, n.s., ii, 34; Temple, pt. ii, 8.
25 *Ormond MSS*, n.s., ii, 20, 36; T. Carte, *The Life of James, Duke of Ormond* (Oxford, 1851), ii, 129.
26 *Ormond MSS*, n.s., ii, 20.
27 *Ormond MSS*, n.s., ii, 23.
28 Richard Bagwell, *Ireland under the Stuarts and during the Interregnum* (London, 1909), i, 351, 353, 355.
29 Bellew, 'John Bellew of Willistown', 231.
30 Clarke, 179.
31 J.T. Gilbert, *History of the Irish Confederation and the War in Ireland (1641–9)* (Dublin, 1882–91), i, 269–79.
32 Russell and Prendergast, *The Carte MSS*, Appendix A, No. 67 cited in Clarke, 187.
33 Carte, ii, 225–6; Clarke, 191–2.
34 Carte, ii, 202–22; Clarke, 207.
35 Gilbert, *History of the Irish Confederation*, ii, 47–8, 213–14.
36 Bellew, 231–2.
37 Thomas L. Coonan, *The Irish Catholic Confederacy and the Puritan Revolution* (New York, 1954), 92–3, 155. Coonan's work is extremely sympathetic to the native Irish and their policies and hostile to the Old English and theirs. It also exhibits serious deficiencies in documentation and evidence (see J.C. Beckett's review in *IHS* 11 (1958–59), 52–5). Nonetheless, if used with care, it does provide one of the few detailed narratives of the events under discussion.
38 J. Bossy, 'The Counter-Reformation and the People of Ireland', *Historical Studies* viii (1971), 155–69.
39 R.F. Foster, *Modern Ireland 1600–1972* (London, 1988), 79–80. For strategies and respective troop strengths of the various combatants during this period, see Scott Wheeler, 'Four Armies in Ireland', in Jane Ohlmeyer, ed., *Ireland From Independence to Occupation 1641–1660* (Cambridge, 1995), 43–65.
40 References to finances and supply can be found in *CSPI 1633–1647*, 540, 607, 640, 641, 647, 651–2, 671.

41 For Preston's military campaigns during this period, see Coonan, *The Irish Catholic Confederacy*, 161–2, 198; Carte, ii, 429–30, 439, 477–8, iii, 154.

42 MS. 31,998; MS. 31,715; Coonan, 163; Carte, ii, 518–20.

43 Rolf Loeber and Geoffrey Parker, 'The Military Revolution in Seventeenth-Century Ireland', in *Ireland from Independence to Occupation*, 76.

44 Gilbert, vi, 78–85.

45 Bagwell, ii, 122; Carte, iii, 237, 247.

46 *CSPI 1633–1647*, 540. For a complete account of the complex intrigues surrounding the failed attack on Dublin, an excellent example of the internal divisions which often stalemated Confederate policy, see Patrick J. Corish, 'Ormond, Rinuccini, and the Confederates', in *NHI* iii, 321–2; Coonan, 234–40; Carte, iii, 271–88.

47 Gilbert, VII, 244.

48 MS. 31,966; Bellew, 234; Denis Murphy, S.J., *Cromwell in Ireland: A History of Cromwell's Irish Campaign* (Dublin, 1897), 22.

49 *Ormond MSS*, n.s., i, 211.

50 A full account of the breach of Rathmines can be found in Murphy, *Cromwell in Ireland*, 25–31.

51 MS. 31,966; Bellew, 234.

52 Murphy, 86.

53 At the end of May 1649, Ormond's forces – 14,500 foot and 3,700 horse – had but four pieces of artillery (Murphy, 23); Cromwell, on the other hand, brought a train of modern artillery with his force of 12,000. P.J. Corish, 'The Cromwellian Conquest, 1649–53', in *NHI* iii, 337. See Corish, 339 for Ormond's strategy.

54 Bagwell, ii, 233–43; *The Earl of Castlehaven's Memoirs of the Irish Wars* (1684, rpt. Delmar, New York, 1974), 166–9.

55 Bellew, 236.

56 S.R. Gardiner, 'The Transplantation to Connaught', *English Historical Review* 14 (1899), 730.

57 C.H. Firth, R.S. Rait, *Acts and Ordinances of the Interregnum, 1642–1660* (London, 1911), 598–603.

58 As Gardiner pointed out, it would have been impossible to enforce the death sentences ordered under the first five qualifications of the Act, which would have encompassed 'something like half the Irish male population'. Instead, a clause in the *Act for the Satisfaction of the Adventurers*, passed on September 26, 1653, directed that land in Connacht be reserved 'for the habitation of all the Irish nation comprehended in the qua''fications' of the *Act for the Settling of Ireland*, neatly including the qualifications which required pardon for life and estate. If those in the five qualifications had not been executed, they were to be transplanted ('The Transplantation to Connaught', 708–9, 715–16). R.C. Simington speculates on a secret compromise: the repeal of the death sentences for a reduction in the amount of land available for the transplantees to accommodate the increased demands of the Commonwealth army. Another factor: Ormond and the earls of Castlehaven, Inchiquin, and Clanricard – among those in the five qualifications – had, on occasion, been of service to the Commonwealth (*The Transplantation to Connaught, 1654–58* IMC, 1970, xxiv). Gardiner's point is still a strong one – execution of the penalties provided for, in both a figurative and literal sense, would have virtually eliminated the former ruling class of Ireland.

59 John P. Prendergast, *The Cromwellian Settlement of Ireland*, 3rd ed. (1865; rpt. Dublin, 1922), 147.

60 Petitions of Bellew and others are in MS. 31,966.

61 Bellew, 235.

62 Bellew, 234–5.

63 The following information concerning the lands set out to John Bellew and those in his, and

subsequently his eldest son's possession in the Restoration period is taken from R.C. Simington, ed. *The Transplantation to Connacht, 1654–58* (Dublin, 1970), 73, 78, 172, 177, 217 and *Books of Survey and Distribution*, ed. R.C. Simington (Dublin, 1944–67): V. i-County of Roscommon, 60–61; V. ii – County of Mayo, 21; V. iii – County of Galway, 167, 244, 268–70, 282.

64 *Transplantation to Connacht*, 73, 172, 177, 217; *Books of Survey and Distribution*, iii, 279–80. John Bellew of Castletown was under age when his father Sir Christopher died, sometime after 1642. 'To shun the disasters and calamities in that nation', he was sent to France, but returned to Ireland with Ormond and was in command of a troop of horse. On the Restoration, his petition for the return of his lands was granted. *CSPI 1660–1662*, 48–9, 222.

65 *Transplantation to Connacht*, 268; *Books of Survey and Distribution*, iii, 177; MS. 31,901.

66 MS. 31,948.

67 S.J. Connolly, *Religion, Law, and Power*, 15.

68 Bellew, 236.

69 *CSPI 1660–1662*, 250.

70 Bellew, 236–7.

71 J.G. Simms, 'The Restoration, 1660–85', in *NHI* iii, 422.

72 Cited in J.C. Beckett, *A Short History of Ireland*, 83.

73 Karl S. Bottigheimer, 'The Restoration Land Settlement in Ireland: a Structural View', *IHS* 18 (1972), 18–21. See also, L.J. Arnold, 'The Irish Court of Claims of 1663', *IHS* 24 (1985), 417–30.

74 MS. 31,994(A).

75 MS. 31,947.

76 *CSPI 1666–1669*, 344.

77 For a complete account of the complex land dealings of Bellew and Taaffe, necessarily generalized here, see O'Sullivan, 'Land Ownership Changes in the County of Louth in the 17th Century', Chapter V.

78 MS. 31,947.

79 *15th Report from the Commissioners ... respecting the Public Records of Ireland* (1825), Appendix, 'Abstracts of Grants', 247; *Books of Survey and Distribution*, ii, 21.

80 There is some uncertainty as to the location of Castle Bellew, since there were castles in both Clonoran and Clonoranoughter. The Bellew family papers provide less than definitive confirmation: at least one letter from Mary Bellew to her husband John was written from Clonoran; yet in 1684, a description of Bellew lands in Galway mentions the creation of the manor of Clonoranoughter 'alias Castlebellew'. Since the sites are roughly adjacent, however, it may well be, as has been suggested, they were one and the same. Gerard J. Lyne, 'Three Certified Gross Survey Transcripts for County Galway', *Analecta Hibernica*, no. 35 (1992), 171–2, n. 48, 49; MS. 31,947; O'Sullivan, 289.

81 *15th Report of the Commissioners ...*, 321; MS 31,989.

82 Entered in *Books of Survey and Distribution* as 'Sir Nicholas Plunkett a lease'. This and Christopher Bellew's other lands in Tiaquin are in V. iii, 268.

83 See Sir William Petty, *Hiberniae delineatio, atlas of Ireland* (London, 1685; rpt. Newcastle on Tyne, 1968) for Corgarrowes and H. Moll's 1701 map of Galway in the NLI for Mount Bellew.

84 Charles McNeill, 'Reports on MSS in the Bodleian Library Oxford', Rawlinson MSS A, Folio 275: Royal Nomination of Sheriffs, October 6, 1686 in *Analecta Hibernica* 1 (1930), 37.

85 John D'Alton, *Historical and Genealogical Illustrations of King James' Irish Army List* (1689, 2nd. ed. (Dubin, 1860), i, 35; J.G. Simms, *Jacobite Ireland* (London, 1969), 89–90.

86 G.E.C., i, 101.

87 D'Alton, *King James' Irish Army List*, ii, 305. An impression of the haste with which they

were recruited and armed is given by Major-General Pusignan, a commander of the French troops who accompanied James: 'I have seen the regiments of Bellew, of 'Gormestown', and of 'Louth', who have not a sword and very few muskets. The companies are stronger in pikes than in muskets, and of those very few are in a state to fire. In fine I cannot exaggerate what they want in this country'. (*D'Avaux's Negotiations*, 82 cited in D'Alton, ii, 306–7).

88 *CSPI 1693*, 133; D.Alton, ii, 526.

89 Peter Beresford Ellis, *The Boyne Water: The Battle of the Boyne*, 1690 (New York, 1976), 31–2; John Cornelius O'Callaghan, *History of the Irish Brigades in the Service of France* (Glasgow, 1870), 79.

90 D'Alton, ii, 306; O'Callaghan, 79–80.

91 J.G. Simms, *Jacobite Ireland*, 189–93; 212–15.

92 The chief casualties of the Williamite settlement – those Catholics who had their estates confiscated – were primarily those who had submitted directly after the battle of the Boyne or who took advantage of the articles providing for passage to France and fought for Louis XIV. J.G. Simms, *The Williamite Confiscation in Ireland, 1690–1701* (London, 1956), 161. Of the latter group, even some of these obtained pardons (see the information on Richard Bellew in the text following).

93 J.G. Simms, 'Irish Jacobites: Lists from TCD MS N.1.3.' in *Analecta Hibernica* 22 (1960), 21–2, 90; J.G. Simms, *Williamite Confiscation*, 76; D'Alton, ii, 305.

94 J.G. Simms, 'Irish Jacobites', 105, 132; Simms, *Williamite Confiscation*, 76; *G.E.C.*, i, 102. For Richard Bellew's brief military career in France, see Chapter III.

95 Cited in O'Sullivan, 345.

96 Simms, 'Irish Jacobites', 90.

97 *CSPI 1693*, 133.

98 Ibid., 331.

99 Simms, 'Irish Jacobites', 131.

100 Ibid., 107; MS. 31,889.

101 Simms, *Williamite Confiscation*, 162; Appendix D, 195.

CHAPTER 2: 'THE GAVEL, THAT INFERNAL ACT'

1 MS. 27,108.

2 Osborough, 'Catholics, Land and the Popery Acts of Anne', 28–9, 35–8; T.P. Power, 'Converts,' in *Endurance and Emergence*, 108, 110–11.

3 James Anthony Froude, *The English in Ireland in the Eighteenth Century* (1881; rpt. New York, 1888) i, 374.

4 In 1772, Catholics were permitted to take a 61-year lease of 50 acres of bog with ½ acre of arable land adjoining, if they reclaimed the land within 21 years.

5 As cited in Power, 110. See also Eileen O'Byrne, ed., *The Convert Rolls* (IMC: Dublin, 1981), xiii, hereafter referred to as *Convert Rolls*.

6 As indicated above, the Convert Rolls have been published, but for problems with the source (methods of enumeration, completeness, etc.), see O'Byrne, *Convert Rolls*, vii–xv; Power, 103–5. An earlier analysis is that of Francis Finegan, 'The Irish "Catholic Convert Rolls"', *Studies* 38 (1949), 73–82.

7 J.G. Simms, 'Connacht in the Eighteenth Century', *IHS* 11 (1958–59), 118.

8 Archbishop Synge of Tuam to Archbishop Ware of Canterbury, 15 April 1725, in William P. Burke, *Irish Priests in Penal Times, 1660–1760* (Waterford, 1914), 247.

9 Charles O'Connor Don, *The O'Conors of Connaught; An Historical Memoir* (Dublin, 1891), 242, 295–6; Osborough, 24.

10 *Rambles through Ireland* (Cork, 1798) as cited in Simms, 'Connacht in the Eighteenth Century', 118.

11 Finegan, 'The Irish "Catholic Convert Rolls"', 77. Finegan counts 460 recognizable Galway names in the rolls from 1703–99 (75); Power, 395 from 1703–1800 (104).
12 *Burke's Landed Gentry of Ireland*, 4th ed. (1958), s.v. French of Monivea, 272; Prendergast, 152–3; Denis A. Cronin, *A Galway Gentleman in the Age of Improvement: Robert French of Monivea, 1716–79 Maynooth Studies in Local History: Number 2* (Dublin, 1995), 10–12.
13 *Convert Rolls*, App. II, 304.
14 Gerald Dillon, 'The Dillon Peerages', *Irish Genealogist* 3 (1958), 98–9.
15 *NLI Reports on Private Collections*, No. 4: The Dillon Papers, 34–5, 80; *Convert Rolls*, 77.
16 *Burke's Peerage and Baronetage*, s.v. Bellew, 237.
17 There are frequent references to 'uncle Dominick' by Michael and Patrick Bellew, Christopher Bellew's sons, in the family correspondence; and Christopher *Kelly* Bellew, Dominick's son, addresses Michael Bellew as 'cousin' in his letters to him.
18 Registry of Deeds, Dublin. Book 119, A-B (1786–93) 367–554–5; Case on Behalf of Michael Dillon Bellew for Advice of Nicholas Ball, Esq., 30 October 1830.
19 Nat.Arch. *Thrift Abstracts*: 1457–2300, No. 1796.
20 Osborough, 25.
21 W.E.H. Lecky, *History of Ireland in the Eighteenth Century* (1892; rpt. London, 1913) i, 347–50; Froude, *The English in Ireland in the Eighteenth Century* i, 602–8.
22 Thomas U. Sadleir, 'The Burkes of Marble Hill', *Galway Archaeological and Historical Journal* 8, (1913–4), 1–5.
23 Martin J. Blake, 'The Families of Daly of Galway with Tabular Pedigrees', *Journal of the Galway Archaeological and Historical Society* 13 (1927), 140; Simms, 'Connacht in the Eighteenth Century', 131.
24 Patrick Melvin, 'The Galway Tribes as Landowners and Gentry', in Gerald Moran, ed., *Galway: History and Society* (Dublin, 1996), 326–8.
25 Relevant papers include a draft will of Henry Dillon, and among Christopher Dillon Bellew's papers, 'my father's intended answer to Andrew French's bill', providing a summary of events from the Bellew side. See also Andrew French's letters, MS. 27,106.
26 *15th Report from the Commissioners ...* (1825), Appendix, 'Abstracts of Grants', 242.
27 Ibid., 320.
28 There are three Garrett Dillons and one Gerald Dillon entered on the *Convert Rolls* (76).
29 The complexities of the litigation, correspondence, etc. concerning this property can be traced in MSS. 31,900; 27,131; 27,123; 27,134; 27,170; 27,181; 27,194; also Hon. Mrs. Gerald Bellew, 'Some Notes on the Family of Bellew of Thomastown, Co. Louth', *County Louth Archaeological Journal* 5 (1923), 193–7 and among the Bellew family legal papers, 'Caleghan's opinion' (1735) and Exchequer Bill of Bellew-McCartan (1740). There are discrepancies in the sources as to the exact genealogy of Roger Bellew's female heirs; I have followed the account in the legal sources.
30 Registry of Deeds, Dublin. Book 11, A-B (1768–84) 333–491–225542 (13 November, 1780).
31 Philip Savage indeed conformed. *Convert Rolls*, 252.
32 MS. 27,106.
33 Osborne, 37–8.
34 MS. 27,112.
35 There is no specific reference to total acreage in the Bellew papers. This estimate is derived from, first, Tadhg MacLochlainn, *A Historical Summary on the Parish of Ahascragh Caltra and Castleblakeney* (Ballinasloe, 1979), 33. This is an antiquarian history and, despite the acknowledged assistance of Mrs. L.H. Grattan-Bellew, is somewhat unreliable, in at least its discussion of the Bellew family genealogy. Nonetheless, the estimate of 10,000 acres is supported by U.H. Hussey de Burgh, *Landowners of Ireland* (Dublin, 1878), 29, which shows Sir H.C. Grattan-Bellew, Bt. with 10,516 acres in county Galway. Although this is a nineteenth-century evaluation, very little acreage was added to the Galway estate after a few purchases by Christopher Dillon Bellew in the early nineteenth century. See also Opin-

ion of Frederick W. Walsh Esq. on the Abstract of the Title of Thomas A. Grattan-Bellew, Esq. to Estates in the Counties of Galway and Roscommon, 1884.

36 See, for example, maps of Shankill to the south; Gorteen to the north; and leases of Christopher Bellew, Michael Bellew's father, to lands in Ballyaderrany to the northeast. MSS. 31,905; 31,967; 31,968–70.

37 *NLI Reports on Private Collections*, No. 47: The Mahon Papers, 250; MS. 27,108.

38 MS. 31,905.

39 MS. 27,118.

40 Abstract of the Title of Michael Bellew of Mount Bellew in the County of Galway, Esq. to the following lands being lately part of the estates of Sir Patrick Bellew of Barmeath in the County of Louth, Bt.

41 *Ibid.*; Registry of Deeds, Dublin. Book 119, A-B (1786–93) 381–497–252582.

42 *Life of Theobald Wolfe Tone*, ed. William Theobald Tone (Washington, D.C., 1826) ii, 231.

43 Bellew commercial enterprises are discussed in Chapter 4.

44 The Bellew estate, business, and household accounts referred to in the remainder of this chapter are in a number of MSS, some of which are extensive, i.e., hundreds of items. Wherever possible, I have given dates to facilitate location. Unless otherwise noted, see MSS. 27,476–7; 31,931; 27,461–3; 27,475.

45 *The Journal of John Wesley*, ed. Nehemiah Curnock (New York, 1910) iv, 170–1.

46 *Rutland MSS* (London: HMC, 1894) iii, 243.

47 Edward Wakefield, *An Account of Ireland, Statistical and Political* (London, 1812) i, 32.

48 MS. 31,947.

49 John O'Donovan, *The Economic History of Livestock in Ireland* (Dublin and Cork, 1940), 94–6.

50 L.M. Cullen, *An Economic History of Ireland Since 1660*, 2nd ed. (London, 1987), 64–6.

51 O'Donovan, *Economic History of Livestock in Ireland*, 98–9; Arthur Wollaston Hutton, ed. *Arthur Young's Tour in Ireland (1776–1779* (London, 1892) ii, 106–7 (hereafter referred to as *Young's Tour*).

52 O'Donovan, 93, 101–2.

53 *Young's Tour* i, 283.

54 MS. 31,920.

55 *Young's Tour* i, 275, 283.

56 MS. 27,112.

57 Hely Dutton, *A Statistical and Agricultural Survey of the County of Galway* (Dublin, 1824), 16–17; 118–19; Wakefield, *An Account of Ireland* i, 317.

58 *Young's Tour* i, 246.

59 Dutton, *Statistical and Agricultural Survey of Galway*, 115.

60 O'Donovan, 100.

61 MS. 27,133.

62 Cullen, *Economic History of Ireland Since 1660*, 66.

63 MS. 27,138.

64 For the development of the Irish provisions trade and the participation of members of the Bellew family in it, see Chapter 4.

65 O'Donovan, 172, 175, 177; Wakefield ii, 338.

66 Sile Ní Chinnéide, 'Coquebert de Montbret's Impressions of Galway City and County in the Year 1791', *Journal of the Galway Archaeological and Historical Society* 25 (1952), 4; Dutton, 118–19; Wakefield ii, 310–11.

67 O'Donovan, 144; *Young's Tour* i, 283.

68 *NLI Reports ...*, No. 47: The Mahon Papers, 792.

69 In the eighteenth century, all cattle were referred to as 'black', regardless of color. Since the general term 'cattle' was applied to sheep and horses as well, 'black cattle' was used to differentiate cows from the other two. O'Donovan, 169–70.

70 *Young's Tour* ii, 254.
71 *NLI Reports*, No. 4: The Dillon Papers, 75–6.
72 Cronin, *A Galway Gentleman in the Age of Improvement*, 20.
73 MSS. 31,968; 27,108; 31,921.
74 *NLI Reports ...*, No. 47: The Mahon Papers, 794.
75 David Large, 'The Wealth of the Greater Irish Landowners', *IHS* 15 (1966), 28–9.
76 Thomas Newenham, *A View of the Natural, Political and Commercial Circumstances of Ireland* (1809) as cited in Large, 'Wealth of the Greater Irish Landowners', 30.
77 Cullen, *Economic History of Ireland*, 78–9, 82.
78 F.H.A. Aalen, *Man and the Landscape in Ireland* (New York, 1978), 34–7.
79 *Young's Tour* i, 261–71.
80 Dutton, *A Statistical Survey*, 18.
81 As cited in Constantia Maxwell, *Country and Town in Ireland under the Georges* (London, 1940), 188–90.
82 Cullen, *Economic History of Ireland*, 48–51.
83 George O'Brien, *The Economic History of Ireland in the Eighteenth Century* (Dublin and London, 1918; rpt. Philadelphia, 1977), 221.
84 *Young's Tour* i, 277; Cullen, *Economic History of Ireland*, 61.
85 *Young's Tour* i, 271–2. For a detailed description of French's participation in the linen industry, see Cronin, 28–33.
86 MS. 27,106. For an account of the activities of Andrew French and Michael Bellew's merchant brother Patrick in marketing flaxseed, see Chapter 4.
87 MS. 27,108.
88 Cullen, *Economic History of Ireland*, 53, 75.
89 MSS. 27,133; 27,138; 31,915.
90 MS. 27,218.
91 Dutton, 423; Cullen, *Economic History*, 108, 120. By the late 1790s, the bleach yard and mill at Monivea were no longer in use. (Cronin, 32).
92 L.M. Cullen, 'Catholic Social Classes Under the Penal Laws', in T.P. Power and Kevin Whelan, eds., *Endurance and Emergence*, 61–3. For a brief historical survey of eighteenth-century graziers, see David Seth Jones, *Graziers, Land Reform, and Political Conflict in Ireland* (Washington, D.C., 1995), 24–9.
93 The term 'middleman' should be used with care, because it is frequently used, especially by Young, as a term of blanket opprobrium; moreover, it is often an inadequate term to describe the complexity of leaseholding and the variety of leaseholders in eastern county Galway. See, for example, Cullen, 'Catholic Social Classes', 59 and D. Dickson, 'Middlemen', in T. Bartlett and D. Hayton, eds., *Penal Era and Golden Age* (Belfast, 1979), 162–85.
94 *Young's Tour* i, 275–6, 283; ii, 47.
95 Rent accounts and leases can be found in MSS. 31,915; 31,918; 31,919.
96 MS. 27,108.
97 MS. 27,108.
98 MS. 27,137.
99 Lecky, *History of Ireland in the Eighteenth Century* i, 361–2, 367; Connolly, *Religion, Law and Power*, 211–12.
100 James J. Donnelly, Jr., 'The Rightboy Movement, 1785–88', *Studia Hibernica* 17–18 (1977–78), 136–7, 145.
101 Dutton, 71; Wakefield, 1, 259–61, 382–3.
102 Donnelly, 'The Rightboy Movement', 124–5; Cullen, *Economic History*, 83.
103 Wakefield, ii, 754.
104 Wakefield, i, 32.
105 MS. 27,106.

106 Ibid.
107 MS. 31,967. For a recent geographic analysis of landowner investment in country house and park construction that stresses economic as well as status considerations, see L.J. Proudfoot, 'Spatial Transformation and Social Agency: Property, Society and Improvement, *c*.1700 to *c*.1900', in B.J. Graham and L.J. Proudfoot, eds., *An Historical Geography of Ireland* (London, 1993), 246–8.
108 Maxwell, *Country and Town under the Georges*, 101.
109 Ibid., 106–7.
110 MS. 31,909.
111 Dutton, 434.
112 Ibid., 442.
113 *Young's Tour* ii, 148.
114 Maxwell, 31. A comparison of the sums recorded in the wage books and Maxwell's citation of servants' wages from the north of Ireland for the same period show servants in the Bellew household receiving anywhere from £1–3 less per year; disparities are even greater in wages paid kitchen help.
115 MS. 27,145.
116 *Young's Tour* ii, 149–50.
117 Miscellaneous architectural plans, drawings, etc. are in MS. 31,994.
118 MS. 27,135. The artificial lake was completed in the early nineteenth century under the direction of Hely Dutton. Bellew's, and Dutton's, success was noted by Prince Pückler-Muskau in his tour through Ireland in 1832: He considered that it was a 'perfect study for the judicious distribution of masses of water ...' Edward Malins & the Knight of Glin, *Lost Desmesnes: Irish Landscape Gardening, 1660–1845* (London, 1976), 67.
119 *Burke's Guide to Country Houses*, ed. Mark Bence-Jones (London, 1978) 1-Ireland, xxiii.
120 Descriptions of Mount Bellew house are taken from the following: *Burke's Guide to County Houses* 1, s.v. Mount Bellew, 212; J.P. Neale, *Views of the Seats of Noblemen and Gentlemen in England, Wales, Scotland, and Ireland* (London, 1820) 3, s.v. Mount Bellew, n.p.; *The Architecture of Richard Morrison and William Vitruvius Morrison* (Irish Architectural Archive: Dublin, 1989), 127–8.
121 MS. 27,216; Peter Harbison, Homan Potterton, Jeanne Sheehy, *Irish Art and Architecture: from Prehistory to the Present* (London, 1978), 197–8.
122 Maxwell, 20.
123 William Hamilton Maxwell, *Wild Sports of the West* (1832; rpt. London, 1973), 260.
124 Registry of Deeds, Dublin. Book 119, A-B (1786–93) 367–554–5 (6,7 February, 1786).
125 MS. 31,957 summarizes evidence from the trials of the murderers. An even more melodramatic (if possible) story of the murder is in *The Recollections of Skeffington Gibbon, from 1796 to the Present Year 1829 ...* (Dublin, 1829), 8–12. I am indebted to Patrick Melvin for drawing my attention to this account.
126 MS. 27,112.
127 Richard Cumberland, *Memoirs of Richard Cumberland* (London, 1807) i, 278–9.
128 Wakefield i, 805; ii, 760.
129 *Young's Tour* ii, 154–5.
130 For the artistic interests and English tours of Robert French, see T.C. Barnard, 'The Worlds of a Galway Squire: Robert French of Monivea, 1716–79', in *Galway: History and Society*, 282–4.
131 Neale, *View of the Seats ...* 3, s.v. Mount Bellew, n.p.
132 Dutton, vii.
133 M. Pollard, *Dublin's Trade in Books 1550–1800* (Oxford, 1989), 218; MS.27,293. For other orders, catalogues, and lists, see MSS. 31,992–3; 27,467; 27, 296–7.
134 A.D. Leeman, *A Systematic Bibliography of Sallust* (Leiden, 1965), 15–16; W. Seyfarth, *Ammianus Marcellinus: Res Gestae* (Leipzig, 1978) 1, x-xiv. Apuleius' *Opera Omnia* was

indeed a rarity, probably one of the few in the British Isles; it was edited by P. Colvius in 1588. C. Giarratano and P. Frassinetti, *Apulei Metamorphoseon* (Turin, 1960), lv. I am indebted to Paul B. Harvey, Jr. for this information and these citations.

135 Richard C. Cole, 'Private libraries in Eighteenth-Century Ireland', *Library Quarterly* 44 (1974), 241. There are, however, some inaccuracies in Cole's description of Bellew's holdings, and one rather thinks the family would have been slighted to be categorized primarily as 'merchants'.

136 MS. 27,104.

137 MS. 27,297.

138 David Irwin, *English Neo-Classical Art: Studies in Inspiration and Taste* (London, 1966), 89, 119–21, 123.

139 An inventory of the Bellew collection is in MS. 31,992.

140 Irwin, *English Neo-Classical Art*, 38; *Henry Fuseli, 1741–1825* (London, 1975), 61–2.

141 Neale, *Views of the Seats* 3, s.v. Mount Bellew, n.p.; *Burke's Guide to Country Houses* 1, s.v. Mount Bellew, 212.

CHAPTER 3: 'WE MUST PART OUR NATIVE LANDS'

1 MS. 27,106.

2 O'Callaghan, 7–8; Lecky, i, 248.

3 O'Callaghan, 79–81. Bellew's colonelship of the regiment was brief, however. Another commander of superior age and influence was appointed in his stead, and Bellew, slighted, returned to Ireland where he succeeded to the barony on the death of his elder brother in 1694. Under threat of attainder, he conformed, took his seat in the Lords, and received a pension of £300 a year from Queen Anne. The barony of Duleek became extinct with the death of his son in 1770.

4 Beckett, 95.

5 J.G. Simms, 'The Irish on the Continent, 1691–1800', *NHI* iv, 630; for the various subsequent transmogrifications and name-changes of these regiments, see Harman Murtagh, 'Irish Soldiers Abroad, 1600–1800', in Thomas Bartlett and Keith Jeffrey, eds., *A Military History of Ireland* (Cambridge, 1996), 298.

6 Daniel Corkery, *The Hidden Ireland* (Dublin, 1925) as cited in J.G. Simms, 'The Irish on the Continent', 637. None of this, however, saved him from being made a scapegoat for the lack of French success in India; on his return from his regiment's Indian campaign, he was executed.

7 Lecky, i, 250; Richard Hayes, *Biographical Dictionary of Irishmen in France* (Dublin, 1949), s.v. Lally, Thomas, 146; Darcy, Patrick, 52; Kirwan, Richard, 145; and Lynch, Isidore, 158.

8 O'Callaghan, 81n.; D'Alton, II, 254; John O'Hart, *The Irish and Anglo-Irish Landed Gentry When Cromwell Came to Ireland* (1884; rpt. Shannon, 1968), appendix, 532.

9 Christopher Duffy, *The Wild Goose and the Eagle: A Life of Marshal von Browne 1705–1757* (London, 1964), 2–3; O'Callaghan, 191.

10 Marquis MacSwiney of Mashanglass, 'Notes on Some Irish Regiments in the Service of Spain and Naples in the Eighteenth Century', *Proceedings of the Royal Irish Academy* 37, Sect. C, No.9 (1927), 160–1; Murtagh, 'Irish Soldiers Abroad', 296.

11 Duffy, *The Wild Goose*, 87–8; Lecky, i, 251.

12 *Spanish Knights of Irish Origin: Documents from Continental Archives*, ed. Micheline Walsh (IMC: Dublin, 1960), i, 114–16; MS. 27,139.

13 Duffy, *The Wild Goose*, 87–8; Lecky, i, 251; Simms, 'The Irish on the Continent', 643. The family of Lacy had generals in Austrian, Russian, and Spanish service.

14 Duffy, *The Wild Goose*, 1, 3, 6–7; O'Hart, appendix, 522; G. Franks, 'Field Marshal Ulysses Maximilian Browne', *JRSAI* 71 (1941), 121–9.

15 J.G. Simms, 'Connacht in the Eighteenth Century', *IHS* 2 (1958), 127; Christopher Duffy, *The Army of Maria Theresa: The Armed Forces of Imperial Austria, 1740–1780* (New York, 1977), 19, 23. Unless otherwise, or specifically, noted, the following discussion of the organization of the Austrian army is based on Duffy, *The Wild Goose*, 5, 10–11, 147–8 and Duffy, *Army of Maria Theresa*, 24–5, 27, 29, 34–5.
16 *Memoirs of the House of Taaffe*, 33, as cited in Duffy, *The Wild Goose*, 6.
17 This tradition was in part born of necessity since the Austrian lower nobility and gentry, unlike their continental counterparts, were loath, despite Imperial pressure and incentives, to enter military service for most of the eighteenth century. Duffy, *Army*, 24, 29.
18 *Annual Register 1765*, as cited in O'Callaghan, 601–2.
19 A reference to either Lieutenant-General Edward D'Alton, proprietor of a regiment of Galician infantry, or General of Artillery Count Richard D'Alton, proprietor of a regiment of Hungarian infantry. Lt. Col. Cavenagh, 'Irish Colonel Proprietors of Imperial Regiments', *JRSAI* 57 (1927), 117–26.
20 MS. 27,118.
21 Duffy, *The Wild Goose*, 147–8.
22 MS. 27,118.
23 All correspondence from John Bellew to Michael Bellew is contained in MS. 27,118.
24 This discussion of Imperial foreign policy aims in the last quarter of the eighteenth century is based on C.A. Macartney, *The Hapsburg Empire 1790–1918* (London, 1968), 116–18, 130–50.
25 Paul P. Bernard, *Joseph II and Bavaria: Two Eighteenth-Century Attempts at German Unification* (The Hague, 1965), 108.
26 Bernard, *Joseph II and Bavaria*, 121.
27 K. Roider, *Austria's Eastern Question 1700–1790* (Princeton, 1982), 169–70.
28 Duffy, *The Wild Goose*, 28.
29 M. de la Colonie, *The Chronicles of an Old Campaigner*, as cited in Duffy, *The Wild Goose*, 27.
30 Stanford J. Shaw, *Between Old and New: The Ottoman Empire under Sultan Selim III 1789–1807* (Cambridge, Mass., 1971), 30; Duffy, *Army*, 94.
31 Duffy, *Army*, 54; Béla K. Király, *Hungary in the Late Eighteenth Century: The Decline of Enlightened Despotism* (New York, 1969, 106, 140.
32 Description of Hungarian events is based on Király, *Hungary in the Late Eighteenth Century: The Decline of Enlightened Despotism* (New York, 1969), 106, 140.
33 This may be a reference to the military academy established by Maria Theresa for the education of officer cadets. Duffy, *Army*, 29–30.
34 This was a serious financial consideration; cavalry mounts, especially for cuirassiers, were very expensive. Duffy, *Army*, 35; 103–4. When Bellew lost one of his horses to glanders, he had to go on foot for a time; its eventual replacement cost him 15 guineas.
35 Macartney, *The Hapsburg Empire*, 117.
36 Murtagh, 'Irish Soldiers Abroad', 310.
37 Duffy, *The Wild Goose*, 15, 17, 138; *Army*, 27.
38 Duffy, *The Wild Goose*, 15; *Army*, 28; *Annual Register 1766*, as cited in O'Callaghan, 602.
39 Founded in 1629, this Franciscan establishment was supported by both the Imperial House and the financial aid of Irish soldiers in Imperial service, e.g. an ambitious building project in 1704 was financed by Count Sigismund Maquire, the Imperial General of Artillery at Olmutz. The House educated priests for the Irish mission and served to link the Irish in central Europe with their fellows on the continent and in Ireland until its suppression by Joseph II in 1786. Brendan Jennings, 'The Irish Franciscans in Prague', *Studies* 28 (1939), 210–22.
40 One other member of the Bellew family in the Louth branch was in Austrian service, only one segment of a rather tumultuous career. Matthew Bellew, the younger brother of Dominick

Bellew, Catholic bishop of Killala, had served in the Imperial army and, during the siege of Belgrade in 1789, was injured by the explosion of a mine. Retiring from Austrian service, he entered the Russian army, where he rose to the rank of major. He returned to Ireland in March 1796; William Bellew, a son of Sir Patrick, reported his landing in Dublin after losing his money to a French privateer on his passage. He appears to have considered returning to Russia, but made his way to Killala, where Bishop Bellew had a residence. In 1798, in the French invasion under Humbert, he offered his services to the French commander and was appointed general of the Irish auxilaries. Ill-health, however, resulted in his replacement (the Protestant bishop of Killala, Joseph Strock, attributed it to drunkenness, but his opinion of all who joined the French was a low one). He was taken prisoner by General Trench's loyalist forces in the capture of Killala and hanged for his part in the rebellion. Efforts to implicate his brother the bishop were unsuccessful; Dominick Bellew appears to have been wholly unsympathetic to the rebel cause and defended himself against these charges successfully. Richard Hayes, *The Last Invasion of Ireland: When Connacht Rose* (1937; rpt. Dublin, 1979), 22, 33, 80, 175, 260–1, 318; MS. 27,120.

41 The former reference is to George Robert Fitzgerald, a notorious Mayo member of the Ango-Irish gentry, who owed the nickname 'Fighting Fitzgerald' to his excessive predilection for duelling. In the course of a highly eccentric career, he murdered an under-tenant and was hanged in June, 1786. His trial and death caused a public sensation. Constantia Maxwell, *Country and Town in Ireland under the Georges* (London, 1940), 52–5; Mary MacCarthy, *Fighting Fitzgerald and Other Papers* (London, 1930), 81–181.

42 *Young's Tour*, i, 68.

43 Lecky, i, 148.

44 John Brady and Patrick J. Corish, 'The Church under the Penal Code', in *A History of Irish Catholicism* 4, ed. P.J. Corish (Dublin, 1971), 74–5.

45 *A Report from the Lords Commissioners ... into the Present State of Popery in this Kingdom ... within the Counties of Mayo and Galway ...* (Dublin, 1731). Included in *Report on the State of Popery, 1731* in *Archiv.Hib.* 3 (1914), 126–7.

46 From the 1780s and perhaps earlier, Catholics from the gentry class could, by connivance, attend Trinity, much as English Catholics often spent time at Oxford or Cambridge, but like their English counterparts, couldn't receive degrees without taking oaths of conformity. Moreover, the strong Protestant associations of Trinity continued to keep the numbers of Catholics there to a minimum, even after it had been officially opened to them in 1793; as well, restrictions on fellowships and scholarships awarded to Catholics continued into the first half of the nineteenth century. Lecky, ii, 512; M.D.R. Leys, *Catholics in England 1559–1829: A Social History* (New York, 1961), 163; R.B. McDowell, *Ireland in the Age of Imperialism and Revolution 1760–1801* (Oxford, 1979), 418; James Johnson Auchmuty, *Irish Education: A Historical Survey* (Dublin, 1937), 81, 134–5.

47 A.C.F. Beales, *Education Under Penalty: English Catholic Education from the Reformation to the Fall of James II 1547–1689* (London, 1963), 133. Indeed, the lay element grew to predominance there; from 1750 to 1794, three-quarters of Douai students did not go on to the priesthood. P.R. Harris, 'The English College, Douai, 1750–1794', *Education Under Penalty*, 169, 176.

48 While the Jesuits of St Omers provided training for their younger members and recruited others, by the end of the seventeenth century, only one in four students went on to a religious vocation; St Gregory's was a predominantly lay school from the start. Beales, *Education Under Penalty*, 169, 176.

49 For courses of study and daily routine, see Beales, 132–3; Harris, 'English College, Douai', 86–7, 90; *Douai College Documents 1639–1794*, ed. P.R. Harris, *CRSP* (Record Series), LXIII (1972), 139–41; and A.S. Barnes, *The Catholic Schools of England* (London, 1926), 80–2. For the similarity in curricula, see Beales, 133; *CRSP* LXIII, 141.

50 The Bellew papers contain several examples of the younger Bellew sons' exercises in Latin,

written also, no doubt, to impress their father and elder brother with their progress; Luke Bellew sent home a Latin poem and 'Henricius Bellew' a letter to his 'frater carissime'. MSS. 27,132 and 27,121.

51 Beales, 135; *CRSP* LXIII, 142.
52 The number of students enrolled remained constant around 110 for most of the century. *CRSP* LXIII, 146.
53 *CRSP* LXIII, 120, 123, 270; *The Douay College Diaries: The Seventh Diary 1715–1778*, ed., Edwin H. Burton and Edmond Noland, *CRSP* XXVIII, 187, 198, 223–4, 260, 263, 267.
54 *CRSP* XXVIII, 267–8.
55 *St Omers and Bruges Colleges, 1593–1773: A Biographical Dictionary*, ed., Geoffrey Holt, *CRSP* (Record Series LXIX (1979), 33.
56 Beales, 135, 158, 164.
57 *CRSP* LXIX, 95, 166–7, 209.
58 Barnes, *The Catholic Schools of England*, 63, 70–7. The specified age of admission at St Omers was 14. When the college was in France, the preparatory school was located in various places near St Omers. Beales, 159; *CRSP* LXIX, 2.
59 *CRSP* LXIX, 85, 195.
60 *CRSP* LXIII, 151, 266, 356.
61 *CRSP* LXIII, 359; MS. 27,110.
62 Barnes, 78–9.
63 MS. 27,132.
64 Cathaldus Giblin, 'Irish Exiles in Catholic Europe', in *A History of Irish Catholicism*, 4, ed., P.J. Corish (Dublin, 1971), 11–13, 16–17.
65 Correspondence from Luke Bellew to his brother Christopher Dillon Bellew is contained in MS. 27,132.
66 MS. 27,133.
67 Beales, 41, 115.
68 See Harris, 'English College, Douai', 83, 85–6; *CRSP* LXIII, 141.
69 *CRSP* LXIII, 141.
70 Ibid., 246, 248, 251.
71 Maurus Lunn, 'The Patronal Title of St Gregory's at Douai', *Downside Review* 87, no. 288 (July, 1969), 278–81.
72 Beales, 176, 180.
73 *CRSP* LXIII, 121, 123, 126, 145, 263.
74 *CRSP* LXIX, 13, 85.
75 *CRSP* LXIII, 269; MS. 27, 110; *Catalogue des écoliers* of the Collège Académique.
76 Maureen Wall, *Catholic Ireland in the Eighteenth Century*, 18–60; Brady and Corish, 'The Church under the Penal Code', 27.
77 Wall, *Catholic Ireland in the Eighteenth Century*, 22–3; James O'Boyle, *The Irish Colleges on the Continent: their Origin and History* (Dublin, 1935), 17–18.
78 For the numbers of priest-students at the different Irish Colleges, see Brady and Corish, 6–8.
79 Patrick Boyle, 'The Irish College at Bordeaux', *Irish Ecclesiastical Record*, ser. 4, 22 (1907), 137; L. O'Murray, 'The Poets and Poetry of Kilkerley', *County Louth Archaeological Society Journal* 4, no. 2 (December 1917), 192.
80 O'Boyle, *Irish Colleges*, 235; Boyle, 'Irish College at Bordeaux', 135; Brady and Corish, 6–8.
81 Another example of this attitude is reflected in the history of St Gregory's school in Douai. In 1781, it was decided by the English Benedictine Congregation that the newly expanded house should also serve as the general novitiate for all boys intended for orders as well as a school for lay students. English and Irish gentry parents, apparently fearing too ecclesiastical an establishment, ceased sending their children there, and it became necessary to admit

foreign, i.e. French, boys. Enrollment in the 1780s, the period when Luke Bellew and his two Taaffe cousins attended the school, reflects this; by 1785, the school had become two-thirds French. Barnes, 83–4.

82 Ms. 27,133.

83 Giblin, 'Irish Exiles', 17; O'Boyle, *Irish Colleges*, 234; Boyle, 'Irish College at Bordeaux', 133.

84 Edward MacLysaght, 'Report on Documents Relating to the Wardenship of Galway', *Analecta Hibernica*, No. 14 (1944), 60, 66–7; Dáire Keogh, *'The French Disease'*: the *Catholic Church and Radicalism in Ireland 1790–1800* (Dublin, 1993), 18.

85 Hayes, s.v. Dillon, Edward, 64.

86 This was Arthur Richard Dillon, son of Lieutenant-Colonel Arthur Dillon, who led Dillon's Regiment to France in 1690. Born in 1721 at St Germain, he entered orders and became, as a result of Louis xv's patronage, bishop of Evreux, then archbishop of Toulouse and later Narbonne, and President of the Estates of Languedoc. Hayes, s.v. Dillon, Arthur Richard, 63–4.

87 MS. 27,133.

88 Although even here, some irritating distinctions were made between Protestants and Catholics. Catholics were excluded from army medical positions and the offices of state physician or surgeon, barred from medical professorships at Trinity and the School of Physick, and denied the rank of Fellow in the College of Physicians. Lecky, iii, 26.

89 Hayes, s.v. Cantwell, Andrew, 26–7; Comyn, Michael, 40; Garvan, Callaghan, 102; and Higgins, John, 125.

90 MS. 27,133.

91 Hayes, s.v. O'Shee, Robert Richard, 261; MS. 27,108.

92 MS. 27,133.

93 This was Francis James Walsh, the son of Philip Walsh, who settled at St Malo in 1685 and made a fortune in shipbuilding, privateering, and the slave trade. Francis also went into business as a shipbuilder at Cadiz and participated in the profitable slave trade. He was created Count Walsh de Serrant by Louis xv in 1754 and after 1763 acted as Prince Charles Edward's representative to the French and Spanish courts. Hayes, s.v. Walsh, Francis James, 307.

94 In 1807, among the six Catholic laymen on the Board of Trustees was Sir Edward Bellew, 6th baronet. *Wilson's Dublin Directory* (1807), 133.

95 G.A. Hayes-McCoy, 'The Red Coat and the Green', *Studies* 37 (1948), 400. From 1762, British regiments on the Irish establishment were permitted to enlist Irish Catholics; it appears Catholic recruits were quietly accepted in some regiments even earlier. However, the offer of several prominent Catholics, Sir Patrick Bellew among them, to raise six Catholic regiments for British service in Portugal in 1762 was rejected. The need for manpower in the war against revolutionary France brought a change in official attitudes, and Catholic Irish enlistments were welcomed. Hayes-McCoy, 400–1; O'Callaghan, 160, 598–9, 608, 630.

96 Hayes, s.v. Dillon, Arthur, 60–1; O'Callaghan, 50–1.

97 Hayes, 261; MS. 27,127.

98 Hayes, 221.

99 MS. 27,127.

100 Commission of Thomas Bellew, gent., as ensign in the 36th Regiment of Foot, 22 April 1842; *Burke's Peerage and Baronetage*, s.v. Bellew, 236–7, Grattan-Bellew, 238; Engraving of 'Tombs on Cathcart's Hill near Sebastopol Crimea erected subsequently to December 3rd 1855' with inscriptions, R.G. Branston, engraver, Dublin: MS. 31,996.

101 MS. 27,112. The school in Staffordshire may have been Sedgley Park, the most important Catholic school in the Midlands. Begun in 1762, it catered to boys of the middle and mercantile classes. Barnes, 102–3.

102	Harris, 'English College, Douai', 91–2.
103	Giblin, 142.
104	O'Boyle, 226; Giblin, 25; Hayes, 64.
105	MS. 27,110.
106	Louvain Papers 1606–1827, ed., Brendan Jennings (*IMC*, Dublin, 1968), 511–12, 515–21, 529–85, 596–605, 614–29.
107	J. Healy, *Maynooth College: its Centenary History* (Dublin, 1895), 657, as cited in Brady and Corish, 48.
108	MS. 27,106.

CHAPTER 4: COMMERCE AND TRADE

1	Discussions of the penal laws' effect on Catholic business and trade can be found in T. Arkins, 'The Commercial Aspect of the Irish Penal Code', *Studies* 1 (June, 1912); Maureen Wall, 'The Catholics of the Towns and the Quarterage Dispute in Eighteenth-Century Ireland', *IHS* 8 (1952) and 'The Rise of a Catholic Middle Class in Eighteenth Century Ireland', *IHS* 11 (1958). Both of Wall's essays have been reprinted in *Catholic Ireland in the Eighteenth Century*, 61–84; references below are to the latter edition. David Dickson provides a re-assessment of Wall's interpretation in 'Catholics and Trade in Eighteenth-Century Ireland: An Old Debate Revisited', in *Endurance and Emergence*, 85–100.
2	*A Great Archbishop of Dublin, William King, D.D.*, ed., C.S. King (London, 1906) as cited in Wall, 76; Arkin, 'The Commercial Aspect of the Penal Code', 266; *Egmont MSS* (London, *HMC*, 1920–23) 1, 356 as cited in Francis G. James, *Ireland in the Empire 1688–1770* (Cambridge, Mass., 1973), 229–30.
3	Dickson, 'Catholics and Trade in Eighteenth-Century Ireland', 87–8.
4	L.M. Cullen, 'The Irish Merchant Communities in Bordeaux, La Rochelle and Cognac in the eighteenth century', in L.M. Cullen and P. Butel, eds., *Négoce et industrie en France et en Irlande aux XVIIIe et XIXe siècles* (Paris, 1980), 53 and 'Merchant Communities Overseas, the Navigation Acts and Irish and Scottish Responses', in L.M. Cullen and T.C. Smout, eds., *Comparative Aspects of Scottish and Irish Economic and Social History 1600–1900* (Edinburgh, 1977), 170–1.
5	This discussion of Galway's trade up to the Cromwellian conquest is based on M.D. O'Sullivan, *Old Galway: The History of a Norman Colony in Ireland* (Cambridge, 1942), 400–14.
6	See also O'Donovan, 25.
7	*Calendar of Carew MSS*, 6, 176; *CSPI* 1611–1614, 475.
8	T.C. Barnard, *Cromwellian Ireland: English government and Reform in Ireland 1649–1660* (Oxford, 1975), 55–7.
9	James Hardiman, *The History of the Town and County of Galway* (Dublin, 1820; rpt. Galway, 1975), 136–9, 167–70.
10	Lecky, i, 346–7, 350; Hardiman, *The History of the Town and County of Galway*, 183–5.
11	Cullen, *Economic History*, 18–19.
12	O'Donovan, 147.
13	L.M. Cullen, *Anglo-Irish Trade 1660–1800* (Manchester, 1968), 14.
14	Raymond Gillespie, 'The Irish Economy at War', *Ireland from Independence to Occupation*, 179–80.
15	Cullen, *Economic History*, 12, 54–6; *Anglo-Irish Trade*, 1819.
16	See Crotty, *Irish Agricultural Production*, 16, Table 1 for the rise in provisions exports between 1665–1758 and 277, Table 65B for average annual exports in the eighteenth century.
17	Cullen, *Anglo-Irish Trade*, 16; O'Donovan, 106; O'Brien, 221.

19 Hardiman, 183 note z.
20 For a masterful overview of what he has not altogether facietiously termed a 'Galway mafia', see L.M. Cullen, 'Galway Merchants in the Outside World, 1650–1800', in Diarmuid O'Cearbhaill, ed., *Galway, Town and Gown, 1484–1984* (Galway, 1984), 63–89, on which this general account is based.
21 Cullen, 'Galway Merchants in the Outside World', 69; Francis G. James, *Ireland in the Empire 1688–1770*, 300; Aubrey Gwynn, ed., 'Documents Relating to the Irish in the West Indies', *Analecta Hibernica* 4 (1932), 146.
22 From *C.O.* 1/42/193–243 as cited in Richard S. Dunn, *Sugar and Slaves: The Rise of the Planter Class in the English West Indies, 1624–1713* (Chapel Hill, 1972), 69, 126–7.
23 Extracts from Martin J. Blake, *Blake Family Records*, 2nd Series (London, 1905) in Gwynn, 273–7.
24 Cyril Hamshere, *The British in the Caribbean* (Cambridge, Mass., 1972), 155.
25 Richard B. Sheridan, *Sugar and Slavery: An Economic History of the British West Indies 1623–1775* (Baltimore, 1973), 175, 180.
26 Richard B. Sheridan, 'The Rise of a Colonial Gentry: A Case Study of Antigua', *Economic History Review*, 2nd series, 13 (1960–61), 348–9, 354–6.
27 Cullen, 'Merchant Communities Overseas', 167.
28 R.B. McDowell, 'Ireland in the 18th Century British Empire', *Historical Studies* 9 (1974), 52.
29 Cullen, 'Merchant Communities Overseas', 171.
30 Richard Pares, *Merchants and Planters*, *Economic History Review* Supplement 4 (Cambridge, 1960), 40.
31 Frank Wesley Pittman, *The Development of the British West Indies 1700–1763* (New Haven, 1917), 358–9; Lowell J. Ragatz, *The Fall of the Planter Class in the British Caribbean 1763–1833* (London, 1928; rpt. New York, 1963), 127.
32 From *C.O.* 10/1 as cited in Noel Deerr, *the History of Sugar* (London, 1949), i, 177. For Dominica's early history, see Nellis M. Crouse, *French Pioneers in the West Indies 1624–1664* (New York, 1940), 4–5, 258; and Richard Pares, *War and Trade in the West Indies 1739–1763* (Oxford, 1936; rpt. London, 1963), 196–7.
33 *Acts of the Privy Council, Colonial Series* 4, 580–609.
34 *Acts of the Privy Council, Colonial Series* 4, 587–9; Thomas Atwood, *The History of the Island of Dominica* (London, 1791; rpt. London, 1971), 3–4.
35 *Journal of the Commissioners for Trade and Plantations*, January 1768–December 1775 13, 274; Ragatz, *The Fall of the Planter Class*, 116.
36 Deerr, *History of Sugar* i, 177.
37 D.L. Niddrie, 'Eighteenth-Century Settlement in the British Caribbean', *Institute of British Geographers*, no. 40 (December, 1966), 80.
38 John Byres, *Plan of the Island of Dominica, References to the Plan of the Island of Dominica* (London, 1776) in the John Carter Brown Library, Providence, R.I. All subsequent references to acreage and land ownership are from Byres unless otherwise noted. Patrick L. Baker, in *Centring the Periphery: Chaos, Order and the Ethnohistory of Dominica* (Montreal, 1994), 63–4, calculates numbers and percentages for landownership and leasing by the French and 'British' (Baker subsumes both Irish and Scots names under that general heading); calculations and statistics for the Irish are my own.
39 R.B. Sheridan, *Sugar and Slavery*, 456–7.
40 Registry of Deeds, Roseau, Dominica; *Acts of the Privy Council, Colonial Series* 5, 281.
41 Sheridan, *Sugar and Slavery*, 456.
42 *The Report of the Commission of the Legislature of Dominica, appointed to enquire into ... the Condition, Treatment, Rights & Privileges of the Negro Population of that island* (London, 1823; rpt. in *West Indian Slavery: Selected Pamphlets*, Westport, Conn., 1970), Pamphlet No. 5, 40.

43 D.L. Niddrie, 'Eighteenth-Century Settlement in the British Caribbean', 76.

44 *Acts of the Privy Council, Colonial Series* 4, 587.

45 Atwood, *History of the Island of Dominica*, 283–4.

46 Scott, 'State of the Island of Dominica 12 July 1765' in *Shelburne Papers* 77: 121, William L. Clements Library, University of Michigan, Ann Arbor.

47 Atwood, 73–4.

48 Ragatz, 129–30.

49 For the history of the maroons in Dominica, see Michael Craton, *Testing the Chains: Resistance to Slavery in the British West Indies* (Ithaca, 1982), 140–5, 224–33.

50 Atwood, 74.

51 Sheridan, *Sugar and Slavery*, 179–80, 464.

52 A 'Michael Barnewall Bellew' is listed as one of the appraisers of Francis Bellew's lands; however, this does not seem to be his eldest brother (in fact, unlike his son, Christopher Dillon Bellew, who is almost always referred to by both first and middle names, there is no middle name given for Michael Bellew in the correspondence or legal documents contained in the family papers). The Michael Barnewall Bellew listed may be one of the younger brothers of Michael Bellew's cousin, Christopher Kelly Bellew. Since the latter sometimes spoke of going to Jamaica and claimed a familiarity with America, it is tempting to speculate that the link might have been his younger brother, who had either been attracted by possibilities in Dominica, like Francis, or been elsewhere in the Indies and available for the appraisal.

53 It is difficult to determine exactly where Francis Bellew died. While the reference to 'aforesaid island' suggests Dominica, his prerogative will, filed 13 February 1769 and proved 27 June 1773, lists him 'of Cork, late of the island of St Christopher'. *Betham's Genealogical Abstracts, Prerogative Wills (Phillips MSS)* 6, 164. Nat. Arch.

54 The appraisal is included in MS. 31,967, which contains surveys of lands around Mount Bellew.

55 As of this writing, the deed books on Dominica which might provide information on whether the lands were sold, written off, or abandoned are inaccessible.

56 *Dominica Letterbook, 1777–1786*: Letters of Charles Winstone, William L. Clements LIbrary, University of Michigan, Ann Arbor.

57 Deerr, 199–202; Sheridan, *Sugar and Slavery*, 492.

58 For financial and political connections, see Sir Lewis Namier and John Brooke, *The History of Parliament: The House of Commons 1754–1790* (New York, 1964), 2, q.v. Colebrooke, 235–7; 3, q.v. MacLeane, 93–4, Stewart, 480–81.

59 The following discussion of the Galway members of the Irish merchant colonies in St Malo, La Rochelle, Nantes and Bordeaux is based upon the exhaustive studies of Richard Hayes, ('Irish Associations with Nantes', *Studies* 28 (1939); 'Irish Links with Bordeaux', *Studies* 27 (1938); *Old Irish Links with France: Some Echoes of Exiled Ireland* (Dublin, 1940); and *Biographical Dictionary of Irishmen in France*) and, more recently, L.M. Cullen ('Galway Merchants in the Outside World' and 'The Irish Merchant Communities of Bordeaux, La Rochelle, and Cognac in the Eighteenth Century').

60 Cullen, 'Galway Merchants in the Outside World', 76.

61 MS. 27,109.

62 Hayes, *Biographical Dictionary*, s.v. O'Quinn, Patrick, 253. The Quins were relatively untypical of Bordeaux merchants in their involvement in colonial trade; L.M. Cullen speculates that this involvement may have derived from their Galway background. They also maintained their sole Irish trading ties with Galway ('Galway Merchants in the Outside World', 87; 'The Irish Merchant Communities of Bordeaux, La Rochelle, and Cognac in the Eighteenth Century', 55, 57).

63 Cullen, 'The Irish Merchant Communities of Bordeaux, La Rochelle, and Cognac in the Eighteenth Century', 60.

64 *Betham's Genealogical Abstracts, Prerogative Wills* (*Phillips MSS*) 6, 116. Luke Bellew died while on a trip to England, presumably on his brandy business. I am indebted to Prof. L.M. Cullen for this information.

65 Richard Hayes, 'Ireland's Links with Compostella', *Studies* 37 (1948), 328.

66 Jean O. McLachlan, *Trade and Peace with Old Spain, 1667–1750: A Study of the Influence of Commerce on Anglo-Spanish Diplomacy in the first half of the Eighteenth Century* (Cambridge, 1940), 6–10.

67 Cullen, 'Merchant Communities Overseas', 170; 'Galway Merchants in the Outside World', 84–5.

68 'Irish Wills from Barcelona', 2nd series, *Irish Genealogist* 6 (1983), 471–2.

69 Around 1740, five-sixths of the manufactures consumed in Spain were supplied by foreign countries, and nine-tenths of Spanish- American trade was in foreign hands. Clarence Henry Haring, *The Spanish Empire in America* (1947; rpt. New York, 1963), 295, n.3. This imbalance in trade with America would not be completely reversed until the end of the eighteenth century. Antonio Garcia-Baquero Gonzalez, *Comercio Colonial y Guerras Revolucionarias: La decadencia económica de Cádiz a raiz de la emancipación americana* (Seville, 1976), 59.

70 Antonio Garcia-Baquero Gonzales, *Comercio Colonial*, 48–9; *Cádiz y el Atlántico (1717– 1778: El Comercio colonial español bajo el monopolio gaditano* (Seville, 1976) 1, 482; Clarence Henry Haring, *Trade and Navigation between Spain and the Indies in the Time of the Hapsburgs* (Cambridge, Mass., 1918), 111–12.

71 Haring, *Trade and Navigation Between Spain and the Indies*, 108–9; Garcia-Baquero, *Cádiz y el Atlántico* 1, 199–232, *Commercio Colonial*, 98.

72 Jaime Vicens-Vives, *An Economic History of Spain*, trans. by Frances M. López-Morillas (Princeton, 1969), 487–8.

73 Garcia-Baquero, *Cádiz y el Atlántico* 1, 489, 491–4.

74 Richard Hayes, 'An Unpubished Franco-Irish MSS', *Studies* 28 (1939), 480–2.

75 W.H. Hargreaves-Mawdsley, *Eighteenth-Century Spain 1700–1788: A Political, Diplomatic, and Institutional History* (1979; rpt. Totowa, N.H., 1979), 93, 100, 124.

76 McLachlan, *Trade and Peace with Old Spain*, 25, 212–13 n. 121; Garcia-Baquero, *Cádiz y el Atlántico* 1, 404–5, 427 n. 59, 428, 432 n. 69.

77 Marquess MacSwiney of Mashanglass, 'Two Distinguished Irishmen in the Spanish Service: Sir Toby Burke and Dr. John Higgins', *Studies* 28 (1939), 77.

78 McLachlan, 140–41, 212–14 n. 121.

79 Garcia-Baquero, *Cádiz y el Atlántico* 1, 492–3, 495 (Garcia-Baquero does not distinguish between England and Irish merchants); Cullen, 'Merchant Communities', 169.

80 Julian Walton, 'Census Records of the Irish in Eighteenth-Century Cadiz', *Irish Genealogist* 6 (1985), 748–56.

81 Major William Dalrymple, *Travels through Spain and Portugal in 1774, with a short account of the Spanish Expedition against Algiers in 1775* (London, 1777), iii, 12, 170.

82 *Spanish Knights of Irish Origin*, i, 114–16. Correspondence cited concerning the house of Lynch and Bellew is in MSS. 27,140; 27,143; 27,148; 27,133; 27,139.

83 Cullen, *Anglo-Irish Trade*, 19; Garcia-Baquero, *Comercio Colonial*, 58; Cullen, *Economic History*, 58.

84 The conversion of the Spanish dollar/peso to the English pound is based on the eighteenth-century equations of 1 Spanish dollar=20 *reales de vellon*, and £1=100 *reales de vellon*. (Richard Herr, *The Eighteenth-Century Revolution in Spain* (Princeton, 1958), 147 n. 3; Dalrymple, *Travels Through Spain*, 20). Thus, 1 Spanish dollar/peso=1/5 England pound. (This, incidentally, agrees with Dalrymple's estimate that 1 Spanish dollar was the rough equivalent of 4*s.*6*d.*)

  The noting of denominations in the Bellew correspondence concerning the assets of the House of Lynch and Bellew and of Patrick Bellew himself ranges from English and Irish pounds to Spanish dollars/pesos and *reales*, and it is sometimes difficult to determine – or decipher – which is being used.

85 Economic historians have commonly asserted that free trade brought no appreciable diminition of Cadiz's trade with the New World (Vicens-Vives, 579–80; Juan Plaza Prieto, *Estructura económica de España en el siglo XVIII* (Madrid, 1975), 443–7). However, gaps in trade statistics, particularly from Cadiz, and difficulties in assessing the relative impact on the regional Spanish economies and on trade as opposed to industry may modify this interpretation somewhat. See John Fisher, 'Imperial "Free Trade" and the Hispanic Economy, 1778–1796', *Journal of Latin American Studies* 13 (1981), 21–48.

86 Herr, *The Eighteenth-Century Revolution in Spain*, 98, 380; Garcia-Baquero, *Comercio Colonial*, 50, 99.

87 MS. 27,133; J. Mannion, 'The Waterford Merchants and the Irish-Newfoundland Provisions Trade, 1770–1820', in *Négoce et industrie en France et en Irlande aux XVIIe et XIXe siècles*, 27, 39; O'Brien, *Economic History*, 169–71; McDowell, 'Ireland in the 18th-century British Empire', 52.

88 MS. 27,138.

89 This discussion of Irish flaxseed trade with the American colonies is based on F. G. James, 'Irish Colonial Trade in the 18th Century', *William and Mary Quarterly*, 3rd series, 20 (1963), 581–3; T.M. Truxes, 'Connecticut in the Irish-American Flaxseed Trade, 1750–1775', *Eire-Ireland* 12 (1977), 34–62; Virginia D. Harrington, *The New York Merch-ants on the Eve of the Revolution* (New York, 1936), 166, 174–5; Arthur L. Jensen, *The Maritime Commerce of Colonial Philadelphia* (Madison, Wisc., 1963), 85–6; P.L. White, *The Beekmans of New York in Politics and Commerce 1647–1877* (New York, 1956), 235–64.

90 Cullen, *Economic History*, 61–2. The role of Galway landlords, including the Bellews, in the linen industry in Connacht is discussed in Chapter 2.

91 *Young's Tour in Ireland* i, 277; MS. 27,106.

92 Correspondence concerning Patrick Bellew's flour trade is in MSS. 27,133 and 27,138.

93 MS. 27,130.

94 The following general discussion of the growth and development of flour milling in this period is based upon L.M. Cullen, 'Eighteenth Century Flour Milling in Ireland', *Irish Economic and Social History* 4 (1977); *Economic History*, 92–5.

95 MSS. 27,108 and 27,115.

96 The building containing the works referred to, whether a building already on the estate or erected in 1776, has been recently torn down. Fortunately, the plaque has been preserved and set in a stone in Bellew Park in the town of Mount Bellew.

97 Wall, *Catholic Ireland in the Eighteenth Century*, 79; Cullen, 'Galway Merchants Overseas', 77–8.

98 MS. 27,109.

99 Correspondence from Christopher Bellew to Christopher Dillon Bellew concerning flour milling is in MSS. 27,109 and 27,145.

100 Correspondence from 1789–92 between Michael Bellew and Bartholomew Costello and the Lynches concerning the settlement of Patrick Bellew's Spanish estate is in MSS. 27,140, 27,148, and 27,143.

101 His voluminous correspondence with Michael Bellew and Christopher Dillon Bellew concerning business and other matters is in MSS. 27,109, 27,130, 27,139, and 27,145

102 This discussion of the Irish provisions trade in the last half of the eighteenth century is based on Cullen, *Anglo-Irish Trade*, 18–20, 28, 47, 71, 91–8; *Economic History*, 58–9, 103; Crotty, *Irish Agricultural Production*, 17–18; O'Donovan, *Economic History of Livestock*, 109–10.

103 See Crotty, 21, Table 4 for the rise in prices of Irish farm produce from the third quarter of the eighteenth century through the war period.

104 The following discussion of Irish banking facilities, including the discounting of bills and

the commercial crisis of 1796–97 is based, unless otherwise noted, upon Cullen, *Economic History*, 73, 95; *Anglo-Irish Trade*, 98–9, 173, 179–81, 201.

105 As cited in Constantia Maxwell, *Dublin under the Georges, 1714–1830*, 3rd ed. (1936; rpt. London, 1956), 278.

106 In 1795, the unofficial Change of Dublin, where wholesale bills were purchased, was in Crampton Court near Dublin Castle; bills on London were purchased at the Royal Exchange. Maxwell, *Dublin Under the Georges*, 283.

107 The enterprises of Thomas Wyse of Waterford in hardware manufacturing and Myles Keon of Keonbrook in the Dublin wine business were both failures. Wall, 79.

108 M.D.R. Leys, *Catholics in England 1559–1829: A Social History* (New York, 1961), 183–4, 201. For the seventeenth-century coal mining operation of Sir Basil Brooke of Madeley and Sir John Winter in the Forest of Dean, and the timber imports of the Lancashire families of Chaloner, Speke, and Gerstang, see 172–4.

109 MS. 27,108.

CHAPTER 5: THE GENTRY AND CATHOLIC RELIEF

1 J.G. Simms, 'Irish Catholics and the Parliamentary Franchise, 1692–1728', *IHS* 12 (1960–61), 28–37.

2 Hugh Boulter, *Letters* (Oxford, 1759) i, 188 as cited in Francis Godwin James, *Ireland in the Empire, 1688–1770* (Cambridge, Mass., 1973), 231.

3 Oliver J. Burke, *Anecdotes of the Connaught Circuit* (Dublin, 1885), 161; R.W. Linker, 'The English Roman Catholics and Emancipation: The Politics of Persuasion', *Journal of Ecclesiastical History* 27 (1976), 158.

4 Colum Kenny, 'The Exclusion of Catholics From the Legal Profession in Ireland, 1537–1829', *IHS* 25 (1987), 353–4.

5 MS. 27,108.

6 Cronin, *A Galway Gentleman in the Age of Improvement*, 48.

7 These may be traced in detail in Bartlett, *The Fall and Rise of the Irish Nation*, Chapters 4, 6–9 and the chapters contributed by R.B. McDowell to *NHI*, iv.

8 For a recent study, see C.D.A. Leighton, *Catholicism in a Protestant Kingdom: A Study of the Irish Ancien Regime* (Dublin, 1994).

9 Eamon O'Flaherty, 'The Catholic Convention and Anglo-Irish Politics', *Arch.Hib.* 40 (1985), 14–15.

10 MS. 27,108.

11 Thomas Wyse, *Historical Sketch of the Late Catholic Association of Ireland* (London, 1829), i, 83; Matthew O'Conor, *The History of the Irish Catholics from the Settlement in 1691, with a View of the State of Ireland from the Invasion by Henry II to the Revolution* (Dublin, 1813), i, 282.

12 For a more detailed account of the opposition to the proposal, see Wall, *Catholic Ireland in the Eighteenth Century*, 119.

13 For an account of O'Conor's entanglements in the penal laws and his difficulties in maintaining his lands in Roscommon, see Chapter 2.

14 Bartlett, *The Fall and Rise of the Irish Nation*,63; Patrick Fagan, *Divided Loyalties: The Question of the Oath for Irish Catholics in the Eighteenth Century* (Dublin, 1997), 126. See Fagan, *passim*, for an analysis of the knotty question of – and the divisions occasioned by – oaths and addresses of loyalty for Catholics.

15 *The Letters of Charles O'Conor of Belanagare*, ed. Catherine Coogan Ward and Robert E. Ward (Ann Arbor, Mich., 1980), i, 89.

16 The manuscript containing the minutes of the proceedings of the Catholic Committee from 1772 to August of 1792 has been edited. See 'The Minute Book of the Catholic Committee,

1773–92', ed. R. Dudley Edwards, *Arch.Hib.* 9 (1942), 1–172, hereafter cited as 'Minute Book'. A useful account of Catholic Committee activities based in part on the minute book is Maureen MacGeehin Wall's unpublished M.A. thesis 'The Activities and Personnel of the General Committee of the Catholics of Ireland, 1767–1784', University College Dublin, 1952.

17 For the role of the Committee in the fight against the imposition of quarterage, see Wall, *Catholic Ireland in the Eighteenth Century*, 61–72.
18 *Letters of Charles O'Conor*, i, 151–2; Bartlett, 356, n. 96.
19 Under its provisions, Catholics were permitted to take a 61-year lease of 50 acres of bog with a one-half acre of arable land adjoining if they reclaimed the land within 21 years.
20 Wall, 'The Activities and Personnel of the General Committee', 106–9.
21 'Minute Book', 31.
22 John Curry, *An Historical and Critical Review of the Civil Wars in Ireland* (Dublin, 1786), ii, 287–93.
23 Ibid.
24 Bartlett, 84.
25 'Minute Book', 32–3.
26 Nat. Arch. Index to Catholic Qualification Rolls, 1778–1790.
27 'Minute Book', 42–3, 45.
28 Wall, *Catholic Ireland in the Eighteenth Century*, 136–7.
29 The lord indeed 'could be had for money'. Viscount Strangford in 1782 offered one of the contestants in an estate case his vote for £200 (the Irish Lords then had appellate jurisdiction). Strangford was subsequently debarred from sitting in parliament, making a proxy, or sitting and voting on a trial of a peer. Edith M. Johnston, *Great Britain and Ireland 1760–1800: A Study in Political Administration* (Edinburgh, 1963), 266.
30 'Minute Book', 70.
31 T. Bartlett, ed., *Maccartney in Ireland, 1768–72* (Belfast, 1979), 330; Sydney to Rutland, 28 September 1784, Sydney MSS, NLI, as cited in Wall, 'The Activities and Personnel of the General Committee', 162, n. 1.
32 Patrick Rogers, *The Irish Volunteers and Catholic Emancipation* (London, 1934), 115–21; Lecky, ii, 359–62. For full-length studies of the earl-bishop, see J.R. Walsh, *Frederick Hervey, Fourth Earl of Bristol and Bishop of Derry* (Maynooth, 1972) and W. Childe-Pemberton, *The Earl-Bishop: the Life of Frederick Hervey, Bishop of Derry and Earl of Bristol* (London, 1924).
33 As cited in Rogers, *The Irish Volunteers and Catholic Emancipation*, 70.
34 Rogers, 75.
35 Wall, *Catholic Ireland in the Eighteenth Century*, 149.
36 James Kelly, 'The Parliamentary Reform Movement of the 1780s and the Catholic Question', *Arch.Hib.* 43 (1988), 98–9, 106.
37 For accounts of the Grand National Convention, see Rogers, 99–133; Lecky, ii, 364–73.
38 Kelly, 'The Parliamentary Reform Movement', 100–1.
39 'Minute Book', 86–7.
40 Lecky, ii, 403–4.
41 HMC. *Charlemont MSS*, i, 125.
42 'Minute Book', 87–8.
43 As cited in Rogers, 123.
44 Wall, 'Activities and Personnel of the General Committee', 167.
45 Ibid., 176; Rogers, 151.
46 P.R.O. 30/8/328 as cited in R.B. McDowell, *Ireland in the Age of Imperialism and Revolution 1760–1801* (Oxford, 1979), 317.
47 HMC. *Rutland MSS*, iii, 140–2.
48 Kelly, 108–10.

49 Wall, *Catholic Ireland in the Eighteenth Century*, 150.
50 'Minute Book', 92–3; Wall, *Catholic Ireland in the Eighteenth Century*, 156; Kelly, 112–13.
51 Wall, 'The Activities and Personnel of the General Committee', 190.
52 'Minute Book', 110–11.
53 *King's Inn Admission Papers 1607–1867*, ed. E. Keane, P.B. Phair, T.U. Sadleir (*IMC*: Dublin, 1982), 31.
54 MS. 27,127.
55 Subsequent correspondence cited from Christopher Kelly Bellew to Michael Bellew from 1790–1794 is in MS. 27,135.
56 References to Christopher Kelly Bellew's service to the Catholic Committee and accounts of Committee meetings from January 20, 1790 to March 1, 1791 in which he participated are in 'Minute Book', 113–16.
57 For the account of the meeting presented by the delegation to the Catholic Committee, see 'Minute Book', 126–9.
58 HMC. *Fortescue MSS*, ii, 39.
59 'Minute Book', 151.
60 Kenmare to Hobart, 15 March 1791, H.O. 100/33, #237.
61 Westmorland to Dundas, 26 July 1791 as cited in Lecky, iii, 10.
62 Rogers, 226–7.
63 *The Drennan Letters 1776–1819*, ed. D.A. Chart (Belfast, 1931), 61.
64 Edward Cooke to Hobart, 5 December 1791, H.O. 100/33 as cited in Albert J. Hamilton, 'The Movement for Irish Roman Catholic Relief, 1790–1793'. Ph.D. Dissertation, University of Notre Dame 1967, 116.
65 *King's Inn Admission Papers*, 31. In June of 1791, he boasted to his cousin Michael Bellew that 'I shall be the first Catholic called to this Bar since the first institution of the penal laws'.
66 *The Drennan Letters*, 71.
67 The proceedings of the Catholic Committee meeting can be reconstructed from 'Minute Book', 140–2; Sir Hercules Langrish to Westmorland, 19 December 1791, Langrishe to Hobart, 20 December 1791, H.O. 100/34 as cited in Hamilton, 'The Movement for Irish Roman Catholic Relief', 120–4.
68 Francis Plowden, *An Historical Review of the State of Ireland* (Philadelphia, 1806), iv, Appendix, no. LXXXVI.
69 'Minute Book', 144–8.
70 For a full account of the tortuous negotiations – and mutual frustration – between the British cabinet and the Irish government, see Bartlett, 121–45.
71 He did so in 1792, along with William Bellew, son of Sir Patrick. *King's Inn Admission Papers*, 31–2.
72 Westmorland to Lord Melville, 2 May 1792. Westmorland MSS, NLI.
73 *Correspondence of Edmund Burke*, ed. Thomas W. Copeland (Cambridge, 1958–78), vii (1792–94), 9–10.
74 'Minute Book', 166–7.
75 For Tone's career as Catholic agent, see Marianne Elliott, *Wolfe Tone: Prophet of Irish Independence* (New Haven, Conn., 1989), Chapters 11–15.
76 R.B. McDowell, *Ireland in the Age of Imperialism and Revolution*, 397.
77 *Memoirs of Theobald Wolfe Tone*, ed. William T.W. Tone (London, 1827), ii, Appendix, 410–15.
78 Keogh, *'The French Disease': The Catholic Church and Radicalism in Ireland 1790–1800*, 60.
79 'Minute Book', 160–1.
80 *Life of Theobald Wolfe Tone*, ed. William T.W. Tone (Washington, D.C., 1826), i, 457.

81 Christopher Bellew's correspondence with his cousin Christopher Dillon Bellew from 1792 is in MSS. 27,145 and 27,144. William Drennan commented to his brother-in-law Samuel McTier that 'a Dr. Ryan made a most elegant harangue indeed'. *Drennan Letters*, 94.

82 The following account of the Convention and Christopher Dillon Bellew's role in it is based on *Life of Theobald Wolfe Tone*, i, 224; *Memoirs of Theobald Wolfe Tone*, i, 110–12. Tone's notes, summaries of speeches, and memoranda taken during the sitting of the Convention are generally reliable as to events and language; his comments about personalities should be assessed with care.

83 O'Flaherty, 'The Catholic Convention', 28–9.

84 *Correspondence of Edmund Burke*, vii, 64.

85 *Drennan Letters*, 106–7.

86 Elliott, *Wolfe Tone*, 174, 196.

87 *Drennan Letters*, 70–1.

88 Hobart to Evan Nepean, 13 January 1793, H.O. 100/42, #111–12.

89 As cited in Lecky, iii, 132.

90 *Parliamentary Debates*, xiii, 203–19, 273–5, 278, 327–8 as cited in Lecky, iii, 147, 161, 163–9.

91 *Life of Wolfe Tone*, i, 267, Appendix, 428; *Memoirs of Wolfe Tone*, i, Appendix, 428.

92 For a view of the English Catholics' participation in the movement for emancipation (which reflected much of the same conservative-activist split), see R.W. Linker, 'The English Catholics and Emancipation: The Politics of Persuasion', *Journal of Ecclesiastical History* 27 (1976), 151–80.

EPILOGUE

1 MS. 27,126.

2 MS. 27,106.

3 Kevin Whelan, 'The Regional Impact of Catholicism', in William J. Smyth, Kevin Whelan, eds., *Common Ground: Essays on the Historical Geography of Ireland* (Cork, 1988), 272–3.

4 MS. 27,227. This occasioned some friction with the local priest, as the monks complained of the neglect of the religious education of the local children. According to their reports, one girl was unable to answer a question about how many gods there were, and many children were unable to make the sign of the cross.

5 MS. 27,104.

6 MS. 27,127.

7 See, for example, MS. 31,926.

Bibliography

PRIMARY SOURCES: MANUSCRIPTS

National Library of Ireland, Dublin
    Bellew of Mount Bellew papers
    Westmorland MSS

National Archives, Dublin
    Index to Catholic Qualification Rolls, 1778–90
    Lodge MSS. Transcripts of Convert Rolls
    Philips MSS. Betham's Genealogical Abstracts
    Thrift Abstracts of Prerogative Wills, 1457–2300

Registry of Deeds, Dublin
    Deedbooks for 1768–84; 1786–93

Genealogical Office, Dublin
    MSS 3; 178; 179

Public Record Office, London
    Home Office Records, H.O. 100

John Carter Brown Library, Providence, R.I.
    Plan of the Island of Dominica

William L. Clements Library, University of Michigan, Ann Arbor
    Shelburne Papers
    Dominica Letterbook, 1777–1786

PRIMARY SOURCES: PRINTED

1. *Record Publications*

Calendar of State Papers, Ireland, 1603-1670, 13 vols, 1870–1910.
Journal of the Commissioners for Trade and Plantations, 1704–1782, 14 vols, 1920–1938.
Acts of the Privy Council of England, Colonial Series, 6 vols, 1908–12.

2. *Publications of the Irish Manuscripts Commission*

Analecta Hibernica
    i   (Report on MSS in the Bodleian Library, Rawl. MSS), 1930
    iv   (Documents Relating to the Irish in the West Indies), 1932
    xiv   (Report on Documents Relating to the Wardenship of Galway), 1944
    xxii   (Irish Jacobites: Lists from TCD MS. N.1.3.), 1960
Books of Survey and Distribution, i, county of Roscommon; ii, county of Mayo, iii, county
    of Galway, ed.,, R.C. Simington, 1949–62.
The Convert Rolls, ed., Eileen O'Byrne, 1981.
Dowdall Deeds, eds McNeill, C. and Otway-Ruthven, A.J., 1960.
King's Inn Admission Papers 1607–1867, ed., E. Keane *et al.*, 1982.
Louvain Papers, 1606–1827, ed., Brendan Jennings, 1968.
Spanish Knights of Irish Origin, i, ed., Micheline Walsh, 1960.
Transplantation to Connacht, 1654–58, ed., R.C. Simington, 1970.

3. *Publications of the Historical Manuscripts Commission*

Charlemont MSS., v. 1–2, 1891–1894.
Fortescue MSS., v. 1–10, 1892–1927.
Ormonde MSS., ser. 36, v. 1–2, 1895–1899.
Ormonde MSS., ser. 36, n.s., v. 1–8, 1902–1920.
Rutland MSS., ser. 24, v. 1–4, 1888–1905.

4. *Other Documentary Material*

Ainsworth reports on MSS in private custody:
    Dillon papers (No. 4); Mahon papers (No. 47), National Library of Ireland.
Archivium Hibernicum, ix. (Minute Book of the Catholic Committee, 1773–92), 1942.
Catholic Record Society
    xxviii (The Douay College Diaries: The Seventh Diary, 1715–1778), 1928;
    lxiii   (Douay College Documents 1639–1794), 1972;
    lxix   (St. Omers and Bruges Colleges 1593–1773: A Biographical Dic-
           tionary), 1979.
Fifteenth Report from the Commissioners ... respecting the Public Records of Ireland (1825).
Firth, C.H. and Rait, R.S., *Acts and Ordinances of the Interregnum, 1642–1660*, 3 vols,
    London, 1911.
Gilbert, J.T., *History of the Irish Confederation and the War in Ireland (1641–9)*, 7 vols,
    Dublin, 1882–91.

5. *Pamphlets, Correspondence, and Other Contemporary Writings*

Address to the Roman Catholics of Ireland, Theobald McKenna, Dublin, 1792.
Arthur Young's Tour in Ireland (1776–1779), ed., Arthur Wollaston Hutton, 2 vols, London,
    1892.
Atwood, Thomas, *The History of the Island of Dominica*. London, 1791; rpt. London, 1971.
Boulter, Hugh, *Letters ...*, 2 vols, Oxford, 1769–70.
Brewer, James Norris, *The Beauties of Ireland*, 2 vols, London, 1826.
Carr, John, *The Stranger in Ireland*. London, 1806.
Carte, T., *The Life of James, Duke of Ormond*, 6 vols, Oxford, 1851.
Correspondence of Edmund Burke, ed., Thomas W. Copeland, 10 vols, Cambridge, 1858–1978.

Cumberland, Richard, *Memoirs of Richard Cumberland*, 2 vols, London, 1807.

Curry, John, *An Historical and Critical Review of the Civil Wars in Ireland*, 2 vols, Dublin, 1786.

Dalrymple, Major William, *Travels through Spain and Portugal in 1774 ...* London, 1777.

The Drennan Letters 1776–1819, ed., D.A. Chart, Belfast, 1931.

Dutton, Hely, *A Statistical and Agricultural Survey of the County of Galway*. Dublin, 1824.

The Earl of Castlehaven's Memoirs of the Irish Wars, 1684; rpt. Delmar, N.Y., 1974.

Hardiman, James, *The History of the Town and County of Galway*. Dublin, 1820; rpt. Galway, 1975.

The Ireland of Sir Jonah Barrington: Selections from his Personal Sketches, ed., Hugh B. Staples, London, 1967.

The Journal of John Wesley, ed., Nehemiah Curnock, 8 vols, New York, 1909–1916.

Journal of Sir Simonds D'Ewes, ed., Wallace Notestein, New Haven, 1923.

The Letters of Charles O'Conor of Belanagare, ed., Catherine Coogan Ward and Robert E. Ward, 2 vols, Ann Arbor, Michigan, 1980.

Life of Theobald Wolfe Tone, ed., William Theobald Wolfe Tone, 2 vols, Washington, D.C., 1826.

Maccartney in Ireland, 1768–72, ed., T. Bartlett, Belfast, 1979.

MacNeven, W.J., *Pieces of Irish History ...*, New York, 1800.

Maxwell, William Hamilton, *Wild Sports of the West*, London, 1832.

Memoirs of the Political and Private Life of James Caulfield, Earl of Charlemont, Francis Hardy, London, 1810.

Neale, J.P., *Views of the Seats of Noblemen and Gentlemen in England, Wales, Scotland, and Ireland*, 6 vols, London, 1820.

O'Conor, Matthew, *The History of the Irish Catholics*, Dublin, 1813.

Parnell, Sir Henry, *A History of the Penal Laws against the Irish Catholics*, 4th ed., London, 1825.

Plowden, Francis, *Historical Review of the State of Ireland ...*, 4 vols, Philadelphia, 1806.

Proceedings at the Catholic Meeting of Dublin, Dublin, 1792.

Proceedings of the General Committee of the Catholics of Ireland, Dublin, 1793.

A Report from the Lords Commissioners...into the Present State of Popery in this Kingdom ... within the Counties of Mayo and Galway ..., Dublin, 1731.

The Recollections of Skeffington Gibbon, from 1796 to the Present Year 1829 ..., Dublin, 1829.

Temple, Sir John, *The Irish Rebellion ...*, London, 1646.

Transactions of the General Committee of the Roman Catholics of Ireland during the Year 1791, Dublin, 1792.

Vindication of the Cause of the Catholics of Ireland, Dublin, 1793.

Wakefield, Edward, *An Account of Ireland, Statistical and Political*, 2 vols, London, 1812.

Wyse, Thomas, *Historical Sketch of the Late Catholic Association of Ireland*, 2 vols, London, 1829.

SECONDARY SOURCES

Aalen, F.H.A., *Man and the Landscape in Ireland*, New York, 1978.

Arkins, T., 'The Commercial Aspect of the Irish Penal Code', *Studies* 1 (1912), 257–73.

Auchmuty, James J., *Irish Education: A Historical Survey*, Dublin, 1937.

Bagwell, Richard, *Ireland under the Stuarts and during the Interregnum*, 3 vols, London, 1909.

Baker, Patrick L., *Centring the Periphery: Chaos, Order and the Ethnohistory of Dominica*, Montreal, 1994.

Barnard, T.C., *Cromwellian Ireland: English Government and Reform in Ireland 1649–1660*, Oxford, 1975.

——. 'The Worlds of a Galway Squire: Robert French of Monivea' in Gerard Moran, ed., *Galway: History and Society* Dublin, 1996, 271–96.

Barnes, A.S., *The Catholic Schools of England*, London, 1926.

Bartlett, Thomas, *The Fall and Rise of the Irish Nation: The Catholic Question 1690–1830*, Dublin, 1992.

Beales, A.C.F., *Education under Penalty: English Catholic Education from the Reformation to the Fall of James II, 1547–1689*, London, 1963.

Beckett, J.C., *A Short History of Ireland*, 5th ed., London, 1973.

Bellew, Hon. Mrs. Gerald, 'John Bellew of Willistown, County Louth and Clonoran, County Galway, 1606-1679', *Journal of the County Louth Archaeological Society* 6 (1928), 229–37.

——. 'Some Notes on the Family of Bellew of Thomastown, County Louth', *Journal of the County Louth Archaeological Society* 5 (1923), 193–7.

Bernard, Paul P., *Joseph II and Bavaria: Two Eighteenth-Century Attempts at Unification*, The Hague, 1965.

Blake, Martin J., 'The Families of Daly of Galway with Tabular Pedigrees', *Journal of the Galway Archaeological and Historical Society* 13 (1927), 140.

Bossy, John, 'The Counter-Reformation and the People of Catholic Ireland, 1596–1641', *Historical Studies* 8 (1971), 153–70.

Bottigheimer, Karl S., *English Money and Irish Land: The 'Adventurers' in the Cromwellian Settlement of Ireland*, Oxford, 1971.

——. 'The Restoration Land Settlement: A Structural View', *Irish Historical Studies* 18 (1972), 1–21.

Boyle, Rev. Patrick, 'The Irish College at Bordeaux', *Irish Ecclesiastical Record* 22 (1907), 127–45.

Brady, John and Corish, Patrick J., *The Church under the Penal Code* in *A History of Irish Catholicism*, v, iv, ed., P.J. Corish, Dublin, 1971.

de Burgh, U.H. Hussey, *Landowners of Ireland*, Dublin, 1878.

Burke, Oliver J., *Anecdotes of the Connaught Circuit*, Dublin, 1885.

Burke, W.P., *Irish Priests in Penal Times 1660–1760*, Waterford, 1914.

Burke's Guide to County Houses, vol. I – Ireland, ed., Mark Bence-Jones. London, 1978.

Burns, Sir Alan, *History of the British West Indies*, London, 1954.

Burns, Robert E., 'The Irish Penal Code and Some of its Historians', *Review of Politics* 21 (1959), 276–99.

Canny, Nicholas, *The Formation of the Old English Elite in Ireland*, Dublin, 1975.

Cavenagh, Lt.Col., 'Irish Colonel Proprietors of Imperial Regiments', *Journal of the Royal Society of Antiquaries of Ireland* 57 (1927), 117–26.

Clark, Samuel and Donnelly, James S. Jr., ed., *Irish Peasants: Violence and Political Unrest, 1780–1914*, Madison, Wisc., 1983.

Clarke, Aidan, *The Old English in Ireland, 1625–1642*, Ithaca, N.Y., 1966.

——. 'The Breakdown of Authority 1640–41' in *A New History of Ireland*, ed., T.W. Moody *et al.*, Oxford, 1976. iii, 270–88.

Cole, Richard C., 'Private Libraries in Eighteenth-Century Ireland', *Library Quarterly* 44 (1974), 231–47.

Coonan, Thomas L., *The Irish Catholic Confederacy and the Puritan Revolution*, New York, 1954.

Connolly, S.J., 'Religion and History', *Irish Economic and Social History* 10 (1979), 66–80.

——. *Religion, Law and Power: the Making of Protestant Ireland, 1660–1760*, Oxford, 1992.

Corish, Patrick J., 'Ormond, Rinuccini, and the Confederates' and 'The Cromwellian Conquest, 1649-53' in *A New History of Ireland*, ed., T.W. Moody *et al.* Oxford, 1976, iii, 317–35; 336–52.

Cronin, Denis A., *A Galway Gentleman in the Age of Improvement: Robert French of Monivea, 1716–79*, Dublin, 1995.

Crotty, Raymond D., *Irish Agricultural Production: its Volume and Structure*, Cork, 1966.

Crouse, Nellis M., *French Pioneers in the West Indies, 1624–1664*, New York, 1940.

——. *The French Struggle for the West Indies, 1665–1713*, New York, 1943.

Cullen, L.M., *Anglo-Irish Trade 1660–1800*, Manchester, 1968.

——. 'Catholics Under the Penal Laws', *Eighteenth Century Ireland* 1 (1986), 23–36.

——. *An Economic History of Ireland since 1660*, London, 1972.

——. 'Eighteenth-Century Flour Milling in Ireland', *Irish Economic and Social History* 4 (1977), 5–25.

——. *The Emergence of Modern Ireland, 1600–1900*, London, 1981.

——. 'Galway Merchants in the Outside World' in Diarmuid O'Cearbhaill, ed., *Galway, Town and Gown, 1484–1984*, Galway, 1984, 63–89.

——. 'The Irish Merchant Communities of Bordeaux, La Rochelle, and Cognac in the Eighteenth Century' in L.M. Cullen and Paul Butel, eds, *Négoce et industrie en France et en Irlande aux XVIII ᵉ et XIX ᵉ Siecles* Paris, 1980, 51–64.

——. 'Merchant Communities Overseas, the Navigation Acts and Irish and Scottish Responses' in L.M. Cullen and T.C. Smout, eds, *Comparative Aspects of Scottish and Irish Social History 1600–1900* Edinburgh, 1977, 165–76.

Curtin, Nancy J., '"Varieties of Irishness": Historical Revisionism, Irish Style', *Journal of British Studies* 35 (1996), 195–219.

D'Alton, John, *Historical and Genealogical Illustrations of King James' Irish Army List 1689*, 2nd ed., Dublin, 1860.

Deerr, Noel, *The History of Sugar*, 2 vols, London, 1949.

Dickson, David. 'Catholics and Trade in Eighteenth-century Ireland: An Old Debate Revisited' in T. Power and K.Whelan, eds, *Endurance and Emergence: Catholics in Ireland in the Eighteenth Century*, Dublin, 1990, 185–200.

——. 'Middlemen' in T. Bartlett and D. Hayton, eds, *Penal Era and Golden Age: Essays in Irish History, 1690–1800*, Belfast, 1979, 162–85.

Dillon, Gerald, 'The Dillon Peerages', *The Irish Geneologist* 3 (1958), 98–100.

Donnelly, James J. Jr. 'The Rightboy Movement, 1785–88', *Studia Hibernica* 17–18 (1977–78), 120–202.

Duffy, Christopher. *The Army of Maria Theresa: The Armed Forces of Imperial Austria, 1740–1780.* New York, 1977.

——. *The Wild Goose and the Eagle: A Life of Marshal von Browne, 1705–1757*, London, 1964.

Dunn, Richard S., *Sugar and Slaves: The Rise of the Planter Class in the English West Indies, 1624–1713*, Chapel Hill, N.C., 1972.

Elliott, Marianne, *Wolfe Tone: Prophet of Irish Independence*, New Haven, Conn., 1989.

Ellis, Peter B., *The Boyne Water: The Battle of the Boyne, 1690*, New York, 1976.

Fagan, Patrick, *Divided Loyalties: The Question of the Oath for Irish Catholics in the Eighteenth Century*, Dublin, 1997.

Finegan, Francis, 'The Irish Catholic "Convert Rolls"', *Studies* 38 (1949), 73–82.

Fisher, John, 'Imperial "Free Trade" and the Hispanic Economy, 1778–1796', *Journal of Latin American Studies* 13 (1981), 21–56.

Foster, R.F., *Modern Ireland 1600–1972*, London, 1988.

Froude, James Anthony, *The English in Ireland in the Eighteenth Century*, 3 vols, London, 1881.

García-Baquero González, Antonio, *Comercio Colonial y Guerras Revolucionarias: La decadencia económica de Cádiz a raiz de la emancipacion americano*, Seville, 1972.

——. *Cádiz y el Atlántico (1717–1778): El comercio colonial español bajo el monopolio gaditano*, Seville, 1976.

Gardiner, S.R. 'The Transplantation to Connaught', *English Historical Studies* 14 (1899), 700–34.

Giblin, Cathaldus. *Irish Exiles in Catholic Europe* in *A History of Irish Catholicism*, v, iv, ed., P.J. Corish, Dublin, 1971.

Gillespie, Raymond, 'The Irish Economy at War' in Jane Ohlmeyer, ed., *Ireland from Independence to Occupation* Cambridge, 1995, 160–80.

Graham, B.J. and Proudfoot, L.J., *An Historical Geography of Ireland*, London, 1993.

Hamilton, Albert J., 'The Movement for Irish Roman Catholic Relief 1790–1793', Ph.D. Diss., University of Notre Dame, 1967.

Hamshere, Cyril, *The British in the Caribbean*. Cambridge, Mass., 1972.

Harbison, Peter *et al.*, *Irish Art and Architecture: from Pre-History to the Present*, London, 1978.

Haring, Clarence Henry, *Spanish Empire in America*, New York, 1947.

——. *Trade and Navigation between Spain and the Indies in the Time of the Hapsburgs*, Cambridge, Mass., 1918.

Harrington, Virginia. *The New York Merchants on the Eve of the Revolution*, New York, 1935.

Harris, P.R., 'The English College, Douai, 1750–1794', *Recusant Studies* 10 (1969), 79–95.

Hayes, Richard, *Biographical Dictionary of Irishmen in France*, Dublin, 1949.

——. 'Irish Associations with Nantes', *Studies* 28 (1939), 115–26.

——. 'Irish Links with Bordeaux', *Studies* 27 (1938), 291–306.

Hayes-McCoy, G.A., 'The Red Coat and the Green', *Studies* 37 (1948), 326–32; 396–408.

Herr, Richard, *The Eighteenth-Century Revolution in Spain*, Princeton, N.J., 1958.

Hone, Joseph, *The Moores of Moore Hall*, London, 1939.

Irish Architectural Archive, *The Architecture of Richard Morrison and William Vitruvius Morrison*, Dublin, 1989.

Irwin, David, *English Neo-Classical Art: Studies in Inspiration and Taste*, London, 1966.

James, Francis G., *Ireland in the Empire 1688–1770*, Cambridge, Mass., 1973.

——. 'Irish Colonial Trade in the Eighteenth Century', *William and Mary Quarterly* 20 (1963), 574–84.

Jennings, Rev. Brendan, 'The Irish Franciscans in Prague', *Studies* 28 (1939), 210–22.

Jensen, Arthur L., *The Maritime Commerce of Colonial Philadelphia*, Madison, Wisc., 1963.

Johnston, Edith Mary, *Great Britain and Ireland, 1760–1800: A Study in Political Administration*, Edinburgh, 1963.

——. *Ireland in the Eighteenth Century*, 2nd ed., Dublin, 1980.

Kelly, James, 'The Parliamentary Reform Movement of the 1780s and the Catholic Question', *Archivium Hibernicum* 43 (1988), 95–117.

Kenny, Colum, 'The Exclusion of Catholics From the Legal Profession in Ireland', *Irish Historical Studies* 25 (1987), 337–57.

Keogh, Dáire, *'The French Disease': The Catholic Church and Radicalism in Ireland 1790–1800*, Dublin, 1993.

Király, Béla, *Hungary in the Late Eighteenth Century: The Decline of Enlightened Despotism*, New York, 1969.

Large, David, 'The Wealth of the Greater Irish Landowners, 1750–1815', *Irish Historical Studies* 15 (1966–67), 21–47.

Lecky, W.E.H., *History of Ireland in the Eighteenth Century*, 5 vols, London, 1892.

Leighton, C.D.A., *Catholicism in a Protestant Kingdom: A Study of the Irish Ancien Regime*, Dublin, 1994.

Leys, M.D.R., *Catholics in England, 1559–1829: A Social History*, New York, 1961.

Linker, R.W., 'The English Roman Catholics and Emancipation: The Politics of Persuasion', *Journal of Ecclesiastical History* 27 (1976), 151–80.

Loeber, Rolf and Parker, Geoffrey, 'The Military Revolution in Seventeenth-Century Ireland' in Jane Ohlmeyer, ed., *Ireland from Independence to Occupation 1641–1660*, Cambridge, 1995, 66–88.

Lunn, Dom Maurus, 'The Patronal Title of St. Gregory's at Douai', *Downside Review* 87 (1969), 278–81.

Macartney, C.A., *The Hapsburg Empire 1790–1918*, London, 1969.

MacCurtain, Margaret, *Tudor and Stuart Ireland*, Dublin, 1972.

McDowell, R.B., *Ireland in the Age of Imperialism and Revolution 1760–1801*, Oxford, 1979.

——. 'Ireland in the Eighteenth-Century British Empire', *Historical Studies* 9 (1974), 49–63.

——. 'Parliamentary Independence, 1782–9' and 'The Age of the United Irishmen: Reform and Reaction, 1789–94' in *A New History of Ireland*, eds T.W. Moody and W.E. Vaughn, Oxford, 1986, iv, 265–373.

McLachlan, Jean O. *Trade and Peace with Old Spain, 1667–1750*. Cambridge, 1940.

MacLysaght, Edward, *Irish Life in the Seventeenth Century*, 4th ed., Dublin, 1979.

——. *More Irish Families*, Dublin, 1960.

McParland, Edward, 'Sir Richard Morrison's Country Houses: The Smaller Villas-I', *Country Life* 153 (1973), 1462–66.

Macswiney, Marquis of Mashanglass, 'Notes on Some Irish Regiments in the Service of Spain and Naples in the Eighteenth Century', *Proceedings of the Royal Irish Academy* 37 (1927), 158–74.

Mahoney, Thomas H.D., *Edmund Burke and Ireland*, Cambridge, Mass., 1960.

Malins, Edward and the Knight of Glin, *Lost Desmesnes: Irish Landscape Gardening, 1660–1845*, London, 1976.

Mannion, John. 'The Waterford Merchants and the Irish-Newfoundland Provisions Trade, 1770–1820' in L.M. Cullen and Paul Butel, eds, *Négoce et industrie en France et en Irlande aux XVIIe et XIXe siècles*, Paris, 1980, 27–44.

Marczali, Henry, *Hungary in the Eighteenth Century*, Cambridge, 1910.

Maxwell, Constantia, *County and Town in Ireland under the Georges*, London, 1940.

——. *Dublin under the Georges, 1714–1830*, 3rd ed., London, 1936.

Melvin, Patrick, 'The Composition of the Galway Gentry', *Irish Genealogist* 7 (1986), 81–96.

——. 'The Galway Tribes as Landowners and Gentry' in Gerard Moran, ed., *Galway: History and Society*, Dublin, 1996, 319–74.

Messenger, John C., 'The Influence of the Irish on Montserrat', *Caribbean Quarterly* 13 (1967), 3–25.

Murphy, Dennis, *Cromwell in Ireland: A History of Cromwell's Irish Campaign*, Dublin, 1897.

Murtagh, Harman, 'Irish Soldiers Abroad, 1600–1800' in Thomas Bartlett and Keith Jeffrey, eds, *A Military History of Ireland*, Cambridge, 1996, 294–314.

Ní Chinnéide, Síle, 'Coquebert de Montbret's Impressions of Galway City and County in the Year 1791', *Journal of the Galway Archaeological and Historical Society* 25 (1952), 1–14.

Niddrie, D.L., 'Eighteenth-Century Settlement in the British Caribbean', *Institute of British Geographers* No. 40 (1966), 67–80.

O'Boyle, Rev. James, *The Irish Colleges on the Continent: Their Origin and History*, Dublin, 1935.

O'Brien, George, *The Economic History of Ireland in the Eighteenth Century*, Dublin, 1918.

O'Callaghan, John Cornelius, *History of the Irish Brigades in the Service of France*, Glasgow, 1870.

O'Conor Don, Rt. Hon. Charles Owen, *The O'Conors of Connaught: An Historical Memoir*, Dublin, 1891.

O'Donovan, John, *The Economic History of Livestock in Ireland*, Cork, 1940.

O'Flaherty, Eamon, 'The Catholic Convention and Anglo-Irish Politics, 1791–3', *Archivium Hibernicum* 40 (1985), 14–34.

O'Hart, John, *The Irish and Anglo-Irish Landed Gentry: When Cromwell Came to Ireland*, 1884; rpt. Shannon, 1968.

O'Sullivan, Harold, 'Land Ownership Changes in the County of Louth in the 17th Century', Ph.D. dissertation, Trinity College Dublin, 1992.

O'Sullivan, M.D., *Old Galway: The History of a Norman Colony in Ireland*, Cambridge, 1942.

Osborough, W.N., 'Catholics, Land, and the Popery Acts of Anne' in T. Power and K. Whelan, eds, *Endurance and Emergence: Catholics in Ireland in the Eighteenth Century*, Dublin, 1990, 21–56.

Pares, Richard, *Merchants and Planters. Economic History Review*, Suppl. 4, Cambridge, 1960.

——. *War and Trade in the West Indies, 1739–1763*, Oxford, 1936.

Perceval-Maxwell, M., *The Outbreak of the Irish Rebellion of 1641*, Montreal, 1994.

Pittman, Frank Wesley, *The Development of the British West Indies, 1700–1763*, New Haven, 1917.

Pollard, M., *Dublin's Trade in Books 1550–1800*, Oxford, 1989.

Prendergast, John P., *The Cromwellian Settlement of Ireland*, 3rd ed., 1865; rpt. Dublin, 1922.

Ragatz, Lowell J., *The Fall of the Planter Class in the British Caribbean, 1763–1833*, London, 1928.

Rogers, Patrick, *The Irish Volunteers and Catholic Emancipation: A Neglected Phase of Irish History*, London, 1934.

Sadleir, Thomas U., 'The Burkes of Marble Hill', *Galway Archaeological and Historical Journal* 8 (1913–14), 1–5.

Shaw, Stanford J., *Between Old and New: The Ottoman Empire under Sultan Selim III 1789–1807*, Cambridge, Mass., 1971.

Sheridan, R.B., 'The Rise of a Colonial Gentry: A Case Study of Antigua, 1730–1775', *Economic History Review* 13 (1960–61), 342–57.

——. *Sugar and Slavery: An Economic History of the British West Indies 1623–1775*, Baltimore, 1973.

Simms, J.G., 'Connacht in the Eighteenth Century', *Irish Historical Studies* 11 (1958–59), 116–33.

——. 'Irish Catholics and the Parliamentary Franchise', *Irish Historical Studies* 12 (1960–61), 28–37.

——. 'The Irish on the Continent, 1691–1800' in *A New History of Ireland*, ed., T.W. Moody and W.E. Vaughan, Oxford, 1986, iv, 629–56.

——. *Jacobite Ireland 1685–91*, London, 1969.

——. 'The Restoration, 1660–85' in *A New History of Ireland*, ed., T.W. Moody *et al.*, Oxford, 1976, iii, 420–53.

——. *The Williamite Confiscation in Ireland, 1690–1703*, London, 1956.

Truxes, Thomas M., 'Connecticut in the Irish-American Flaxseed Trade, 1750-1775', *Eire-Ireland* 12 (1977), 34–62.

Wall, Maureen McGeehin, 'The Activities and Personnel of the General Committee of the Catholics of Ireland, 1767–1784', M.A. thesis, University College, Dublin, 1952.

——. *Catholic Ireland in the Eighteenth Century: The Collected Essays of Maureen Wall*, ed., Gerard O'Brien. Dublin, 1989.

Walton, Julian, 'Census Records of the Irish in Eighteenth-Century Cadiz', *Irish Genealogist* 6 (1985), 748–56.

Wheeler, Scott, 'Four Armies in Ireland' in Jane Ohlmeyer, ed., *Ireland from Independence to Occupation 1641–1660*, Cambridge, 1995, 43–65.

Whelan, Kevin, 'The Regional Impact of Irish Catholicism 1700–1850' in W. Smyth and K. Whelan, eds, *Common Ground: Essays on the Historical Geography of Ireland,* Cork, 1988, 253–77.

White, Philip L. *The Beekmans of New York in Politics and Commerce 1647–1877*, New York, 1956.

MAPS

Moll, H. *Galway*, 1701, National Library of Ireland.

Petty, Sir William. *Hiberniae delineatio, atlas of Ireland*, London, 1685; rpt. Newcastle on Tyne, 1968.

Taylor, George and Skinner, Andrew. *Maps of the Roads of Ireland ...*, London and Dublin, 1778; rpt. Shannon, 1969.

Index

Place names, unless otherwise specified, refer to locations, estates, etc. in co. Galway.